Caught in the Crossfire

Caught in the Crossfire

Scotland's Deadliest Drugs War

Russell Findlay

BIRLINN

This edition first published in 2013 by
Birlinn Limited
West Newington House
10 Newington Road
Edinburgh
EH9 1QS

www.birlinn.co.uk

ISBN: 978 1 78027 163 7

British Library Cataloguing-in-Publication Data
A catalogue record for this book is available from the British Library

Typeset by Iolaire Typesetting, Newtonmore
Printed and bound by Clays Ltd, St Ives plc

Contents

Timeline

June 1983 – Jamie Daniel is jailed for four years at Chichester Crown Court for heroin smuggling.

2 January 1984 – Eddie Lyons Sr is stabbed in Scapa Street, Cadder. His attackers are later jailed after Eddie identified them to the police. He and his family are escorted by police to their new home in Milton.

7 December 1991 – Garry Lyons, the eight-year-old son of Eddie Lyons Sr, dies of leukaemia.

1992 – Eddie Lyons Sr is given control of a disused former school annexe on Ashgill Road, Milton, with the backing of community police officer John Cameron, which he will later run as the Chirnsyde Community Initiative.

1995 – Lyons first receives public funding.

September 1998 – Ellen Hurcombe is elected as a Labour councillor in Milton.

18 April 1999 – Michael Lyons Sr dies of a crack cocaine overdose following a police drugs raid at a high-rise flat in Castlebay Street, Milton.

30 April 1999 – Eddie Lyons Sr is interviewed on STV's evening news bulletin at Chirnsyde, talking about the community's drug problem.

5 August 1999 – Chirnsyde Community Initiative is formed and funding from Glasgow City Council begins. Eddie Lyons Sr is appointed co-ordinator.

24 December 1999 – Steven Lyons attacks Marc McDonnell, prompting a violent vendetta by the Club Boys against the McDonnells.

10 May 2000 – drug dealer Frank McPhie is shot dead in Maryhill, Glasgow, following a dispute with Jamie Daniel.

13 June 2000 – Labour MSP Patricia Ferguson goes on the beat with community police officer John Cameron. They pay a visit to Chirnsyde.

2 September 2000 – outside Chirnsyde, a gang attacks Thomas McDonnell Sr with a knife, golf clubs and a scaffolding pole. Six men – Eddie Lyons Sr, Johnny Lyons, Eddie Lyons Jr, Steven Lyons, Andrew Gallacher and Paul McGuinness – are charged with attempted murder.

10 January 2001 – with the cases against Edward Lyons Sr and Johnny Lyons withdrawn, the trial of the remaining four begins at the High Court in Glasgow but it is abandoned due to witness intimidation.

7 February 2001 – Thomas's wife, Margo McDonnell, writes to the then Lord Advocate Colin Boyd, Strathclyde Police's Chief Constable John Orr and Justice Minister Jim Wallace. She reveals her family's ordeal and the relationship between PC John Cameron and Eddie Lyons Sr.

18 May 2001 – a new trial for the attempted murder of Thomas McDonnell Sr begins against Eddie Lyons Jr, Steven Lyons, Andrew Gallacher and Paul McGuinness.

28 May 2001 – several charges are dropped which leads to Gallacher being acquitted.

4 June 2001 – McGuinness is found guilty of the attempted murder of Thomas McDonnell Sr. The cases against Eddie Lyons Jr and Steven Lyons are not proven.

22 June 2001 – McGuinness is sentenced to eight years in prison for the attempted murder of Thomas McDonnell Sr.

August 2001 – a quantity of cocaine belonging to the Daniel family is stolen from a house party in Milton. The cocaine is sold to the Lyons, sparking war between the two families.

August 2001 – the Daniels torch Chirnsyde, causing £30,000 worth of damage. Two weeks later, Robert Daniel allegedly trashes the Chirnsyde minibus. Vandalism and breach of the peace charges against him are later dropped by prosecutors.

5 September 2001 – the director of Glasgow City Council's Culture and Leisure Department, Bridget McConnell, writes a letter to the director of the council's Education Department, Ken Corsar. In it, she admits knowledge of the fire attack and vandalism at Chirnsyde but urges her colleague to review his decision to stop sending children there.

September 2001 – an attempt to shoot Steven Lyons outside Mallon's pub is made but he is not hit.

22 November 2001 – Bridget McConnell's husband, the Labour MSP Jack McConnell, becomes Scotland's First Minister.

12 December 2001 – PC John Cameron resigns as chairman of Chirnsyde.

12 January 2003 – Kevin 'Gerbil' Carroll is shot and injured outside his mother's home in Milton.

19 January 2003 – the Daniel family are exposed in the *Sunday Mail* newspaper's 'Crime Inc' investigation.

23 January 2003 – Johnny Lyons is shot in Stornoway Street, Milton, but survives.

23 February 2003 – the *Sunday Mail* publishes a story about Eddie Lyons Sr running Chirnsyde under the headline, 'Would you let this man look after your children?'

20 March 2003 – another attempt is made to shoot Johnny Lyons near his home but, this time, he is not hit.

24 September 2003 – the trial of Jamie Daniel for allegedly attacking taxi driver James Gallagher is abandoned at Glasgow Sheriff Court, amid concerns of witness intimidation.

October 2003 – the trial of Stephen Burgess for the shooting of Kevin Carroll is abandoned at the High Court in Glasgow.

10 January 2004 – John Madden, a member of the Chirnsyde-based Club Boys gang, is shot by Kevin Carroll, using a Kalashnikov AK-47. He survives.

5 February 2004 – Steven Lyons is stopped in a vehicle and has £14,980 in cash seized from him under proceeds of crime laws.

14 February 2004 – the Club Boys go on the rampage at Tuscany nightclub, Kirkintilloch. Two men are hit by car and six suffer knife injuries.

20 February 2004 – police seize £185,000 of cannabis and heroin at addresses in Kirkintilloch. The haul is linked to the Lyons.

20 February 2004 – the East Kilbride home owned by Eddie Lyons Sr is searched by police who find £63,000 in cash.

2 March 2004 – campaigner Billy McAllister is arrested for fly-posting leaflets which allege that a corrupt police officer is an associate of the Lyons family.

24 May 2004 – Patricia Ferguson MSP writes a letter addressed to 'Dear Eddie'. In it, she asks Eddie Lyons Sr to nominate a member of the community to attend the official opening of the Scottish parliament.

3 September 2004 – Club Boy Andrew Gallacher is sentenced to four years at the High Court in Glasgow for heroin and cannabis dealing.

January 2005 – two unidentified plain-clothes police officers threaten to plant drugs on Billy McAllister outside Kelvindale Post Office.

25 February 2005 – a senior member of the Club Boys admits dealing cannabis and is sentenced to 30 months imprisonment at the High Court in Edinburgh.

22 June 2005 – a report by Bridget McConnell is presented to councillors. It recommends that they should vote to continue funding Chirnsyde, which they do. The report is also critical of members of the public who have complained.

17 August 2005 – two campaigners who object to Eddie Lyons Sr being funded with public money are given emergency mobile phones over fears for their safety. Two others receive panic alarms.

13 September 2005 – Steven Lyons is found not guilty of three attempted murder charges at Tuscany nightclub. Fellow Club Boy Charles McMurray, who is not charged, tells the court that he was responsible. Ross Monaghan is also cleared at the High Court in Glasgow.

17 October 2005 – after being forced to do so by the Scottish Information Commissioner, Glasgow City Council reveals the names of which police officers provided them with information about Eddie Lyons Sr and Chirnsyde.

1 December 2005 – Robert Daniel is jailed for eight years after he is caught with £300,000 of heroin.

19 January 2006 – the £63,000 seized from the home of Eddie Lyons Sr is forfeited at the High Court in Edinburgh. The Crown Office states that the money was the 'proceeds of drug trafficking'.

16 February 2006 – Billy McAllister wins election to the council ward which includes Milton. The SNP candidate's main policy pledge is to remove Eddie Lyons Sr from Chirnsyde.

18 April 2006 – Eddie Lyons Jr is shot at the front door of his home in Ratho Drive, Cumbernauld. He survives.

July 2006 – Johnny McLean is given an absolute discharge at Glasgow Sheriff Court for keeping his son off school for four years due to his Chirnsyde objections.

15 September 2006 – Glasgow City Council votes to continue funding Chirnsyde on a month-to-month basis after a damning report by accountancy firm Scott-Moncrieff. They also vote to undertake a 'comprehensive scrutiny review'.

6 November 2006 – the gravestone of Garry Lyons is found vandalised. The attack is blamed on Kevin Carroll.

8 November 2006 – Eddie Lyons Jr is struck by his own car when Kevin Carroll ambushes him in Bellshill. Lyons is not shot but his associate Andrew Gallacher suffers bullet wounds.

16 November 2006 – Kevin Carroll and Ross Sherlock are shot by the Club Boys in Auchinairn, Bishopbriggs.

6 December 2006 – a triple shooting at David Lyons' Applerow Motors in Balmore Road, Lambhill, results in Michael Lyons Jr being killed. Steven Lyons and Robert Pickett survive. The Daniel hit men are Raymond Anderson Sr and James McDonald.

7 December 2006 – Eddie Lyons Sr is evicted from Chirnsyde.

2 March 2007 – Raymond Anderson Sr, his son, Raymond Jr, and James McDonald are arrested over the murder of Michael Lyons and the shootings of Steven Lyons and Robert Pickett.

10 March 2007 – Jamie McColl is stabbed to death by James Murphy, a member of the Club Boys.

18 July 2007 – Kevin Carroll is jailed for 18 months for possession of 5.56mm and 9mm ammo. In a plea deal, the more serious charges relating to the Heckler & Koch are dropped.

4 October 2007 – the SNP MSP Bob Doris raises a debate on Chirnsyde in the Scottish Parliament which praises the 'four bampots' who opposed Eddie Lyons Sr's Chirnsyde regime.

19 October 2007 – Club Boy James Murphy is jailed for nine and a half years for the culpable homicide of Jamie McColl.

9 November 2007 – Strathclyde Police state that David Lyons is 'involved in serious and organised crime including the trafficking and supply of class-A drugs'. They make the claim during a council hearing about an associate's used car sales licence application, which is rejected.

31 December 2007 – police raid the home of ex-soldier Andrew Quinn in Dennistoun, Glasgow. They find heroin plus a massive cache or ammunition from the British Army.

15 February 2008 – police from Glasgow and Kent raid Howe Barracks, Canterbury. They smash a gang of soldiers from the Royal Regiment of Scotland's Argyll and Sutherland Highlanders who supply guns, ammunition and explosives to gangsters. Three soldiers, former soldier Quinn and an associate are later jailed for a total of almost 50 years.

25 February 2008 – the trial of Raymond Anderson Sr and James McDonald for the Applerow triple shooting begins at the High Court in Glasgow.

26 February 2008 – Robert Pickett says the 'wrong people' are in the dock. He denies being paid to say this. Lord Hardie later jails him for two years for contempt of court.

2 May 2008 – Anderson and McDonald are found guilty of murdering Michael Lyons and attempting to murder Steven Lyons and Robert Pickett. They are each jailed for a minimum of 35 years, later reduced to 30 on appeal.

17 March 2009 – the Club Boys gun down Kevin Carroll's associate John Bonner in Springburn, Glasgow, using a shotgun. He survives.

12 May 2009 – officers from the Scottish Crime and Drug Enforcement Agency speak to Glasgow council leader Steven Purcell in his office and warn him that he may be blackmailed over his cocaine use.

4 June 2009 – Paul Lyons kills Mark Fleeman in a road-rage incident on the M74.

22 November 2009 – the *Sunday Mail* newspaper reveals that Kevin Carroll's 'alien abduction gang' are suspected of a series of gunpoint kidnappings of rival drug dealers across Scotland.

12 January 2010 – Kevin Carroll orders cocaine dealer Steven Glen to meet him the next day. Glen discusses Carroll's demands with his 'boss' Allan 'Babesy' Johnston.

13 January 2010 – Kevin Carroll is shot dead in the back of an Audi parked outside Asda in Robroyston. It is seven years plus one day since he was shot outside his mother's house.

23 January 2010 – one of the hit men suspected of shooting Kevin Carroll leaves Scotland for Spain.

26 January 2010 – the two guns used to kill Kevin Carroll are found in undergrowth in Coatbridge, Lanarkshire.

2 March 2010 – Steven Purcell announces his decision to quit as leader of Glasgow City Council. The *Sunday Mail* later reveals his cocaine warning from the Scottish Crime and Drug Enforcement Agency.

4 March 2010 – Paul Lyons admits the road-rage murder of Mark Fleeman. He is later jailed for 12 years.

8 March 2010 – justice secretary Kenny MacAskill unveils a new police car – a seized £75,000 Audi linked to Kevin Carroll. Within a fortnight, the Daniels firebomb Maryhill police station twice in a bid to destroy it.

27 April 2010 – Eddie Lyons Sr is spared jail and given 300 hours community service for mortgage fraud at Glasgow Sheriff Court.

18 May 2010 – the funeral of Kevin Carroll takes place but his grave in Bearsden remains unmarked for almost two years.

1 June 2010 – Jamie Daniel is jailed for a year at Glasgow Sheriff Court for a road-rage attack in the city's west end having been arrested and remanded four months earlier.

2 July 2010 – police raid the home of corrupt officer PC Derek McLeod where they find a cannabis farm. He is also accused of passing stolen intelligence to the Lyons.

30 July 2010 – armed police raid the home of Ross Monaghan in Penilee, Glasgow. He is the second hit man to be suspected of shooting Kevin Carroll and is charged with his murder.

2 August 2010 – Ross Monaghan appears in court charged with murdering Kevin Carroll.

23 June 2011 – PC Derek McLeod is jailed at the High Court in Edinburgh for 16 months for leaking information to a suspected Kevin Carroll hit man. He is also jailed for two years and three months for drug dealing but a reporting ban is put in place.

23 March 2012 – the trial of Ross Monaghan for the murder of Kevin Carroll begins at the High Court in Glasgow.

3 May 2012 – the trial of Ross Monaghan collapses and he is acquitted after Lord Brailsford rules that there is insufficient evidence.

Introduction

It was Scotland's dirtiest and deadliest gang war for a generation – the biblical-sounding Daniels against the Lyons.

On one side was the secretive Daniel family, headed by the snarling, glowering presence of Jamie Daniel. After a childhood scarred by tragedy and chronic poverty, he fought his way out of 'The Jungle' in Glasgow's Possilpark, where stealing scrap metal was the precursor to creating a drug importation and distribution network, and built up vast wealth and underworld power. Daniel, his family and their extended gang had a burning hatred of the police and operated firmly in the shadows where they carved out a reputation among the UK's sharpest major organised crime groups. Kevin 'Gerbil' Carroll, the partner of Daniel's daughter, became Scotland's most violent young criminal and ran his own team which dealt drugs but also 'taxed' rival dealers. Carroll's mob posed as police officers to stage abductions at gunpoint. Having suffered sickening acts of torture, the broken and bewildered victims forfeited their drugs, cash or guns.

On the other side was the Lyons family, at the head of which was a cocky, small-time crook called Eddie Lyons Sr. Having been stabbed at the age of 25, he was branded a 'grass' and driven out of his home on the Cadder housing estate under police protection for helping to jail his attackers. The Lyons were rehoused in nearby Milton where Eddie Sr evolved into a self-styled community leader. The loss of his eight-year-old son Garry to cancer brought an outpouring of goodwill and support. With the backing of his friends in the police, he was handed the keys to the council-owned Chirnsyde Community Initiative, a community centre in the heart of Milton. Two of his other sons, Eddie Jr and Steven, along with their tight-knit group of friends became the Club Boys and their gang hut was Chirnsyde – aka 'Eddie's Club'.

Eddie Sr was the smiling, plausible puppet master who outwardly acted like the model citizen, concerned about tackling youth crime, while the Club Boys peddled drugs and inflicted violence on both their enemies and innocents. One father whose sons were being bullied by the Club Boys went to Chirnsyde to plead with Eddie Sr to end the violence. He was knifed and left for dead by a cowardly pack of thugs yet only one Club Boy was convicted for his attempted murder.

The war between the Daniels and Lyons was sparked by an opportunistic theft of cocaine from a safe house in Milton. Few would have predicted that this relatively minor incident in 2001 would have unleashed such an astonishing wave of murder, mayhem and terror spanning over a decade.

When the Lyons were accused of flagrantly peddling the Daniels' stolen white powder, the blue touchpaper was lit. The niggling hostility between the Club Boys and the young Daniel gang members exploded.

What started as being about the cash, territory and power of the north Glasgow drugs trade became very personal with deep, reciprocal loathing. The Daniels regarded the Lyons with derision – they were nothing more than upstarts and grasses, tainted by their father's legacy – but they also underestimated them. The Lyons either didn't understand the Daniels' fearsome reputation or perhaps they didn't care.

More than a dozen shootings took place with one dead on each side. Others died in frenzied street violence while an innocent and loving father's life was stolen in a cowardly road-rage attack.

The devastation was immense and obscene. There were beatings, slashings, abductions, disfigurement and torture. Cars and homes were firebombed in the night as children slept. Devastated families were ripped apart and forced to live under witness protection. Justice was twisted with witnesses bribed and terrorised. Judges responded by handing down record prison sentences. Kevin Carroll's vile desecration of the grave of little Garry Lyons marked a sickening low.

In 2006, proud new father Michael Lyons, 21, was slaughtered by Daniel family mercenaries in a crime which stunned Scotland. Two masked gunmen brought carnage, terror and death to a busy Lyons family-owned garage forecourt in broad daylight. Perhaps most shocking was that the deadly weapons used in the triple shooting had been sold by a rogue band of British Army soldiers who flooded Glasgow's underworld with state-of-the-art guns, ammunition and explosives, much of which has never been accounted for.

Observers firmly believed that the dominant Daniels had the upper hand as the vanquished Club Boys were forced out of Glasgow for their own safety. Daniel gang lieutenant Carroll relentlessly hunted them down. The Lyons were determined to avenge the atrocity inflicted on their brother's grave. They also knew that it was Carroll or them – kill or be killed. Terrified shoppers dived for cover when 29-year-old Carroll had 13 shots pumped into him as he sat in an Audi outside a suburban Asda supermarket.

These dark events were not confined to the underworld. A group of parents were caught in the crossfire. They refused council orders to send their children to Chirnsyde and into the hands of Eddie Sr who was in receipt of over £1million of funding from taxpayers. For many long years, the campaigners were arrogantly dismissed then smeared by those in power who inexplicably backed the perverse Chirnsyde regime.

The campaigners' brave and determined battle revealed a murky nexus between criminals, police officers and politicians. Against the odds, they won their crusade and exposed how the cancerous Daniel v Lyons feud seeped from the city's mean streets into the highest echelons of the political elite, from Holyrood to George Square, the offices of First Minister Jack McConnell and disgraced Glasgow City Council leader Steven

Purcell. Their story will inspire any community that wants to fight back.

Police fear, however, that the violence has not ended and that is simply a matter of time before more blood is spilled. They firmly believe that the war is far from over.

1

Get Out of Town

In the darkness, a convoy of cars and vans snaked along Scapa Street. Inside, three generations of the Lyons family, their belongings hastily packed, had been forced to say an abrupt farewell to the area they called home. Police officers in marked vehicles formed the cortege's protective head and tail. The mood was sombre, almost funereal, but no one was dead – not this time. Many of those who stood watching the procession were satisfied. As the family were removed, the word 'grass' was spat out with venom.

On 2 January 1984, Eddie Lyons had been stabbed. It was the final act in a spate of spiralling violence between members of the Lyons family and the Moran family who lived side by side in Cadder, a small north Glasgow council estate in the shadow of three sprawling burial grounds – St Kentigern's, the Western Necropolis and Lambhill Cemetery.

The original reasons for what started the feud are lost in time but much of it stemmed from the two large families vying for control and respect. The savage attack happened in the Scapa Street home of Eddie Lyons' parents where he then lived. It came days after a Moran family member suffered a severe beating with baseball bats at the hands of the Lyons. Prior to Lyons being stabbed, this had been the most serious incident in this tit-for-tat cycle of violence. As a consequence of the beating, it was decided that Lyons would pay. He was lucky not to have paid with his life.

He was inside when every front window was smashed. From the street, came shouted threats. Two men then burst through the flimsy wooden front door. With Lyons were his younger sister Victoria, their parents Edward and Marion plus another woman. Within minutes, the two knifemen had dispensed their brutal vengeance and fled. Lyons could only lie helplessly gazing upwards in a warm, sticky pool of his own blood and wait for the ambulance and police sirens to grow louder. His father was also injured, although less seriously, by the blade.

In parts of the west of Scotland generations of police officers and politicians have been unable to end the ingrained culture of knife crime, and Lyons could have been just another statistic in the annual death toll but he clung to life. His survival presented him with a choice – either hit back even harder against the Morans and remain silent when the police came calling or throw in the towel and fully co-operate with the detectives of Strathclyde Police. He chose the latter. By the time he had signed each A4 page of his detailed witness statement, he knew that his life would change forever.

Lyons was then 25 years old and had married Josephine when they were both aged 20. At the time of the stabbing, they were already parents to three sons – Eddie Jr who was four, three-year-old Steven and Garry who was two months old.

Lyons was fresh faced and had a permed hairstyle which was typical of that era and its stars such as footballer Kevin Keegan. With a sparkle in his eyes, he was smart, likeable, a quick talker and streetwise but diminutive both in physical stature at around 5 foot 2 inches tall and in reputation – nowhere near the ranks of the dangerous grey men who controlled the city's crime.

Alongside the entrenched knife culture, another blight at the heart of the criminal justice system is the label of 'grass'. It can be unfairly applied to ordinary people who have good reason to speak to the police but is easier to understand when it's given to criminals who inform on rivals or those who take the law into their own hands while simultaneously seeking redress and protection from the authorities. And that is exactly what Lyons had chosen to do. In the underworld, this kind of behaviour is the lowest of the low.

In the weeks following the attack, the Moran family became enraged at his and his family's willingness to speak with the police and point the finger. But Lyons was determined and remained resolute despite suffering intimidation in the lead-up to the trial. In one incident, eight weeks after the stabbing which could have put him a plot in one of Cadder's neighbouring cemeteries, he was terrorised by one of the Morans in West Nile Street, a bustling city-centre street packed with office workers and shoppers.

In what appeared to be a chance encounter, the Moran followed Lyons and gestured that he had a knife in his jacket. Cornered and terrified, Lyons – his blade injuries still raw and healing – had no way of knowing if it was a bluff. The man then punched his passive victim and looked him in the eyes as he spat out the warning: 'Your cards are marked – you are a grass.' It was a terrifying but futile attempt to prevent Lyons from giving evidence.

Lyons' decision to give a detailed statement to the police and then go to the High Court in Glasgow that August to testify against his attackers resulted in two men being jailed. Robert Moran, nicknamed Barra, was sentenced to three years' imprisonment, while his associate Alan Smith, known as Smido, got an 18-month sentence.

For their own safety before the trial, Lyons and his family's co-operation led to them being unconventionally escorted from Cadder by their guardian angels in blue.

The emotive word 'grass' continued to echo in their ears a long time after the humiliation of their enforced exile from Cadder. Throughout 1984 and onwards, 'Lyons grasses' and 'Lyons scum' were sprayed on the streets of Cadder and elsewhere in the city. It was still happening into the 90s. They were reviled.

One Moran family associate said, 'The whole place knew what that family was at the time and nothing has changed. Eddie ran to the cops because his bottle went. That still clings to him and his family like the stench of stale smoke. The cops had to move them out because the whole scheme turned against them. One minute they want to act like gangsters but then go crying to the police when it gets too hot. You can't have it both ways.'

Long before the existence of a witness protection scheme, the three generations of Lyons were taken just under two miles east across the city to the sprawling post-war social housing estate of Milton which is on the other side of the arterial Balmore Road that heads north to affluent suburbs. It wasn't far but it was enough to end the violence, if not the enmity, between the two families.

Initially Lyons spent a short spell in Cathay Street, near to his parents' new home. Then he, Josephine and their growing young family were given a council flat in Liddesdale Road. Their first three sons were joined by daughter Ashley the following year and then Christopher in 1989. A female neighbour remembers Lyons at the time as being 'constantly on the make but plausible'.

Having survived the Moran stabbing, it wasn't long before he was at the centre of a second violent feud and yet another lucky escape from becoming a murder victim. This time, the violence was a result of his family's early foray into drug dealing. His younger brother Michael was making a lot of cash by indiscriminately peddling amphetamines, known as speed, to youngsters. Heroin had begun to hit Glasgow in a major way in the early 1980s but drugs were nowhere near as prevalent as they later became. People in the community united to tackle those involved.

In 1986, the simmering tensions between the Lyons and those who did not want drugs seeping into Milton led to a number of flashpoints, one of which sparked a riot. One Lyons family member used his van as a weapon to drive at a man and knock him down. The hit-and-run attack, which caused the victim serious injuries, was the catalyst for an explosion of violence. Later that night, there was a running battle on the street as the community turned on the Lyons. Scores of people became involved. Many used feet and fists while others grabbed makeshift weapons from garages and kitchen drawers.

Initially, the police were hopelessly overwhelmed until backup brought calm.

Lyons and his brother Michael ended up in hospital. Their injuries were not too serious – cuts and bruises, perhaps the odd broken bone.

Later that night, after peace had been restored, a female neighbour of Lyons went out the back of the Liddesdale Road close to get some coal from the bunker. Standing motionless in the darkness were two men. One had a claw hammer while the other held a shotgun across his body. He snarled at the innocent neighbour, 'Where is he?'

She did not scare easily and was more than capable of standing up to two thugs – even one with a gun. The plucky woman had no idea which 'he' they were referring to, nor did she ask. Instead, she produced her own weapon – a hammer which was stashed in the bunker – and told them to fuck off.

She said, 'I told them I would phone the police and they ran off. Lyons later told me he was in Stobhill Hospital when he heard the report of two men with a gun. He had heard it through the radio of the police officer guarding him. I didn't know who they were looking for but they must have thought I had something to do with Lyons because I came out the same close.'

The duo who had gone hunting for Lyons that night were serious individuals and there is little doubt that they meant business. Had they caught up with him, he would almost certainly have been bludgeoned with the steel hammer, shot or both.

Lyons, however, was safely tucked up under the crisp cotton hospital sheets, being fussed over by nurses and shielded by his police friends. When the officers' radios crackled with a report of a gunman in Liddesdale Road, Lyons would have been extra grateful of his surroundings.

Days after the riot, the violence continued. A taxi driver smashed the windows of Lyons' flat in Liddesdale Road because the family had sold speed to his 14-year-old daughter. The anti-drugs message was clearly not getting through.

It had not taken long since their arrival in Milton for the Lyons family to become hated by many of their new neighbours for bringing violence, fear and drugs to their relatively peaceful community.

The eldest of six children, Lyons was born on St Valentine's Day in 1958. He was followed by David a year later, Victoria in 1961, Michael in 1964, Johnny in 1965 and Deborah in 1970.

Michael and Johnny were more infamous due to their capacity for extreme violence, drug dealing, armed robbery and another prevalent crime of the era – ram-raiding, where thieves smashed stolen cars through shop fronts and made off with the stock.

It was well known that eldest brother Eddie ran with the hares and hunted with the hounds. People in Milton had heard all about what had happened in Cadder. Sometimes, he would personally scrub off 'grass' when it had been daubed on walls but he could never stop the whispers.

Long before the age of digital TV and DVDs, movies were watched on VHS tapes which, in the 1980s, brought Hollywood blockbusters into family homes for the first time. Every high street had at least one video rental shop but the easily copied tapes also sparked a huge black market for pirated ones. Fakes became so prevalent that, to many people, including those who abhorred crime, buying or renting pirated tapes didn't even feel like they were breaking the law.

In Milton, Eddie became the go-to guy. Some of his best customers were policemen. He often joked that the officers at Saracen station were the slowest to return tapes. They didn't have to pay the late fines.

Lyons travelled from house to house where he dropped off and collected the clunky black VHS tapes of the latest releases. He got to know many people in Milton and, like a fishwife, he loved to spend time chatting and garnering gossip and scandal.

A pirate video – such as 1986's big hits like *Top Gun* and *Crocodile Dundee* – cost up to £3 to rent and dozens of tapes went out every day. It was a booming little enterprise and, of course, no tax was paid on the cash income, which was topped up by claiming state benefits, so there was some serious cash coming in.

While Eddie had become a video pirate, the less smart but more violent Johnny earned spectacular hauls from his smash-and-grab ram-raids. He acquired thousands of pounds worth of stolen stock from city-centre boutiques where only footballers and drug dealers could afford the ticket prices.

When the Lyons needed to shift their booty, it was easy. Bargain hunters in Milton became very grateful. As in virtually every housing scheme, being known as the people who could get stuff cheap brought with it some popularity. One resident who lived in the same close as Lyons had a couple of old-fashioned detective friends who served with the Serious Crime Squad. On a quiet night shift, clutching a bottle of Bell's or Famous Grouse, they often popped in to see their old pal. After one of these visits, Lyons came to the door and sheepishly asked his neighbour to warn him whenever his police friends were coming back. Lyons was twitchy about the detectives being so close to his home because of his ducking and diving. Having the Serious Crime Squad in his close was clearly a bit uncomfortable. The neighbour recalled, 'There was always something going on with one of the Lyons. One night two cops came and hit the door looking for Johnny. I told them he lived in the other side of Milton. I had no idea he was actually hiding in my coal bunker. Eddie and Johnny were very close. Johnny was the mental case who would do serious damage. Michael wasn't much better. Eddie was perceived as the puppet master who would get his daft brothers to do his dirty work when required then act all innocent when it suited him.'

By the end of the 1980s, Eddie and Josephine were settled in Milton with their five children. They had now moved from the Liddesdale Road flat to a house in Torogay Street. Later, bulletproof windows would be installed at the property.

They were the type of family that most sensible people wanted nothing to do with. The boys were nice lads but, having the father and uncles they did, some of their friends feared for their future. However, even those who knew them well could not have foreseen how badly things would turn out.

Unfortunately for the rest of Milton – where many of the streets bear the names of idyllic Scottish islands – the Lyons were not going anywhere. At least not for a while . . .

2

Scrap and Smack

While the Lyons family were being escorted out of Cadder in the wake of the Moran feud, the Daniel family had already carved out a much worse reputation for criminality and violence in north Glasgow.

Jamie Daniel – one of ten children – was born in October 1957, four months before Eddie Lyons entered the world. He and his siblings were raised in grinding poverty in the city's Possilpark district, known as Possil, which is around a mile south of Milton. While many areas of Glasgow were ravaged by post-industrial decline, Possil suffered more than most. At one time it was an idyllic suburban pasture which in 1872 had a population of just 10 people. That exploded to over 10,000 within two decades thanks to Walter Macfarlane's massive Saracen foundry – 80 acres in size – which created ornate, decorative ironworks for export around the British Empire and beyond. The Saracen foundry finally closed in the mid 1960s, leaving an employment vacuum that has never been filled. The respectable, working-class neighbourhood soon became a byword for inner-city crime, rotting social housing and despair.

In 1967, when Jamie was aged 10, his father David, a former coal miner and labourer, died of cancer. His widowed mother Agnes, then just 41 years old, was left to raise her large brood alone. It was a brutal, harsh existence. The family's cramped tenement flat, now demolished, was at 8 Finlas Street at its corner with Fruin Street in a bleak part of Possil known to residents and police officers as 'The Jungle' or 'The Jungo', a nickname which didn't require an explanation.

Jamie started off as a violent, petty criminal involved in car thefts, loan-sharking and stealing scrap metal. He was part of a streetwise family of scavengers who were battling for survival. But, in 1969, two years after the death of their father, the second-eldest brother, Billy, battered a policeman to death. George Gates, 50, was a security guard at a colliery in Stepps, Lanarkshire, and had only been a special constable for four months when he was killed.

The off-duty officer had bought a late-night newspaper and, while he made his way home, he witnessed Billy, then aged 19, along with 17-year-old friends James Moffat and Robert Brown, stealing copper cable worth £53 from waste ground in Possil's Closeburn Street. He was standing with his hands in his pockets when Billy lashed out with a heavy, wooden table leg. He delivered at least five thudding blows to the police officer's head. Billy then melted into the gathering crowd and stood and watched as the ambulance arrived and his blood-soaked victim lying in the gutter was taken to Stobhill Hospital, where he died.

The subsequent trial at the High Court in Glasgow bore two of the hallmarks seen in some of the family's future brushes with the justice system – witness intimidation and an attempt to buy the right result.

Three men stood trial – Billy Daniel plus Moffat and Brown. One 17-year-old female witness told the jurors that she had been warned to keep her mouth shut by youths – possibly some of those in the dock – in the moments after the fatal attack. For Billy however, her evidence was nowhere near as damaging as that given by his two co-accused friends. They had told the police everything. While all three were on remand together within the brick walls of the forbidding Victorian-era prison of Barlinnie in the city's east end, Billy decided to wage a campaign of threats, pleas and bribes in a bid to force them to change their statements.

First, Billy offered to pay Moffat's mother £10 a week for life if he lied and admitted the killing, thereby absolving him. It was a significant sum in those days but one which clearly didn't take inflation into account. When that offer was rejected, Moffat was then warned that, if he 'grassed', he would be attacked either in custody or on the outside. Moffat was sent a magazine with the photo of a man whose face had been marked with a crudely drawn slash mark. Other messages intercepted by the authorities included the following written threat: 'Moffat and Brown were born two grasses but their days are marked. They grass a poor, lonely guy for murder. If that guy gets done he will do life.' It was in vain. Billy, then aged 20, was found guilty while trial judge Lord Johnston directed the jury to find Moffat and Brown not guilty.

Billy's mother Agnes said after the verdict, 'I am heartbroken. Since Billy's father died of cancer two years ago, he had been the breadwinner for the family. He always had big ideas and had started his own scrap business. I thought this would keep him fully employed and out of trouble.'

The jailing of his elder brother impacted heavily on 12-year-old Jamie. The experience would also have helped shape his visceral, lifelong hatred for those who co-operated with the police.

Seven years later, a second tragedy struck the family when one of the brothers – Robert – drowned in July 1976. In a remarkable echo of Billy's murder of the police officer, it happened while Robert was also in the process of stealing scrap metal and when he died he was aged 20, the same age Billy had been at the time of his jailing.

Robert and three accomplices, aged 19, 21 and 22, had driven into a restricted area of Rothesay Dock in the shipbuilding town of Clydebank, a few miles west of Glasgow. Police swooped on the gang as they were in the process of the hard and dirty job of gathering their illicit haul. Robert, however, had no intention of joining his brother in prison. While the other three men were handcuffed by the police officers and bundled into the van, Robert had leapt into the River Clyde. Even though it was July, the dirty, dark water was cold and unforgiving. He swam furiously towards the opposite bank but the glimmering lights of Renfrew to the south did not appear to get any closer. Halfway across, as his limbs became leaden and the bitter cold sapped away his remaining energy, he was dragged under the inky black surface.

Justice for his friends was swift. The very next morning – eight days before Robert's body was pulled from the Clyde – his three fellow scavengers were convicted of theft at Dumbarton Sheriff Court. The punishment meted out to two of them was never recorded but the third, Paul Fitzpatrick, was fined £40 which, although a substantial sum of money in those days, was obviously insignificant when measured against the cost of the wasted life of Robert, a father whose two sons would never get to know him. Robert Jr was 18 months old when his dad drowned, while James had not yet reached his first birthday. Their mother, a young sewing machinist called Ann McGeouch, had met Robert Sr while she lived in The Jungle's Fruin Place. She was now another young widow.

Some in the family firmly believe that the pursuing officers deliberately caused Robert's death or that they could have tried harder to save him, which may help explain the source of their long-lasting, anti-police hatred.

Some officers cruelly coined the sarcastic and hateful nickname 'Mark Spitz' for Robert, after the legendary US swimmer of the era. One retired detective said, 'The Daniel family despised the police. The feeling was mutual.'

One of Daniel's sisters, Annette, also followed a path of career criminality. Scrap metal was for the boys. Annette had her eye on the glittering retail environment. Petty shoplifting led to a long rap sheet and evolved into a very lucrative and well-organised 'business'.

Annette formed Scotland's largest shoplifting gang with Jean McGovern, a member of another north Glasgow crime family. Their ever-changing team of thieves, mainly respectably dressed middle-aged women, targeted high streets across the UK to the despair of retailers, in brazen, systematic and relentless organised thefts. Thousands of pounds worth of stock can be swiped in a matter of minutes. Any other shoplifter who encroached on Annette and Jean's domain was soon scared off by the names of the two families.

The Daniel family arrived in Glasgow at the end of the century when Daniel's great-grandfather John Daniel, born in 1869, left behind the rural Aberdeenshire farming village of Methlick for work as a railway stoker in the industrial power-house of Glasgow.

He married Martha Potter in January 1900 in his adopted city. He was killed the following year, aged 31, when he was crushed to death between the buffers of a railway engine and carriage while coupling them at Parkhead Forge. John left behind a 10-month-old son, David, who grew up to become a labourer in steelworks and on the docks. David's wife Christina Reid gave birth to Jamie Daniel's father, also David, in 1925.

In an area dependent on the metal industry, the family's scavenging for scrap should come as no surprise. Foundries, along with shipbuilding, railway locomotive manufacture and numerous other industries, had turned Glasgow into the second city of the British Empire with the fourth-largest population in Europe behind London, Paris and Berlin. The foundry industry was decimated by both the Second World War – when iron procurement became a priority for insatiable military rather than ornate civic projects – and the decline of the Empire.

While the death of heavy industry – accelerated by Margaret Thatcher's Conservative government of the 1980s – played a part in the problem, another blight was about to spread through-out these same bruised communities. In the late 1970s, Glasgow had perhaps 50 heroin addicts. The head of Strathclyde Police drug squad, Jack Beattie, used to claim that he knew each of these rare individuals by name. The beginning of the 1980s marked an explosion of heroin importation that redrew Britain's urban landscape. Glasgow's few dozen junkies soon became several hundred. Before long, the grey army of addicts num-bered many, many thousands. The city's ever-rising heroin death toll became almost as common a feature in the news-papers as the match results of Celtic and Rangers football teams. Countless parents mourned the loss of a son or daughter while society, the police and courts had to learn how to cope with the heroin-fuelled crime wave which swept the city.

One former resident said, 'I grew up in Possil in what became known as The Jungle. While, for many, it seems Possil was an idyllic place it was far from that from the early 80s onwards. The heart was pulled out of Possil with the closure of the remaining industry in the area. The area in which I stayed became a dumping ground for so-called problem families. The houses were allowed to fall into decay. The fabric of the area was allowed to decay. Heroin ravaged a generation.'

Jamie Daniel soon realised there was much more money to be made in smack than there was in scrap. He and his brothers flaunted their sudden wealth in the ultimate boy-racer cars of the time – Ford Escort XR3is and RS Turbos. Often they would tow expensive speedboats behind them, a peculiar sight in their landlocked jungle.

Possil was a hard place and few would challenge the Daniel family's dominance although there were other families and individuals who did not shrink away from them. The biggest early threat to their position came when a feud developed between the Daniels and drowned brother Robert's fellow scrap thief Paul Fitzpatrick who was in league with another Possil criminal called Derek Ferguson, nicknamed Deco.

Many years later, in 2011, Ferguson's name and photo – distinctive due to part of an ear being missing – were released by the Serious and Organised Crime Agency in its list of the UK's ten most wanted criminals thought to be hiding in Spain. Ferguson was being hunted over the fatal shooting of barman Thomas Cameron, 49, in 2007. Police also suspect that he killed Billy Bates, a 43-year-old heroin-dealing former friend, also from Possil, whose body was found in an oil drum in the River Clyde weeks after the shooting.

The feud between the Daniel family and Fitzpatrick and Ferguson soon fizzled out but it illustrated that, like any criminals, they would always come up against someone brave enough – or reckless enough – to take them on, no matter how big their reputation might be. However, they remained the most dangerous beasts in this particular jungle and commanded its streets with fear. They could plunge their corner of Possil into darkness as they had a key for a pavement box which allowed them to turn off the street lighting, often to give cover for discreet nocturnal meetings and plots.

At the beginning of the 1980s, Jamie Daniel was only in his mid 20s but he was at the vanguard of the incredibly lucrative new heroin phenomenon which redrew the UK crime map by forcing traditional criminals either to embrace the drugs trade or to wither away while their rivals grew rich. Young men like Daniel had no intention of being left behind. However, he learned an early lesson in the consequences of getting caught.

When the stabbed Eddie Lyons was being escorted out of Cadder and preparing to testify in court, Daniel had spent a year in his cell at HMP Coldingley near Woking, in Surrey, 420 miles south of Glasgow. In June 1983, seven years after the drowning of Robert, he had been convicted of heroin smuggling at Chichester Crown Court along with his co-accused Ijaz Ahmed, 41, also from Glasgow, who was jailed for eight years.

By this time, Daniel was the father of two children – a son, Francis Green, who was then nine months old, and a three-year-old daughter, Kelly Green, who became known by her nickname of Kelly Bo. Given the string of children he fathered to different women in later years, it seems unlikely Daniel would have played happy families with his children's mother, a dental receptionist called June Green who was originally from Fruin Street, had he remained free.

A 1983 report in the *Sunday Mail* newspaper by veteran journalist Nick Hunter offered the only brief record of Daniel's fate. The report stated:

A new drugs squad has been set up. And – unlike the police – they are not restricted by force boundaries.

The highly trained seven-man squad are Customs and Excise officers based in Glasgow. They have been brought together despite massive cuts in Customs service.

Already the squad have scored a major success in the international fight against hard drugs.

Last week, in a case so far unreported in Scotland, two

Glasgow men were jailed for a total of 12 years at Chichester Crown Court.

Ijaz Ahmed, 41, of Willowbank Crescent, got eight years after being found guilty of three charges of drugs smuggling and James Daniel, 25, of Finlas Street, was sentenced to four years on one charge of drug smuggling through Heathrow Airport.

The squad, while working closely with local customs officers and police drugs squads, have the whole of Britain as their beat.

Remarkably, Jamie Daniel's name would not appear again in the media for another 20 long years.

3

Wee Tough Guy

Eddie Lyons had come close to meeting a violent end twice in his 20s but in 1991, when he was 33, death was not to be avoided again. His and Josephine's third son Garry had died.

The brave boy had lost his determined fight against leukaemia, cancer of the blood. His disease had been diagnosed at the age of two. He managed to cling to life just long enough to celebrate his eighth birthday before he succumbed exactly one month later. Garry underwent all sorts of operations and had chemotherapy treatment which caused his hair to fall out. He had a tumour removed from his stomach but the cancer was everywhere.

It would have taken a heart of flint not to feel sympathy for his mother and father, in raw agony as they watched their child's miniature coffin descend into the steely, winter earth. A few days before Christmas 1991, Eddie Lyons stood in solidarity with family and friends, their ranks swollen by others from the Milton community – good people who wanted to pay their respects including neighbours, teachers and police officers. Not only had two parents lost a son but Eddie Jr, then aged 12, Steven, who was a year younger, Ashley, aged six, and two-year-old Christopher had lost a brother.

The people of Milton acted with a spontaneous and overwhelming kindness of spirit. As the family was paralysed with grief, they took solace from the soothing words and deeds of those around them. A procession of well-wishers made their way to the family's home in Torogay Street to do whatever they could to help them cope with the devastating loss. A brass plaque in memory of the lost pupil was unveiled in the foyer of the now-demolished St Augustine's Primary School.

The night before his burial, Garry's body was taken from his home to St Augustine's chapel where the vigil was held. The priest's soft assurances about Garry's suffering being over and of how he would find eternal peace in heaven brought comfort to those of Christian faith.

The death of Garry also seemed to mark a turning point for Lyons and what the future held for him. He wished God had taken him instead and many really did believe him when he said, through his tears, that he was going to change his ways – there would be no more scams, no more violence. The man who could cause trouble in an empty house vowed that he was going to become a better person – it was the least he could do for his little fighter. To those around him, it seemed as though he was sincere and his resolutions were not some attempt to con people. As the years passed, that sincerity seemed to lessen and then gradually wash away – eventually to be forgotten.

Many who knew Lyons remain puzzled. Was his resolution merely caused by the emotions he had felt over Garry's passing away? Or perhaps, even with his very best intentions, as life eventually began to get back to normal, he was ultimately unable to change. Perhaps he didn't try hard enough.

One former friend recalls the poignancy. He said, 'Lyons said, at the time, that God should have taken him instead of Garry. That comment stuck with me for years. Garry was a lovely boy – they all were at that age until their father got his claws into them. He said, at that point, that he would just rent out his videos and stay out of serious trouble. This might sound harsh but, if I ever saw him again, I'd tell him the only good thing to come out of such a tragedy was that it prevented Garry becoming tainted by his influence.'

As if the premature death of a young child was not enough to deal with, Lyons was presented with the problem as to where his son should be buried. The question had not arisen because of some familial quandary over the location of the plots of previously deceased relatives. Rather, Lyons harboured a genuine fear of what might happen to his son's grave at the hands of his many enemies. The obvious resting place was the vast expanse encompassing the trio of cemeteries which were sandwiched between Milton to the west and Cadder to the south. They were just a mile or so from Garry's Torogay Street home. But due to the long shadow cast by the family's violent feuds, Lambhill was ruled out over fears that Garry's plot could be desecrated by any number of those who still held grudges. Instead, the funeral cortege made its way up Balmore Road towards a small cemetery in Bishopbriggs, which is a well-to-do suburb past the city's northern boundary. The Bishopbriggs graveyard was twice as far away from Torogay Street as Lambhill cemetery was. For Lyons to be confronted with such a dark dilemma – being forced to ask himself where his child could rest in peace – was part of the bitter legacy from those past petty feuds that had spiralled into bloody violence.

Most of the mourners who attended Garry's funeral were oblivious to the reason behind the choice of cemetery. All they could see was a family tortured by grief. Through a blur of tears, they watched as Garry was laid to rest, his grave marked by an imposing, black granite headstone, inlaid with a photo of him with his parents. It was also inscribed with the epitaph: 'To the wee tough guy . . . Love You Forever'.

A friend said, 'What it said on the gravestone was spot on. He was very ill but he was never wrapped up in cotton wool – he had an amazing spirit.'

Each year on 7 November – Garry's birthday – his parents, brothers, sister and other family members gathered at the graveside to remember happy times with the innocent little boy who lay in peace . . . or at least he would do so for the next 15 years.

4

Eddie's Club

The middle-aged man in the dinner suit shrieked as the blade sliced through the smooth black suit, white cotton shirt and pink flesh of his back. Dripping blood, Bobby Dempster scrambled over the wall of the tenement backcourt to safety. The detour on the way to a city-centre boxing show had ended in an ambush.

The man's friend – and no relation – was James Dempster, nicknamed 'Demmy'. He was less fortunate and, instead of facing a knife, he was blasted at close range with a gun.

Demmy, then in his mid 30s, was also known as 'The Marshal' in the grim world of illegal dog fighting which secretly flourished in north Glasgow. A friend of the Lyons family, he had played a prominent role at Garry's funeral. He drove ahead to ensure other traffic respectfully allowed the cortege a smooth journey to the cemetery in Bishopbriggs. Now he had taken a bullet from the Lyons. He managed to scramble back to his Ford Escort XR2i and drive himself to the A&E department at Stobhill Hospital.

Earlier that night in 1992, Demmy had told two friends – one of whom was Bobby Dempster – that he was going to deal with Johnny Lyons. He would fight him on the street, one-on-one with no interference and no weapons – what is known in Glasgow as 'a square go'.

The sobbing sincerity of Eddie Lyons Sr following the death of his son Garry had not lasted long. Within a year of Garry's funeral, the family were back to their old ways. Yet again, Eddie was the cause of the violence. He was a natural troublemaker who often stirred things up and enjoyed playing people against each other, often for no apparent reason. Eddie and Johnny had mocked Demmy by branding him as a lightweight, a figure of fun. Word got back to Demmy who warned that he would take it as a joke – this time. Eddie wasn't willing to back down and the jibes around Milton continued. Demmy's simmering anger reached boiling point during a phone call with Eddie. Demmy made some comments that the Lyons were not in his league and he was willing to forgive and forget. It was his way of giving Eddie a way out, a chance to back down peacefully, but Eddie just couldn't help himself. The gist of Eddie's goading taunts was that Johnny would sort out Demmy who angrily responded by telling his tormentor that suited him fine. As he drove to the boxing show, he took a detour to Johnny's haunt at the corner of Liddesdale Road and Scalpay Place. Demmy surmised that Johnny would lose face and run away – if he was stupid enough to still be there. There was little doubt that, in a straight fight, 26-year-old Johnny would have been easily defeated by the older man. That might be why Johnny had a different idea. It did not involve a square go but an ambush.

Johnny was with two youths. One of them was an impressionable boy nicknamed 'Jolly' due to his surname of Rodgers and the other was Victor Gallagher Jr whose dad, Victor Sr, was a brother of Josephine Lyons, the wife of Eddie Sr. The two youngsters had the blades while Johnny had the gun. When Demmy pulled up at the corner, Johnny was grinning from the vantage point of a first-floor window of a tenement close. Demmy bounded up the stairs to reach his target only to be thrown backwards by the blast which reverberated around the gloomy hallway. The gun was pointed at him a second time, at point blank range, but it misfired with a click.

Meanwhile, Dempster in his penguin suit fled through the back and over the wall. Gallagher – who inflicted the knife wound – was ignorant of who the men were which would explain his bravado as he bragged about what he had done. Not long afterwards, Demmy moved out of Glasgow but his burning hatred of the family barely diminished.

Others with close connections to the Lyons family were also

involved in the most serious of criminality. Peter Hetherington was the husband of Eddie's sister Victoria. In the spring of 1992, a 21-year-old security guard called Derek Ure was shot dead during an armed robbery in the upper Clydeside town of Greenock. Hetherington, then aged 31 and also from Milton, was arrested but walked free from the High Court in Paisley due to a lack of evidence. His alleged accomplice Mark Vass secured a not proven verdict – a unique aspect of Scots Law which critics believe allows far too many guilty people to go free. With no regard to the murdered man's devastated family, Vass smirked as he also walked away as a free man. Vass was also suspected of the 1991 murder of 23-year-old Andrew Smith in Maryhill but never charged. However, three years after his not proven verdict, a different kind of justice caught up with him when he was shot dead at the age of 33 by rival criminal Eamonn Docherty.

Some in the police and the underworld suspected that a third masked man who took part in the Greenock armed-robbery-turned-murder was Johnny Lyons but there was not enough evidence to prosecute him.

Eddie was by now a prominent figure in Milton who thrived in his role of self-styled community leader and busybody – a Mr Fix-It with his fingers in many pies and his nose in other people's business. His love of gossiping meant that he was skilled at picking up snippets of information from one person and then adding to it from someone else, eventually building a full picture. Going in and out of people's homes while renting out pirate VHS videos was the perfect cover for finding out what was going on.

One man who Eddie frequently spoke to was community police officer PC John Cameron. The two men's unlikely bond would grow even stronger over the years as would Lyons' relationship with another community police officer, PC Peter Glancey, who was also a youth football coach. PC Glancey was a leading light with the respected north Glasgow-based Arsenal Boys Club which shares a name and colours with the famous London club although it has no official links.

Many in Milton were certain that Eddie was a registered police informant. Even if it was on a less formal basis in those early years, they had no doubt that selective information was whispered into the ear of certain police officers. It's not uncommon for informants to use police officers – unwitting or otherwise – to do their bidding. Why turn on your rivals with knives and guns when passing the right information can inflict damage like serious jail time? To a police officer, winning enough trust to elicit intelligence while simultaneously trying to avoid being used to further the informant's own criminality has always been a tricky balancing act.

Eddie once approached an associate about the presence of heroin dealers in the area. He leaned in and made it simple, 'Tell me where the stash is and I'll tell John.'

Eddie's closeness to PCs Cameron, Glancey and several other officers led to him being sneeringly nicknamed 'the special constable'. Drinkers in Milton pubs would balance an empty pint glass on their head and, to the roar of alcohol-fuelled laughter, do a mocking impression of Eddie by pretending it was a police blue light.

Whatever the roots of the special relationship between Eddie and the police, it would have been largely unremarkable were it not for the seismic event which took place in the aftermath of Garry's funeral when sympathy and goodwill towards the grieving father was in abundance. That was when Eddie took his first step towards legitimacy – with the official backing of Strathclyde Police.

Colston Secondary School in Springburn had been built to educate the children of the workers who had historically made the area Europe's largest manufacturer of railway locomotives. As the industry died, falling pupil numbers led to its closure in 1989. Four years later, the empty building was razed to the ground in a fire attack. Half a mile away from the school was its annexe at 342 Ashgill Road which was shared with Chirnsyde Primary School. The annexe was a significant building with a large sports hall, offices, changing rooms, kitchen, canteen, gym, steam room and computer room. Glasgow City Council later built a floodlit, all-weather sports area on the expanse of open ground which also included a car park and 1970s-style red blaes football pitch.

The building was owned by the council but had lain unused since 1990. It was suggested that this prominent venue in the heart of Milton could be put to good use by Strathclyde Police's community police officers. PC Cameron was instrumental in the process. The plan was that the building could become a drop-in centre for youths. It was an inexpensive and admirable way of building bridges with bored teenagers by giving them a place where they could gather, away from street corners.

By the early 1990s, the venue had been unofficially renamed. It was known simply as 'Eddie's Club'. Eddie had been promoted by the police as the ideal person to become a youth leader. During these early years, the centre was open between 5 p.m. and 10 p.m., seven night a week. For Eddie, it was perfect as he strove to be regarded as an upstanding pillar of the community.

From the outset, there was little observance of red tape as local kids – the sons of Eddie and their pals – had sleepovers in the cavernous building. In later years, raves were also staged which despite the abundance of the 'love drug' ecstasy didn't prevent teenage testosterone leading to violent clashes between the Milton boys and incomers from adjacent Springburn.

In the strict territorial divisions of Glasgow's countless youth gangs, it had become clear from the outset that those from the 'back end' of Milton or elsewhere were not welcome at Eddie's Club. Liddesdale Road runs west to east through Milton. It was deemed to be the dividing line with those streets to the north of it being in the scheme's 'back end'. Chirnsyde lies south-east of Liddesdale Road and is fleetingly visible to passengers looking out the left-hand side of the dozens of daily express trains going from Glasgow Queen Street to Edinburgh. It's as if it were a strategically placed fort for the Club Boys, sitting inside the border of their domain. This was never going to be an inclusive place for all the community. Darker stories emerged including a claim that a teenage girl was gang raped in the toilets. The incident was reported to the police but the alleged victim refused to make a complaint. It was ironic in the extreme that what started out as a police initiative to tackle youth crime would become a breeding ground of serious criminality, a production line for the Lyons crime clan with a notoriety that eventually spread nationwide and overseas. Before long, some in the community viewed this strange, police-backed club as little more than a 'gang hut' for Eddie, his violent teenage boys and their friends.

Around 180 of PC Glancey's Arsenal lads, aged from 8 to 16, used Chirnsyde's facilities. For many who already had little trust of the police, this connection was of no great surprise. Eddie Lyons Jr, then 14, and Steven, 13, were founder members of the 'Club Boys' which took its name from their youth club HQ. Those in the gang included Ross Monaghan, Liam Boyle, Andrew 'Dumbo' Gallacher, Paul McGuinness, Charles McMurray and others who would go on to commit horrific acts of violence and carry out major drug deals connected to, on behalf of or alongside members of the Lyons family.

The council charged a nominal £1-a-year rent which suited the officials because, in return, the community had use of a facility at minimal cost to council budgets and, ultimately, the taxpayer. It would certainly have cost much more to have staffed the venue with council employees. When PC Cameron vouched for Eddie, it carried a lot of weight. Without police backing, it is inconceivable that he would have been handed the keys of a community venue which attracted many young people. At that time, most senior officers would have been oblivious to the idea that they were creating a monster which could come back to haunt the force.

As members of the community later campaigned relentlessly for the removal of Eddie, the police response was muted. How could they admit that Eddie's Club was a toxic breeding ground for crime and violence given that the force had helped to make it happen?

Up until 1995, Eddie ran the centre without any public money. His kitchen in Torogay Street was piled high with cans of fizzy drinks which he sold in the club to raise funds. A coin-operated pool table was installed. The kids occasionally packed shoppers' bags at an Asda supermarket in nearby Robroyston. He and others volunteered their time.

In 1995 there came another major development when Lyons got his first taste of taxpayers' cash thanks to the now defunct Urban Aid regeneration fund for areas of deprivation, which bankrolled it for four years. Lyons was now backed by the police and funded by the taxpayer. He was about to fortify his position by winning political support, specifically the backing of the Labour Party which had long enjoyed a stranglehold on the city. In Glasgow, it was joked that the party's votes were weighed, not counted. Put a monkey in a red rosette and it would win. But this time it was closer than normal with just 34 votes separating Labour's Ellen Hurcombe and the Scottish National Party candidate to be elected councillor for the Ashfield ward.

For Lyons, the result of the 1998 by-election – prompted by the death of the incumbent councillor, 66-year-old former schoolteacher Allan McGarrity while on holiday in Spain – was excellent news. In Hurcombe, he had a loyal ally who had proclaimed, during her campaign, 'I know this area from the ground up. I live here and work here. I know what the problems are and I will be fighting for the area from the inside out.'

Living in the heart of Milton, Hurcombe also knew Eddie and his family. She often received lifts from Lyons in his BMW and the Chirnsyde minibus and, for many years, she faithfully held her surgeries at Chirnsyde where people could come to air their concerns.

One constituent wrote upwards of 50 letters to Hurcombe over the following years, each one raising concerns about Eddie at Chirnsyde and fears about children's safety. He has yet to receive a single reply.

Seven months after Hurcombe's election to Glasgow City Council, tragedy again visited the family when Eddie's brother Michael died of a crack cocaine overdose following a police raid on a drugs factory in a 14th-floor flat in Castlebay Drive in Milton.

When officers with a search warrant burst through the door, it became apparent that 34-year-old Michael had something in his mouth and was not willing to give it up. An ambulance was called but Michael did not respond to the two paramedics who suspected that he was feigning unconsciousness to buy time. He was taken to the A&E unit of Stobhill Hospital where Dr Annette Barnes was given the task of removing the suspected drugs package from his tightly clenched jaws. Two different attempts were made to prise open his mouth but to no avail. Dr Barnes then administered 10mg dose of diazepam, a powerful sedative and muscle relaxant. It had a speedy effect and Michael's jaws dropped open, allowing a nurse to snatch a cellophane bag from his mouth. Dr Barnes administered another drug, flumazenil, in a bid to reverse the effects of the diazepam but Michael suffered a seizure. This prompted the medic to administer a third drug, naloxone, which is often given to those suffering from overdoses. In Michael's case it had no effect. The situation had become a life-and-death emergency and a crash team was called for. They worked tirelessly but the patient's condition continued to deteriorate. At 10.35 p.m. on Sunday, 18 April 1999 – around 34 hours after the police raid – Michael was pronounced dead after suffering heart failure.

His death prompted outrage, perhaps driven only by the pain of their loss, from members of the Lyons family. They very vocally, albeit incorrectly, held the police responsible. One of the police officers who led the raid had been raised in Milton where his parents still lived in Berneray Street. Threats were made that the officer, or his relatives, would face retribution for Michael's death. An approach was made to Eddie to urge his family to keep the peace. He agreed. Some police officers were taken aback at this tactic. They advocated a more robust approach against a criminal rabble uttering threats against an officer and his family, rather than politely asking them to please behave.

Just 12 days after Michael's death, Eddie managed to put his grieving to one side to take part in another incredible public relations opportunity for him and his club. On 6 May 1999, Scotland went to the polls to elect the members of its first parliament in 292 years. In the days leading up to the inaugural election, STV's evening news bulletins carried a series of reports that covered the key issues of the election. Titled 'Holyrood Hopes', the final programme, broadcast on 30 April, was about crime and drugs. Milton was chosen as the type of community that would illustrate the problems and Eddie was selected as an example of someone who was making a difference. The item, seen across central Scotland, began with footage of grinning Eddie playing table tennis in Chirnsyde with his nine-year-old son Christopher and three other children.

The voice-over introduced him, saying, 'Eddie Lyons, a 41-year-old father of five, knows the scheme's problems all too well.'

Eddie then told the reporter, 'It was over two weeks ago we got a phone call from one of the members of the family concerning my brother Michael who overdosed after a drugs bust at the back end of Milton. It transpired that Michael tried to swallow a package which we believe was coke which is basically new to the area of Milton. Michael died roughly two days after on the Sunday.'

Against a backdrop of happy children playing in the sports hall, the voice-over added, 'Eddie's a leading light in the Chirnsyde Community Initiative, a Scottish Office-funded project which has 300 members aged six to 65. It's a thriving, boisterous place, run by local people. Eddie believes such projects are the way ahead.'

Now getting into his stride, Eddie continued, 'Local people are definitely the answer. I mean outsiders, people who work nine to five, I mean they can dictate what they would like to see but at the same time they don't live in the area.'

It concluded with the reporter's comment, 'People in Milton say the scheme's being ruined by a small minority. That's undoubtedly true but it's a huge problem and one the MSPs must target.'

Some Milton residents almost choked on their tea at what they had just seen and heard. Here was Lyons being given a platform to opine about the problem of drugs yet days earlier his own dealer brother had died after a police raid on what was possibly the city's first crack factory, based in the heart of their community. It was outrageous that Lyons had been held up as some kind of expert on how to tackle crime and drugs.

The TV reporter's final comment about a 'small minority' ruining the area brought a wry smile from the same shocked viewers who agreed and could readily identify them – Lyons, his family and their crew.

When the true cause of Michael's death eventually emerged more than two and a half years later, any lingering nonsense about the police having had a hand in it was forgotten. A Fatal Accident Inquiry carried out by Sheriff Craig A. L. Scott established that he 'had ingested approximately 13 to 14 grams of crack cocaine. A single gram of that drug is a potentially fatal overdose.'

'Looking at the matter as a whole,' Sheriff Scott continued, 'it seems to me that the police, the emergency services and the hospital staff all performed to the very best of their ability. It is difficult to escape the obvious conclusion that the only reasonable precaution whereby the death of Michael Lyons might have been avoided would have involved the deceased himself in refraining from consuming such a quantity of lethal drugs in the form of crack cocaine.'

Behind the stark and inescapable legal conclusion was a more significant revelation. Michael Lyons had become Scotland's first crack cocaine death victim. In an era where the noxious brown powder of heroin was king among Glasgow's thousands of drug addicts, crack would thankfully remain rare for many more years. Behind yet another drugs death was the inevitable personal sadness. Michael had left behind a 13-year-old son, Michael Jr, who sobbed in isolation at his father's funeral. His uncle Eddie, with a straight face, earnestly warned mourners about the dangers of drugs. It was decided that heart-broken young Michael was to be raised by his uncle Johnny, the violent armed robber and drug dealer.

Four months after Michael's death came another important development of 1999 when Eddie first received funding from his Chirnsyde landlord Glasgow City Council. His brother's dramatic death had done nothing to stop the relentless march of the community leader – now 'as seen on TV'. It didn't appear to trouble the authorities either as, officially named and constituted with funding from the council's education department, the Chirnsyde Community Initiative was born on 5 August 1999.

Eddie was in charge and he cobbled together a 'management committee' which was required as a funding condition but, in reality, it remained his fiefdom. No matter what the shiny new sign said, to taxi drivers and residents it was Eddie's Club. As the 'co-ordinator', Eddie took a full-time salary. Campaigners were later told that an advert had been placed seeking a co-ordinator and, after candidates had been interviewed, lucky Eddie was hired. A copy of the job advert has never been produced. What qualifications he supposedly had for the new post remain a mystery. Also put on the payroll was Eddie's wife Josephine and her sister Julie Murphy – a near neighbour of Councillor Hurcombe. PC Cameron proudly took up the post as Chirnsyde's chairman.

In those embryonic days, PC Cameron was photographed inside Chirnsyde for local newspaper *The Northender*. As he sat grinning on a rowing machine, he was flanked by then veteran Labour MP for Glasgow Maryhill, Maria Fyfe, who was perched on an exercise bike. Completing the trio was Strathclyde Police's then Assistant Chief Constable Colin McKerracher, who later became Chief Constable of Grampian Police in Aberdeen.

The accompanying article stated: 'The Chirnsyde Community Initiative is an example of partnerships aimed at solving local problems. As chair of the management committee, Constable John Cameron and others, with funding from the Scottish Office and elsewhere, transformed an old dilapidated sports pavilion in Milton, Glasgow, into an attractive resource for the local community.'

A visit from such senior police officers and politicians gave

Lyons massive kudos in official circles and he lapped it up. An Edinburgh newspaper carried a report about adult learning and used Josephine as a positive example. She told how she landed her Chirnsyde job after gaining computer skills at college. The article made no mention of the fact her husband ran the place.

Despite the glowing media coverage, parents who knew exactly what type of people Eddie and his family were chose not to allow their children to go near the place. This led to Eddie asking awkward questions about their non-attendance, causing some parents to feel that they had no choice but to capitulate, albeit with a sense of guilty unease.

Secretary of State for Scotland and the Labour MP for Glasgow Anniesland, the bookish Donald Dewar, had now ushered in the new parliament in Edinburgh following a referendum brought by the landslide general election victory of Tony Blair in 1997. Among the intake of 129 MSPs in the inaugural Scottish parliament was Labour's Patricia Ferguson who landed almost 50 per cent of the votes in the Glasgow Maryhill constituency which includes Milton. That same year, Dewar launched SIPs – social inclusion partnerships – which distributed a multimillion-pound fund intended to help society's most needy, the socially excluded and poverty-stricken, often found in places like the post-industrial schemes of Glasgow.

Eddie was near the front of the queue and soon even more public money came pouring into Chirnsyde via the North Glasgow SIP. In 1999, a cheque for £33,298 arrived. The next year, it was £41,777. Between 1999 and 2006, Chirnsyde raked in a total of £280,768 from SIPs. In the myriad and ever-changing sources of public funding, it may never be known exactly how much was poured in to Eddie's Club but at least £1.4million was eventually accounted for. To Eddie, it must have felt like a dream – money and respectability at a single stroke.

Others in the community regarded it as a nightmare. A man whose family had caused terror and violence for years and continued to do so had been handed their community centre and legitimised with the official backing of Strathclyde Police, the Labour Party, Glasgow City Council and vast sums of public money. Not to mention a prime-time telly plug.

It should have been inconceivable for him to have been held up as a role model for youths by such institutions while he was soaking up public money. Would a man like this have been installed to run a community centre in an affluent middle-class community, no questions asked? Not a chance.

On the brink of the new millennium in the brave new devolved Scotland, Eddie had become bombproof. All he had to do was keep his head down and behave.

5

Fields of Dreams

Johnny McLean liked the view from his living-room window. The green expanse of St Augustine's playing fields was an oasis in the heart of Milton. He and his wife had raised nine children in their council house on Westray Street, overlooking the lush green sports grounds. Thousands of kids – not least Scotland, Celtic and Liverpool legend Kenny Dalglish – first played the beautiful game at St Augustine's. But the playing fields were under threat. In 1998, McLean opened a letter from Glasgow City Council. It contained devastating news. The council planned to sell the land to a developer for £1million. The ten-hectare site – equivalent to around nine full-sized football pitches in size – would be buried under up to 500 new homes. Officials presented a report recommending the deal to councillors who duly voted to grant outline planning approval. The bulldozers and concrete were ready.

Threats to schools, hospitals and playing fields are emotive issues guaranteed to bring out a community's campaigning spirit and few were as impassioned and fervent when it came to fighting their corner as McLean. The letter he received felt little more than an obligatory nod towards sounding out the community. It may have been called a public consultation but it felt like a done deal.

McLean was one of two Westray Street residents who decided to fight and they were determined that St Augustine's would not join the list of 100 playing fields lost over the past five years in a city whose name is usually said to derive from the Gaelic *Glasgu* which translates as 'green hollow' and evolved into 'dear green place'.

On one side of the dispute was McLean and his determined band of residents. Their grass-roots campaign had humble origins and was non-political but it soon gathered the backing of the nation's sporting body Sport Scotland and Sandra White, an SNP member of the new Scottish Parliament. On the other side were Glasgow City Council, PC John Cameron and Eddie Lyons.

At the early stages, a bookmaker offering odds would have viewed it as a one-sided contest with the sale of St Augustine's by far the more likely outcome. It was a campaign which became one of the city's longest-ever planning wrangles and over the two years it often became personal. The reason that Lyons backed the sale of St Augustine's was that the council had earmarked Chirnsyde as an alternative place to fill the void once the playing fields had been lost forever. The council was legally obliged to offer like-for-like sites whenever playing fields were lost so the disappearance of St Augustine's would have turned 'his' club into the undisputed heart of the community.

After one fraught community meeting about the issues, McLean and a neighbour challenged PC Cameron, then Chirnsyde chairman, on why he would not back their campaign. They were furious at his response – he told them simply that it was not what Lyons wanted.

McLean said, 'By that point, the campaign to save St Augustine's was supported by virtually every group and organisation in the area. That night, when we challenged PC Cameron, we explained that it was all about keeping kids active and having the facilities to keep them off the streets, which is what the police should have been pushing for. Instead, he seemed happy to support Lyons who clearly had a vested interest and was empire building.'

Initial thoughts that the council could rubber-stamp the deal and take the developer's cash disappeared very quickly as the strength of feeling became clear. The residents' campaign was backed by Milton Community Council whose chairwoman Pat Curran and member Joe Kerr became important allies. Their knowledge of the slippery, Labour-dominated political process was a great help. The residents came to utterly distrust the council, not least because of the inaccuracies contained within the initial report which had been put before the council's planning committee, the one that had granted outline approval.

The row reached a level of such intensity that the Scottish government 'called in' the council's decision. It appointed John Henderson, a senior reporter in its planning disputes unit, to decide on what should happen. He conducted a nine-day inquiry over August and September 1999 which included visits to St Augustine's and Chirnsyde. One ploy by the council was to set up football goalposts at Chirnsyde the day before his visit in an apparent bid to enhance its status – a case of literally moving the goalposts.

The campaigners, meanwhile, had amassed a petition with 7,000 signatures on it and letters of support from many prominent figures in football including the then Scotland manager Craig Brown, former Milton boy turned professional footballer Tony Higgins and the talisman that was Dalglish, aka King Kenny.

Dalglish wrote to McLean, 'I played football on the playing fields as a young boy and I write to give you my full support in trying to save the pitches.'

Labour councillor Ellen Hurcombe and the MSP Patricia Ferguson later joined the campaign, swept along by the strength of community feeling. The politicians, however, took a back seat and it was Johnny McLean and another resident who were given a place at the top table, alongside the well-paid lawyers, officials and executives, during the public enquiry's closing submissions at the city's Parish Halls.

It was clear that the residents did not trust a word coming from the city council. Community council member Joe Kerr told the hearing, 'It is not surprising that residents in Milton think that their needs have been forgotten and that their objections have gone unheeded. It is disturbing to learn that information given to local residents regarding the future of the pitches has turned out to be untrue.'

One of the residents attacked the council's numerous discrepancies both in the original planning application and the report put before the committee. He said, 'The statements that the site [St Augustine's] is bordered by two-storey tenements and contains only four pitches and that Chirnsyde contains six pitches and is known as a 'sports centre' are seriously misleading, particularly in a public document, and it is significant that they were later corrected in a letter to a Scottish Office. The council's statement that the loss of the pitches "will not change what is already a city-wide problem" is beyond comprehension and the contention that there is little demand for the pitches is totally incorrect. The prospect of financial gain should not have been mentioned as a matter to which councillors should have regard and to suggest that the pitches will fall into disrepair if the application fails is also misleading. The council does not appear to be certain about anything and the evidence of its witnesses has lacked conviction.'

McLean was even more damning in his criticism of the council, not least of Brian Porteous, the deputy director of the culture and leisure department. He said, 'Mr Porteous had made false and conflicting statements. It is misleading to suggest that building houses here will encourage people back into Glasgow, no open space analysis has been carried out, there is no sports centre at Chirnsyde and several council officials have agreed that the committee report was defective.'

Sport Scotland's lawyer was also brutal in his assessment of the council. He stated, 'The planning judgement of the council's sub-committee has been vitiated by the committee report which, in administrative law terms, can be described as outrageous in its defiance of logic.'

The council was forced to hold its hands up, albeit behind a euphemistic veneer of understated language. It conceded that there had been 'minor discrepancies' in the application's plans and that its report to the committee who had voted to grant planning was 'not a perfect document'.

Weeks before the planning reporter was due to reveal his decision, campaigners unearthed a document which had not been disclosed – maybe because it would have been too provocative. It showed that the city council had discovered that part of the Chirnsyde site was endangered by an abandoned 80-metre-deep mine shaft which risked 'collapse of the surrounding ground, which in this case could extend to an area approximately 20 metres in radius'. The council had failed to share its 1996 document with the residents and the planning reporter, much to the anger of the campaigners. MSP Sandra White accused the council of being 'underhand' when it proposed Chirnsyde as an alternative to St Augustine's given this privileged knowledge. She said, 'It's obvious now that there was no way the council could build on this site. It's totally unsuitable for changing rooms or spectator stands, or even for people to gather on the touchline to watch a match.'

A supposedly neutral council spokesman seemed to get personal when asked to explain this revelation: 'Until the public inquiry reports on St Augustine's, and until housing development starts there, there will be no attempt to develop Chirnsyde. These people are making a mountain out of a molehill.'

One month later, in June 2000, the inquiry's findings were revealed. Glasgow City Council was red-carded and St Augustine's playing fields had been saved. The campaigners were ecstatic. It had not even been close. Permission was given to build on the four hectares which were already occupied by buildings but the remaining six hectares were to be retained.

John Henderson was damning in his criticism of the council and ruled that St Augustine's was certainly not 'surplus to requirements' as officials had suggested. Furthermore, the council was ordered to upgrade St Augustine's with three grass football pitches, one synthetic pitch and floodlights. The report also dismissed Chirnsyde as a possible alternative as it was just not up to scratch. Or, put officially, it lacked 'provision of equal community benefit and accessibility'. Not only had the residents won a great victory, the empire-building dreams of Lyons had been dashed. Henderson also praised the residents who had 'correctly and eloquently' criticised the council's controversial report put in front of its planning department.

When the news reached McLean, he said, 'We are delighted. It has been a long hard struggle but the support we have had is tremendous. It is especially gratifying that the council have been ordered to actually redevelop the area and restore the pitches to their former condition.'

In his report, Henderson added, 'The volume of opposition to this application and particularly to the loss of the playing fields from local people and from national sporting organisations and celebrities has been substantial. Local opinion is overwhelmingly in favour of retention of the playing fields and the possibility of compensatory provision being made at Chirnsyde is not acceptable to the community council of local residents. Even although Glasgow has been slow to carry out a survey of its open spaces on which an analysis can be based, it is not disputed that Glasgow is badly off numerically in terms of pitch provision as compared to Aberdeen, Edinburgh and Dundee, that the north western sector is badly off in comparison with other sectors, and that Milton ward is badly off in comparison with other wards. There is clearly therefore not a "long term excess of pitches, playing fields and public open space in the wider area".'

Over a decade later, the redeveloped site continues to thrive in a city which suffers horrific rates of obesity, heart disease and other serious illnesses, often linked to lifestyle. Johnny still likes the view from his living room. The campaigners had every reason to be proud and remain so.

But some in Glasgow City Council did not take the defeat lightly nor did they forget which individuals had been behind their humiliating put-down. If the campaigners thought the fight to save the playing fields had been tough, they had seen nothing yet. The council, it seemed, was itching for a rematch.

6

Paisley Buddies

From the time he was jailed for heroin smuggling in the 1980s, Jamie Daniel's wealth, reach and ruthlessness grew over the next two decades into the new millennium.

The family's name was murmured in almost conspiratorial tones. Unlike Eddie Lyons, Daniel wanted nothing to do with police, politicians or TV crews. He certainly did not yearn to become a community leader. He much preferred being in the shadows where he forged a position at the head of one of Scotland's richest and most secretive organised crime gangs. It kept its roots in Possil while growing a multimillion-pound turnover and developing its involvement in drug and tobacco smuggling, firearms and protection rackets.

The UK heroin boom had been the underworld equivalent of striking oil. The proceeds of dealing in it were money-laundered through a varied array of businesses with interests in hotels, construction, security, private-hire taxis, car washes and even florists. Daniel had come a long way from pinching copper and cars. His survival instincts and anti-surveillance antenna became razor sharp – something he'd learned from his incarceration during the 1980s. He liked nothing better than spotting – then mocking – surveillance officers and cameras. Daniel's empire is impossible to quantify. Long before the Proceeds of Crime Act was introduced in a bid to seize cash and assets from organised criminals, Daniel knew the value of having virtually nothing – homes, businesses, cars – in his own name. The half a dozen Daniel scrap yards which sprang up across Glasgow are regis-tered to other people. Daniel's name is not even to be found on the birth certificates of his many children to various women. He lives and breathes counter-surveillance techniques and was suspicious about mobile phones being bugged and used as tracking devices by the authorities long before many in the criminal fraternity caught up.

Above all else, the Daniels were absolutely ruthless. One young man in his 20s, a private-hire taxi driver from Milton, suffered the family's summary justice when he was instructed to attend a scrapyard meeting to discuss claims by a teenage Daniel girl that he had committed a sex attack on her. He turned up only to be beaten and dragged into a steel container where he was raped by a psychopathic, homosexual criminal who had been recruited for the purpose. Up until then, the victim had enjoyed the thrill of Daniel association. Haunted by his ordeal, he and his parents immediately moved away from their home.

Daniel's personal fortune is estimated at many millions of pounds yet he would haggle over every scrapyard deal and his wealth is not obvious from his scruffy appearance. There is no sugar coating to his raw, snarling demeanour and boiling aggression, where every second word that is spat out seems to be an expletive. Age and ill health in later life have done little to remove the rough edges. There is no midlife desire to be regarded as a legitimate businessman like his peers who donate to political parties and schmooze their way around the city's black-tie charity circuit. His wealth is inconspicuous. He wears grimy overalls rather than fine suits and drives battered vans rather than attention-grabbing supercars.

That low-key image was one of the things that helped Daniel in his steady rise through the underworld. More obviously, he grew bigger by being able to terrorise rivals and operate the logistical headaches of controlling a drug distribution network without getting caught or ripped off. During the ascendancy, the Daniels' violent reputations ensured that they encountered very few challengers in or near their Possil stronghold as other areas frequently became battlegrounds between rivals competing for control of the drugs trade. Such feuds were messy and costly as they disrupted business.

However, there are always challengers. One was another north Glasgow career drug dealer called Frank McPhie. He had beaten murder charges twice – on both occasions due to not proven verdicts. A nasty, dangerous criminal with a long record of armed robbery, he had a passion for dog fighting. While doing an eight-year stretch for drug dealing, he was accused of killing his fellow inmate William Toye, himself a murderer, in his cell in 1997. He got a not proven. McPhie's second alleged murder victim was an up-and-coming 25-year-old criminal called Chris McGrory who was found strangled to death in a van beside a suburban golf course in 1998. Weeks before McGrory's murder, McPhie had been an usher at his wedding. McPhie and the groom's best man Colin McKay – a pit bull breeder – stood trial. Again, it was not proven.

There had been a series of tit-for-tat clashes between McPhie and Jamie's young nephew Robert Daniel Jr – son of the drowned Robert Sr. They concluded with what police have described as one of the most professional underworld assassinations in Scotland. McPhie and three other masked men pounced on Robert outside a Chinese takeaway in King's Place, just off Balmore Road as it runs through Milton. Although Robert suffered serious stab wounds in the attack which centred around a dispute over dog fighting, he survived.

Comments were made that whoever did it would be on the first plane out the country but McPhie had different ideas. He was in no mood to back down – quite the opposite. A meeting between him and Jamie Daniel was arranged. The venue – the back of a parked car. McPhie was up for it. Instead of trying to justify his actions or attempting to smooth things over, he turned to Daniel and told him in no uncertain terms that he was taking over the drugs trade in the area. His tirade, peppered with personal insults about Daniel, was brave and foolish in equal measure. Days later he was dead.

McPhie might have got away with the knife attack on Robert if he had backed down to Jamie Daniel but there was no way he could be allowed to get away with such a brazen challenge to the family and their empire. On 10 May 2000, the 51-year-old was neatly dispatched with a single round from a sniper's rifle. Police are convinced that a disturbance was created with the sole purpose of forcing McPhie to return from some nearby allotments to his home, where he would either seek refuge or, more likely, collect a weapon and rally support. He didn't get past the front door of his communal close. His assassin lay in wait – watching through the telescopic sight's cross hairs from the drying area of high flats opposite his home. Once McPhie filled the sight, the hit man coolly squeezed the trigger.

Jamie Daniel's long-standing lieutenant John McCabe was arrested and charged with the killing but the case was dropped due to a lack of evidence. The police celebrated an apparent breakthrough when they found DNA on the weapon only for it to be matched to a member of the enquiry team. Many believed that the murder bore the hallmarks of an ex-military man or a terrorist veteran of the Troubles in Northern Ireland. They scoffed at the suggestion that a street thug like McCabe possessed the necessary skill. Either way – professional hit man or a lucky shot by McCabe – it was blamed on the Daniels and they had got away with it – a feat which carries maximum kudos in the criminal underworld. To this day, the murder remains unsolved.

However, long before McPhie was so clinically killed, Jamie Daniel had not been content with becoming king of his own small patch. Of course, serious money was made in cornering the Possil and Milton drugs trade but that turnover was eclipsed by two other approaches. The first of these involved importing drugs directly from the European hubs of Amsterdam and Spain and becoming a wholesaler to other gangs across Scotland and even other parts of the UK. London, Liverpool and Manchester are home to gangs who offer wholesale quantities of whatever is required which means the A74 and M74 running north from England remain the main route for drug smuggling into Scotland.

Along with others in Scotland over the years, Daniel has cut out the middlemen by smuggling drugs from overseas in order to maximise profits. He also forged very strong links with members of the British Pakistani communities in Glasgow as well as in the Midlands, Yorkshire and London. These men had access to the world's biggest wholesale heroin market in which raw opium from Afghanistan made the first step of its journey to being jagged into the veins of junkies across Western Europe, by crossing the border into their Pakistani homelands.

Aside from having criminal contacts on a UK and global scale, the second way Daniel made his money was less obvious and almost corporate in its application. He identified housing schemes with the potential for serious drug sales where there were numerous sellers operating but no dominant group in control. He then approached one of the established gangs, often a family similar to his own, with a business proposition. He would guarantee an uninterrupted flow of drugs at good rates. He would also give his new business partners the violent backup – people and firepower – to snuff out all competitors and carve out a monopoly. In exchange, Daniel would take a substantial cut of the generous new profits. Several Daniel-sponsored gangs bloomed.

During the 1990s, Daniel had moved to a CCTV-protected bungalow in the Linwood area of Renfrewshire, near the town of Paisley. That decade saw Scotland's most populous town gripped by a drugs war that claimed many lives and contaminated local politics with its stench.

Daniel was an associate of a notorious criminal from the town called Grant Mackintosh – a career criminal and first cousin once removed of (formerly Sir) Fred 'the Shred' Goodwin, the man who almost brought down the Royal Bank of Scotland with the loss of £24.1 billion in 2008. Mackintosh gloried in the nickname 'Mr P' because of his apparent dominance of his home town but the reality was never that simple. He and Daniel were allies on one side of a feud which had numerous factions.

In addition to partnership and patronage, however, there were also challenges and challengers. Daniel had become the enemy of a criminal gang from Glasgow's Nitshill and Pollok areas which are just to the east of Paisley. This gang was not in the slightest bit fazed by the Daniels' reputation. It was led by a man called Stewart 'Specky' Boyd and his rogues' gallery included Robert 'Piggy' Pickett, George 'Goofy' Docherty and Stewart Gillespie whose cartoonish nicknames belied the murderous violence they were capable of.

Boyd's gang was linked to FCB Enterprise (Security) Ltd, a firm set up in 1987 with almost £200,000 of taxpayers' money from central and local government. Labour Party figures were appointed as its directors. These included councillor Harry Revie, an ally and election agent of then Labour MP for Renfrew West and Inverclyde Tommy Graham. Also on the board were district councillor Olga Clayton and John McIntyre, chairman of the local Labour Party branch.

However, the dominance of Labour Party figures didn't stop the party's Paisley North MP Irene Adams bravely going public in 1995 to sensationally accuse FCB of being a suspected protection racket and front for drug dealing and money laundering. The politician, now Baroness Adams of Craigielea, who has since had her reputation tarnished by the parliamentary expenses scandal, was commended as she stood up to the drugs barons. She suffered death threats for doing so, prompting police protection. Her accusations were the catalyst for a four-year police investigation into the disappearance of £320,000 of public money from FCB. Alleged financial misappropriation was one thing. Murder was quite another.

FCB was based in the town's notorious Ferguslie Park scheme. Boyd and his thugs were linked to the controversial security firm and they had a big problem with a rival drug-dealing family, the Rennies. On 2 November 1995, three Rennie brothers received a visit from a trio of Specky's boys – Gillespie, Pickett and Docherty. Gillespie was giving the orders, Pickett was the shooter and Docherty was the blade man. Incredibly, the hit squad were decked out in matching FCB uniforms. As the Rennie brothers stood outside their homes, Gillespie gave Pickett a handgun, pointed to one of the Rennies and ordered him to 'shoot the fat bastard'. Pickett pointed the gun and pulled the trigger but it clicked and failed to fire. Docherty then stepped in and struck Stewart Rennie with a machete. A blood-bath ensued and the police treated the attacks on the three Rennie brothers as attempted murders.

Following that bloody incident, Gillespie and his pals continued to threaten the Rennies who, in turn, made reciprocal noises. Something had to give. It reached a head six months later when Gillespie, whose brother Billy was an FCB manager, shot Mark Rennie, 26, dead on 23 May 1996. A group of men stood laughing over the dying man. He had been shot in the back as he ran away from the hooded hit man. He didn't have time to produce his own sawn-off shotgun from his jacket sleeve. A post-mortem revealed that the fatal shot had torn through his lung, spleen and heart before exiting from his chest.

Gillespie, 37, was jailed for the murder – and the three attempted murders six months earlier. Jailed for 'life', he was back on the streets just 12 years later. Alongside him in the dock were Pickett, 31, and Docherty, 36, who were each convicted for the earlier attacks on the three brothers. Pickett was jailed for 12 years while Docherty got seven.

The levels of intimidation surrounding the trial led to the creation by Strathclyde Police of a witness protection unit – the use of which became increasingly commonplace in later years due to the rising problem of witness intimidation. It helped to shield and protect crucial and brave witnesses, including the murder victim's lover Margaret Brown, whose testimony allowed justice to be dispensed in the face of serious threats to their safety.

Missing from the dock was the suspected trigger man Boyd who had taken the trip favoured by many of Scotland's serious fugitives with a one-way ticket to Spain. He returned and stood trial for murder the following year but was cleared by a jury.

There were few tears shed at the subsequent demise of Boyd and Docherty. Boyd, a man suspected of involvement in up to nine gangland murders, died in a fireball explosion when he crashed his Audi TT in Spain in 2003. The carnage claimed five other innocent lives. Docherty – another thug who the police firmly believed had got away with murder – was stabbed and run over and killed by a car in 2006 in Glasgow's Tollcross area in a row over drugs.

That wasn't the end of the FCB scandal as, in July 1997, Gordon McMaster, the troubled fellow MP and friend of Adams, took his own life. In a letter to his family and Adam, he accused neighbouring MP Tommy Graham of running a vile anti-gay smear campaign against him. Despite the claims made by Adams, the four-year police investigation into FCB and the missing money resulted in the Crown Office deciding not to prosecute any of those involved. The decision prompted a plea from Adams which – given what happened a decade later with the Lyons family in Glasgow's Milton area – would prove to be prophetic. She said, 'I will be asking the Scottish Office for an assurance that this kind of thing never happens again. It has to be in control and ensure the money is channelled in the right direction. It should never go to people who use it to terrorise the community and further their own ends.'

Daniel's name was never publicly linked to the Paisley quagmire of the 1990s but he had close associations with many of those involved and was suspected of providing drugs and guns to the warring factions through his connections to Mr P. His contacts in the town remain strong.

As the Daniel family later waged a similar battle for control of the drugs trade in Milton, ghosts from Paisley came back to haunt Jamie when Pickett and Docherty formed a deadly alliance with the Lyons. It was an astute move and, for the Lyons, an example of the proverb my enemy's enemy is my friend.

7

Get the Bastard

Throughout the summer of 2000, Eddie Lyons continued to bask in the support of Strathclyde Police and the Labour Party.

By any reasonable measure, the event that took place later that year should have brought his entire house of cards crashing down and destroyed the illusion of Lyons the community leader forever.

The Labour MSP Patricia Ferguson was aware that crime is one of the perennial issues raised by constituents. Like all politicians, she also knew the value of raising her profile by getting her face in the newspapers. To get a first-hand taste of what police officers on the beat encounter, she pounded the streets for three hours one evening alongside two of them – one was PC John Cameron and the other a female officer. Ferguson was featured in the city's *Evening Times* beneath the headline 'My night on the streets with city's thin blue line'.

The trio set off at 8 p.m. from Saracen police station and walked 15 minutes to Milton where their first port of call was Chirnsyde Community Initiative for a guided tour. Ferguson wrote, 'This project has been running for eight years and has developed into a major undertaking.' During the half-hour visit, Ferguson was photographed watching kids using the computers but the article made no mention of the man in charge, Lyons, nor was PC Cameron's role as Chirnsyde chairman disclosed to the readers.

For Lyons, it was more public relations gold. Not only did he have PC Cameron as chairman and Councillor Ellen Hurcombe as a staunch defender but now the area's new Labour MSP had given her tacit seal of approval by popping in for a visit with the media in tow.

What the article also failed to state was that PC Cameron and other community police officers were now using a room at Chirnsyde as a makeshift police station. Official minutes from a Milton Community Council meeting, dated 21 June 2000, revealed that he and three other officers were 'temporarily using [a] refurbished room at Chirnsyde'. In other words, as the Lyons crime family brought waves of misery, drugs and violence to the law-abiding majority in Milton, the head of the family was providing Strathclyde Police officers with a base in the area. Chirnsyde had become a pseudo police station. In addition, PC Peter Glancey was using Chirnsyde as a venue from which to run Arsenal Boys Club. Strathclyde Police could have put a sign above the door.

Due to what happened next, that autumn ought to have been the turning point. In early September, Milton resident Thomas McDonnell Sr came within inches of losing his life. He was stabbed and beaten by a cowardly mob at Chirnsyde as Lyons himself allegedly barked the order to 'get the bastard'. The attack happened because the McDonnell family had finally had enough of the terror campaign they had suffered. Unlike some of the Lyons clan's previous prey, the McDonnells – who were honest, respectable and hard-working – did not seek to resolve the problem through violence.

Head of the family Thomas Sr, then aged 46, was a crane operator while his wife Margo had brought countless babies into the world during her time as a midwife at the city's Royal Infirmary. They were the parents of four sons and two daughters and the McDonnells had no history of disputes with other families. That was until the Lyons came along. The one-sided vendetta waged by the Lyons against the McDonnells stemmed from virtually nothing. It began on Christmas Eve 1999 in the city's Victoria's nightclub when teenage student Marc McDonnell became involved in a row with Eddie Lyons' son Steven, then aged 19. At the end of the night, in the small hours of Christmas morning, two of Steven's Club Boys pals pounced outside the club but the attack didn't last long and those involved safely made their way home. Just like any number of alcohol-fuelled incidents seen every weekend in every UK town and city, it amounted to very little. Such drunken, teenage scraps would usually be quickly forgotten but, for the Lyons, it was only the beginning. Several days later, Marc was back in the city centre shopping when he was approached by three of Steven's cronies who threatened him and attempted to hold him captive until their pal arrived. This marked the beginning of an onslaught of abuse and threats made against Marc and his elder brother Kevin. The brothers lived in fear for months as Steven and his friends cruised the area in cars and frequently attempted to set about them.

Matters escalated in April when Marc, Kevin and their younger brother Michael, who was just 10 years old at the time, drove to a McDonald's restaurant. As they were returning home, a car being driven by Steven's friend Liam Boyle swerved in front of them and screeched to a halt, forcing Kevin to come to a sudden stop to avoid a collision. Boyle – another long-time associate and founder member of the Club Boys – snatched the keys from the ignition and demanded that Kevin got out to fight. The McDonnell boys knew that the Lyons didn't fight fair. Boyle had moments earlier been speaking into his mobile phone, undoubtedly calling for backup. Kevin and Marc – primarily concerned with protecting their younger brother – managed to grab the keys and race back to the family home. Mum Margo was there with three grandchildren when her sons burst in with Boyle close behind. His body became wedged half way through the front door, preventing it from being closed. Suddenly, a BMW appeared and was abandoned in the middle of the road. Out from it sprang Steven and his brother Eddie Jr. Among the volley of threats being hurled were that Kevin would get beaten with baseball bats. Margo screamed at the Lyons boys and Boyle and ordered them to clear off before she called the police.

For Margo, enough was enough and she decided to pay a visit to Lyons at his home in Torogay Street. She expected the community leader to share her concerns. Surely he would agree that a silly feud between kids was now at the point where serious violence seemed inevitable and that he should act decisively to rein in his wayward sons? Did he really want their kids in the morgue and prison?

Lyons stunned her with the response: 'It's just like this, hen. My boys can fight and your boys are going to have to take a hammering. I'll arrange a square go.'

Margo begged him to see sense but it only made him issue another threat – this time indicating that his brother Johnny would get involved. He added, 'Incidentally, we have baseball bats in here and my brother is a nutcase – you don't want him coming to your door because he will smash all your windows in.' Then Lyons said that his only concern was that the McDonnell lads were so fearful of his sons that they may resort to using a knife. Margo felt threatened and was in a state of bewildered shock as she left Lyons' house.

For a further three months, the Lyons boys continued their simmering harassment with verbal threats and occasional violence but the next escalation didn't take place until 29 July 2000 – seven months after the scuffle at Victoria's. Kevin McDonnell had been on a night out in the city centre when Liam Boyle tried to attack him but nothing happened as police officers intervened. Kevin got a taxi home but, having forgotten his front door key, was trying to figure out how to get in when Boyle and another man pulled up outside. In his panic at the approaching pair, Kevin smashed a plant pot which awoke his brother Marc who looked outside to see the blows being rained down. Marc scrambled outside and helped drag Kevin into the safety of their home. Marc suffered a bite wound while Kevin was left battered and bruised.

Up until that point, there had been a reluctance to involve the police given the stigma of being thought to have been involved in an unseemly feud but Margo and her family had reached the end of their tether.

Margo and another mum, whose son had suffered an almost identical pattern of threats and violence from the Club Boys, went to Baird Street police station where they were directed to the Saracen office. They were then told to speak to the very man who could deal with their complaint – Milton community policeman PC John Cameron.

The two mothers met PC Cameron in early August but, having explained their concerns, they immediately sensed that he was unconcerned. PC Cameron revealed to them that he had known Lyons for 20 years and that he was a 'good guy'. He then explained that he had known Eddie Jr and Steven since they were babies and that 'by the way, the boys can fight'. Margo and the other mother were astounded at what they were hearing. The meeting ended with PC Cameron telling them that what they had discussed would remain 'off the record' and took no written details other than the names of the sons. The two mothers refused to be brushed off and they urged PC Cameron to agree to meet them again, next time along with their sons.

At the second meeting, PC Cameron asked the McDonnell boys and the other victims if they wanted what he called 'the feuding' to stop. He also wrongly described the violence as being tit-for-tat when it was actually all one-way traffic from the Lyons. PC Cameron announced that Lyons had the power to bring the problem to an end and offered to go and speak to him. He then made yet another astonishing comment that a 'square go' may resolve matters – the same thuggish solution previously offered by Lyons.

Margo and the other mum were told that PC Cameron would get back to them in five days' time but they didn't hear a single word from him again.

A few days later, at 7 p.m. on Saturday, 2 September 2000, Margo's husband Thomas was almost murdered. At 3 p.m. that day, Kevin and Marc had been at a petrol station in Springburn when three cars drove in and surrounded theirs. They were trapped. A mob swarmed from the cars and launched a flurry of punches and kicks while also trashing the brothers' vehicle in front of witnesses. The craven attack resulted in the police charging five men, including Boyle, with serious assault. It was the final straw for their dad Thomas who decided to visit Lyons in his den – Eddie's Club, the HQ of the Club Boys. He believed that a direct appeal to Lyons was the only way this crazy situation could be defused. He was accompanied by his eldest son Thomas Jr and they brought Kevin along to let Lyons see his fresh injuries. The sons waited outside as he entered the building where he came face-to-face with Lyons who was talking to an elderly couple.

Lyons appeared to be in good spirits and smilingly agreed with Thomas Sr that, yes, he could and would get it sorted. He then told him to wait while he went into his office. Moments later, two cars drew up outside. In the vehicles were Lyons' brother Johnny and his two sons Eddie Jr and Steven, along with their friends Paul McGuinness and Andrew 'Dumbo' Gallacher. Thomas Sr and the detectives who investigated the attack have absolutely no doubt that it was a set-up and that Lyons had summoned them there with a phone call from his office.

They charged at Thomas Sr who was attacked with fists, feet, golf clubs and a scaffolding pole. He was stabbed twice. His sons were also attacked but, mercifully, not stabbed. Like a footballer warming the subs' bench, Uncle Johnny spectated from a car seat, presumably in case he was needed.

Thomas Sr later told detectives and a jury that Lyons had roared, 'GET THE BASTARD!' as the pack swarmed around him.

Beaten to a bloody pulp, he mustered the strength to hobble away from Chirnsyde before he collapsed in a grassy area at the rear of some shops. He later told friends that, had he not got away and had a woman not found him and called an ambulance, he would have been a corpse. As it was, he came within minutes of dying. Being stabbed twice resulted in Thomas Sr losing his spleen. He spent four days in intensive care and the following five in a high dependency unit. Whenever well-wishers turned up to visit as he lay gravely ill in hospital, the police officers protecting him phoned Margo to verify that they were friends not foes seeking to finish the job.

Despite their experience of PC Cameron, the McDonnell family had faith in the police and the courts and they were determined that the cowards who had almost killed Thomas Sr should face justice.

From the outset, the CID team led by Detective Constable Kenny Macleod, who later rose to rank of Detective Inspector, met a wall of silence when they conducted door-to-door enquiries around Chirnsyde. Not a single witness saw anything – or so they claimed. Clearly terrified, they often closed the door without saying a word. An elderly woman later phoned the officers to explain that she was too scared because, if she talked, it would bring trouble to her door. However, what was of much greater concern to the detectives was the issue of the bond between PC Cameron and Lyons. Even before the attempted murder, those in CID had been suspicious. Before the stabbing, most of the CID felt that PC Cameron was too close to Lyons. Their own informants had told them about the cosy connection between the Chirnsyde chairman and co-ordinator.

Early in the enquiry, a decision was taken not to log updates on the shared police computer. All the information about the attempted murder enquiry was kept off the system. Rather than put a block on who could see it – which would have led to questions being asked about why that was being done – they, instead, decided to discuss the information only within a tight circle of trusted colleagues. One of the officers wanted to gain a clearer picture of just how close PC Cameron and Lyons had become so he decided to place his fellow officer under a spot of unofficial surveillance. Having obtained PC Cameron's shift patterns, the detective travelled in his own car and parked outside Chirnsyde.

Cameron arrived there at 9.10 a.m., just after the start of his shift, and did not come back out until 4 p.m. On a following day, the off-duty officer watched as PC Cameron turned up early and waited outside the locked doors. When Lyons turned up, they went in together. When the detective left at 3 p.m., he had still not yet seen PC Cameron come out. Was it any surprise the police couldn't get anyone to talk when one of their own was using the scene of the crime – the mob's gang hut – as an office?

After the savage assault, some of Thomas Sr's suspected attackers went on the run for 10 days but the six wanted men were soon rounded up and charged with multiple offences including attempted murder.

The six accused were Lyons himself along with his brother Johnny, his sons Edward Jr and Steven along with Club Boys pair, Paul McGuinness and Andrew Gallacher. During preparations for the trial, the defence lawyers for each of the accused were entitled to seek a statement from other witnesses. This standard procedure led to a precognition agent acting for one defendant going to Torogay Street to obtain a statement from Lyons at his home. Such agents, often ex-police officers, take statements from potential witnesses in order to see what their evidence will be which then allows the defence lawyers to prepare their cases. The following extraordinary event was to be the tipping point for the CID team and is what prompted DC Macleod to submit a detailed report to senior officers in which he outlined a series of concerns about PC Cameron and Lyons.

When the precognition agent arrived, Lyons refused to co-operate until he could get hold of a certain person. The agent was told to sit and wait while Lyons phoned someone and ordered them to get there straight away. He shouted and swore down the phone and said he would not speak to the agent until his mystery adviser arrived. Lyons made a second call during which he became even more animated.

Shortly afterwards, off-duty PC Cameron arrived. He was instantly recognised by the disbelieving precognition agent. PC Cameron followed Lyons into the kitchen where he was heatedly asked what he should do and say. Lyons eventually calmed down and gave a statement. This episode formed the basis of the internal complaint about the community policeman's links with a prime suspect.

For the McDonnell family, the hell they had been through was about to get worse as a campaign of further intimidation swung into action. Just 24 hours after the stabbing, as their dad's life was hanging in the balance, three of the McDonnell sons were forced into exile for their own safety. They were escorted by police officers to Glasgow Central Station where they were put on a train to live with relatives elsewhere in the country. At one stage, the family were warned that two hit men had been sent from London to shoot them. It was one of a constant barrage of credible threats they received over the following five months, all designed to chip away at their willingness to testify in court. Those of weaker resolve would surely have been crushed under the immense pressure being brought down on the McDonnell family who had been forced to flee what was once a normal happy family home to live in rented accommodation and hotels, constantly fearful that the Lyons would track them down.

The trial was set to begin at the High Court in Glasgow on 3 January 2001. In the days leading up that date, the McDonnells continued to suffer threats as the trial date came and went without a start to proceedings due to legal wranglings. One of the worst moments for the family again involved PC Cameron. They were sickened when they discovered that the officer had agreed to be a character witness for Eddie Lyons Sr during the trial. The officer's name was on lists of defence witnesses submitted to the Crown Office ahead of the trial. It was almost unheard of for any police officer to be a defence witness in any capacity, least of all to give glowing personal testimony to a man accused of attempted murder.

The Crown Office flagged it up with the CID team who, having already submitted their internal report on PC Cameron, again raised concerns with senior officers. When the hierarchy at the force's HQ in Pitt Street found out, PC Cameron was told to forget any notion of giving evidence.

Unbeknown to the CID team, PC Glancey, the other community officer whose boys' football team used the facilities at Chirnside, had agreed to be a defence witness for Eddie Jr.

In the days after the intended trial start date, behind-the-scenes discussions took place between the Crown Office and the raft of defence lawyers and QCs, whose services were all being paid for with taxpayers' money. The purpose of such talks is to allow the prosecution and defence to establish whether an agreement can be reached to plead guilty, thereby avoiding a costly trial. These plea deals also attempt to secure a speedy result while sparing witnesses the ordeal of testifying. The advantage for the accused is that it allows them to plead guilty to usually fewer or less serious charges than those they originally faced. If there are several people charged, a deal often results in some walking free in exchange for others taking the rap. Often expedient, not always palatable.

Such talks take place in Scotland every single day but they are shrouded in secrecy and what is said is never explained to the paying public. In fact, the Crown Office's internal guidelines reveal that secrecy is the official policy.

The 'plea adjustment' document issued to prosecutors states that they 'should generally not disclose the detailed reasons for their acceptance of adjusted pleas . . . The only explanation which should generally be given for the acceptance by the Crown of adjusted pleas is that this was regarded as being, in all the circumstances of the case, in the public interest.' In other words, the public don't need to know why a murder charge becomes a culpable homicide or why one killer walks free while another is convicted. It's none of their business. The guidelines also reveal that prosecutors have 'a duty' to take whatever action 'best serves the public interest in the effective administration of criminal justice'. Victims' rights also take a back seat. Exactly how a decision made by a system which has no public account-ability can be measured against the public interest has never been explained. Similar plea bargaining operates elsewhere but, because the system in Scotland is not accountable or open to scrutiny, it is argued that these cosy chats between lawyers lead to carve-ups in which guilty people walk free.

On this occasion, the discussions centred on a deal offered to Paul McGuinness, who had stabbed Thomas McDonnell Sr. The Crown wanted him to plead guilty in exchange for charges against the others being dropped. It was a neat solution that suited the Crown and the others accused of the crime but, much to the anger of Lyons, McGuinness rejected the offers because he was awaiting sentencing for another offence at the time and feared he'd get a much heavier jail term if the attempted murder rap was also taken into consideration.

Before the trial began, a lack of evidence led to the charges against Lyons and Johnny being dropped. It was a bitter blow for Thomas Sr and his family to see the one they regarded as the smirking puppet master walk free. At least PC Cameron's different loyalties to his employers, Strathclyde Police, and his friend and colleague Lyons would not be tested.

The trial against the remaining four – Eddie Jr, Steven, McGuinness and Gallacher – finally got underway on 10 January despite another wobble when a Crown witness failed to appear, having been intimidated to stay away.

Around a dozen McDonnell family members were kept at a hotel in a secret location to prevent them being targeted. They were escorted there and back by police drivers who used anti-surveillance techniques to prevent their whereabouts being compromised. By the next day, the level of intimidation, in the form of mumbled threats and dirty looks directed at them and their family and friends, had grown to such an extent that a court official went to the family's hotel to take detailed statements about it. To the family's despair, the advocate depute Ruth Anderson – who later became a sheriff – decided to throw in the towel. She abandoned the trial and dropped the charges. One Crown Office official had the audacity to tell the McDonnell family, 'We can't handle this.'

The farce led to McGuinness, the only accused who had been remanded in custody, being released back on to the streets. The CID officers were apoplectic at the Crown's craven surrender to a bilious campaign of witness intimidation. To them – and to the crumpled McDonnell family – it felt like the Lyons had won.

The Crown Office raised a second prosecution, this time against Eddie Jr, Steven, McGuinness and Gallacher. Lyons and Johnny remained in the clear. The McDonnells were told that the second trial would take place at the High Court in Paisley. They were taken to see the court and given details of security precautions but the Crown Office decided that the venue was not suitable as it lacked adequate security so it was back to Glasgow.

Officers from the regional crime squad were drafted in to

ensure the witnesses were adequately protected during the trial, which began on 18 May. Each day, family members were escorted to court, firstly from a hotel in Glasgow then one in the Ayrshire seaside golfing resort of Troon, where they were under 24-hour guard.

But again, on 28 May, a raft of charges was dropped including the entire case against Gallacher who was free to go. That left the two Lyons brothers, Eddie Jr and Steven, and McGuinness in the dock.

The jury returned their verdicts on the remaining charges on 4 June. On the most significant charge of attempted murder, Eddie Jr and Steven celebrated wildly as they were told the case against them was not proven, Scotland's bastard verdict. Eddie Jr would have been immensely grateful to PC Glancey who had taken the oath to give evidence on his behalf. It will never be known whether the friendly policeman's backing had been enough to tip the jurors towards a not proven rather than guilty verdict. McGuinness was found guilty of attempting to murder Thomas Sr and he was jailed for eight years. The others all walked free.

Thomas Sr was a broken man. He and Margo briefly returned to the family home, where panic alarms linked directly to the police had been installed, but the pressure proved too much and they decided to get out. In scenes similar to the Lyons' enforced departure from Cadder 17 years earlier, the police sealed off their street to allow them safe passage from the area they loved and where they had raised their family.

During the time between the first trial collapsing in January and the second one staring in May, Margo wrote to powerful establishment figures in a bid to have her voice heard. The Scottish Parliament's first Justice Minister Jim Wallace, the Lib Dem MSP for Orkney, who is now Baron Wallace of Tankerness; the man in charge of the Crown Office, Lord Advocate Colin Boyd – later elevated to Baron Boyd of Duncansby – and Strathclyde Police's then Chief Constable, Sir John Orr, who months earlier had been knighted, all received copies of her articulate and powerful eight-page letter. In pin-sharp clarity, she detailed the story of what her family had been put through and their experiences with PC Cameron. The letter stated:

Now we feel like we are the ones who have been sentenced. My life is totally disrupted and devastated. My husband is in a very poor state of health. He will probably never work again. We have been forced to move out of our home and into rented accommodation for fear of our lives. This means my whole family are alienated from their respective friends and extended family. I have been off work for six months which has a detrimental effect on my relationship with my employer and colleagues.

My two younger children have had their education disrupted and are extremely traumatised by the whole situation. The children have witnessed several incidents and have to travel 34 miles per day to get to school. Their social lives have ended and they are very isolated.

It is in my opinion that this very unfortunate situation has been made worse by the incompetence of the Crown in not taking this to trial within a sufficiently short time scale. Ruth Anderson was not prepared to give consideration to the peripheral facts surrounding this case and came across as totally incompetent and disinterested.

It appears to me that the witness is the one who had their life totally disrupted and the accused carried on regardless. Why is there no consideration given to the difficulties encountered by those who stand up to these people? If there had been others willing to stand up for their rights, these people would not have been allowed to go on to terrorise a whole community. It is clear from my experience that the reason people don't stand up to them is that there is no support from the judicial system to protect them.

Finally, I would like to point out that as a result of my experience at the hands of the judicial system, if I were ever unfortunate enough to find myself in a similar situation in the future, going to the police and pressing charges would be at the bottom of my list of options.

Thomas Sr spent the following years battling ill health, financial problems, relationship issues and other demons caused by his two ordeals – one at the hands of the Lyons family and the other courtesy of the Crown Office and factions within the police. He and his family watched in silent incredulity as Lyons perversely consolidated his role as a community leader and as a man impressionable teenagers should supposedly look up to. All the while, Lyons was being bankrolled from public funds – the same public money that had failed to ensure the besieged McDonnells were protected from him and his family.

Others who knew Lyons feared for the future. His sons would graduate from Chirnsyde and, for them, a life of gangsterism awaited. Lyons was like the pushy dad who wills his sons to make it as professional footballers because he had failed to do so only, instead of encouraging their footballing skills, Lyons was ensuring they'd make it as proper gangsters. The small-time grass who had been stabbed and chased out of town would do it differently this time, albeit vicariously through the lives of his children. Lyons thought he had struck upon an oh-so-clever formula for success whereby he was the respected, squeaky-clean community leader while the boys did the gangster stuff, but a father grooming his children for a life of crime and violence was not smart – just twisted.

The people of Milton would rightfully have expected that the attempted murder of Thomas Sr would have spelled the end of Lyons' reign at Chirnsyde or at least that it might have led to a few awkward questions being asked by those in authority who apparently had no qualms about Lyons and his regime being suitable for (other people's) children. They were to be disappointed as nothing happened. Yet it was now impossible for the Labour Party, the city council and Strathclyde Police to be able to guarantee the safety of the hundreds of children who used Chirnsyde.

Margo MacDonnell's moving plea for help to the Justice Minister, Lord Advocate and Chief Constable appeared to fall on deaf ears.

The CID team were also bitter at the lack of action. Their dossier on PC Cameron and the complaints made about him by Margo and the other mum led to him being removed from Milton and sent to the affluent suburb of Milngavie but he continued to serve with Scotland's largest police force for many more years. Following his police career, he worked as an Asda supermarket security guard. One officer said of Cameron's treatment, 'I am very loyal to the police but that whole episode was shameful. The senior officers shirked the opportunity and responsibility to do something about it. It was all about preventing a scandal – it was a cover up.'

Not a single word about the bloodbath at Chirnsyde – nor the subsequent trials and terror campaign suffered by the McDonnells – was reported in the media at the time.

For Lyons, it had been a lucky escape. With his unwavering support from the authorities, he could only smile to himself, breathe a sigh of relief and keep taking the money.

8

The Stolen Stash

To the Daniel family, the Lyons were just small-time upstarts and friends of the police. The younger Daniel generation, a similar age to Lyons' sons Eddie Jr and Steven, viewed them with derision – little boys born with silver spoons in their mouths whose upbringing in Milton was a world away from the mean streets of Possil. Their dad was nothing but a grass. They were certainly not even worthy of the description of rivals. There is no doubt that the well-spoken Lyons lads were atypical of the young men more obviously identified as criminals but, like their father, they seemed to have an ability to network and strike partnerships.

Around the turn of the new millennium, the Lyons received a boost when they started doing business with the McGovern gang from Springburn. The five McGovern brothers, Joe, Tony, Tommy, Jamie and Paul, styled themselves 'the McGovernment' as they rose to prominence throughout the 1990s. It was their cousin Jean who had formed the country's biggest shoplifting gang alongside Jamie Daniel's sister Annette. However, their status was smashed with the murder of 35-year-old Tony in 2000 following a fall-out with his former best friend Jamie Stevenson, nicknamed the Iceman. Stevenson later controlled what was arguably the country's largest organised crime gang but he was sentenced to 12 years and nine months for money laundering in 2007.

The relationship between the Lyons and the McGoverns was seen as a direct threat to the Daniels' dominance. Tensions cranked up as the Lyons started to increase their activity in

Milton, often cutting into territory which the Daniels jealously guarded. Clashes were inevitable. But it was a relatively minor incident in the summer of 2001 that lit the fuse which exploded into Scotland's worst gangland feud for a generation.

The biblical-sounding Lyons versus Daniel war was to carry on through that decade and beyond. Along the way, the devastation is impossible to quantify. Three people were murdered, one on each side, while the third was an innocent young father who was just in the wrong place at the wrong time. Other young lives were irreparably damaged or cut short as the countless shootings, slashings, beatings, abductions and acts of torture and violence continued. Cars were torched and homes petrol-bombed as children slept inside. Families were torn apart. Jail sentences of decades were handed down by judges. Brave witnesses who testified in court against both families were forced to see out their lives far from home under police protection and with new identities. The witness protection scheme – a legacy of the 1990s Paisley drugs war trials – had become a slick, nationwide system run by the Scottish Crime and Drug Enforcement Agency, which was ready to spirit people away and turn them into ghosts on behalf of the justice system. However, the incident that was the catalyst for this unprecedented tit-for-tat cycle of violence wasn't a planned putsch but an opportunistic theft that took place one night at a house party in Milton.

Robert Daniel, a nephew of Jamie and the son of Robert Sr who had drowned while evading police during the theft of scrap in 1976, had stashed £20,000 worth of cocaine at a safe house where the police wouldn't know to look. The morning after the night before, in a fug of stale smoke and alcohol, the hungover homeowner got the fright of his life. The package he was supposed to be keeping safe had disappeared. Robert and his associates, who included an extremely violent and highly dangerous 20-year-old called Kevin Carroll, launched their own investigation into what had happened to the cocaine. Those being 'interviewed' were not entitled to have a lawyer present. The Daniel gang's interrogations, rightly or wrongly, identified two brothers from Milton, Paul and Mark Mathers, as the culprits. They were known to be close associates of the Lyons and their Club Boys pals.

Whoever removed the hidden cocaine, it ended up in the hands of the Lyons and, to the fury of the Daniels, it was sold throughout Milton. In later years, the Lyons would insist that they had no idea who the coke had been stolen from – not that the Daniels would have cared even if they chose to believe them.

Stealing drugs was a reckless act. In that criminal world, letting anyone take advantage without suffering any consequence made you weak. The retributions would be instant and final. At least that was the theory. The theft sparked a wave of attacks on the Lyons and their interests, including Chirnsyde, which had the potential to be a headache for Eddie Lyons Sr who wanted no more violence jeopardising his position.

The first incident to take place at the centre was when Daniel youths clambered on to the roof. It took seconds for the flames to take hold and the bright orange glow lit up the 2.30 a.m. darkness. Firefighters raced to the scene and managed to extinguish the blaze before it completely destroyed Eddie's Club but the damage ran into many thousands of pounds.

A fortnight later, on 28 August, Robert Daniel went to Chirnsyde and trashed the centre's minibus which was normally used by Lyons to drive children around. He would use the vehicle to criss-cross Milton between homes, schools and 'his' club, like a courtesy shuttle bus. This act of vandalism was conducted in full view of Lyons and was also allegedly witnessed by PC Glancey, who had given evidence on behalf of Eddie Jr at the Thomas McDonnell attempted murder trial earlier that year.

Robert went to Spain for a short holiday and to allow the heat to diminish but was arrested upon his return to Glasgow and was charged with vandalism and breach of the peace. It was claimed by the campaigners that Robert was offered a police deal which he was happy to accept. Put simply – keep future trouble away from Chirnsyde and you will be in the clear. The Crown Office duly dropped the charges against him. That deal saw Chirnsyde become an exclusion zone from the hostilities but they continued and escalated elsewhere.

Lyons' son Steven became the target of a shooting outside Mallon's pub in Kilfinan Street in the Lambhill area of the city but the shots failed to hit their target. At the time, Steven was in a relationship with the niece of drug dealer Sean Reilly, who was a senior figure in another significant north Glasgow drugs cartel, headed by Willie O'Neill. O'Neill, who later became the manager of celebrated but troubled artist Peter Howson, forged close bonds with the Lyons, further enhancing their standing in the underworld.

Throughout this time, Carroll relentlessly hounded the Lyons and the Club Boys. It was like a blood sport. Every opportunity he got, he terrorised them and there were countless low-level incidents on an almost daily basis. The young Daniels had lost face and the Lyons were seen to be getting away with it. The suspected cocaine thieves, the Mathers brothers, were forced to flee Glasgow over fears for their safety.

The Mathers decided that it would be safe to return home that Christmas but the Daniels were not in the mood for festive forgiveness. At 5 a.m. on Sunday, 23 December 2001, a drive-by gunman sprayed bullets at the windows of their family home on Westray Street, facing the St Augustine's playing fields. A newspaper report stated that the attack was one of several linked to a drugs war but none of the participants were named. At the time, a member of Strathclyde Police's media office said, 'There was damage to the windows and also to the inside of the house which was occupied. We believe it was a drive-by shooting but we have no description of the vehicle or its occupants. We would appeal for witnesses to come forward.'

Despite this public plea for information, neighbours of the Mathers – including Johnny McLean, the man who spearheaded the campaign to save the St Augustine's playing fields from being built over – were amazed when the police did not even make door-to-door enquiries. Why make a public request for witnesses yet not even bother asking the neighbours if they had seen anything? The answer seemed obvious – the police knew the shooting was the work of the Daniel boys and that it stemmed from the theft of cocaine which had been pinned on the Mathers and the Lyons. It was common knowledge. The failure to conduct basic enquiries was perhaps based upon the belief that the likelihood of catching anyone for the drive-by shooting was negligible.

Chirnsyde had now been the scene of an attempted murder, a serious arson attack and vandalism of the minibus. The family's drugs feud with the Daniels had also led to two attempted shootings and other acts of violence. Things were hotting up.

9

See No Evil

Emboldened by the success of the St Augustine's playing fields campaign, the Milton residents decided that something needed to be done about the more serious problem on their doorsteps – Eddie's Club.

The playing fields victory came at the end of June 2000. The attempted murder of Thomas McDonnell at Chirnsyde took place two months later, at the beginning of September. The stabbing was a disgusting and cowardly act which could so easily have ended in a good man, similar to any one of them, bleeding to death in the street – a nagging thought that highlighted the disquiet that had permeated the community for long enough. Even before the McDonnell bloodbath, Johnny McLean had voiced concerns about Eddie Lyons running Chirnsyde and he had a meeting with Glasgow City Council education department officials back in February that year to raise concerns. A letter in reply from Senior Education Officer Christine Higginson was a portent of things to come. She stated, 'I have had your complaints thoroughly investigated and at present can find no evidence to substantiate them.'

McLean garnered significant backing from other like-minded residents who took exception to Lyons becoming a self-styled role model for their children with the backing of the police and the Labour Party, greased with public money. The attempted murder was a game changer. Enough was enough – it was time for action.

McLean and another activist had been refused a place on the Labour-controlled North Glasgow Community Forum because they were wrongly regarded as pro-SNP. Given that the organisation was Labour-controlled, their anti-Lyons stance was another reason for their rejection. Undeterred, they launched a petition that attracted 1,200 signatures from Milton residents which duly swept them on to the board. The next step was for McLean and the other activist to then join the 12-strong Milton Community Council board, which merely required a nomination from another local resident. McLean, the other resident and another local father were joined by an SNP firebrand activist called Billy McAllister who, as a non-resident of Milton, became the frontman. They had a clear understanding of the type of man Lyons was and were motivated to do the best for their children. Branded the 'four bampots' by a Glasgow City Council media spokesman in an attempt to extinguish press interest in their campaign, they embraced the derogatory label in defiance at the smear.

Milton Community Council arranged a meeting at Maryhill police station with Chief Superintendent Alec White, the divisional commander for the area. On the agenda were the concerns about Lyons at Chirnsyde and his connections to PC John Cameron.

Two members of the community council did not show up. It became apparent that they were Lyons loyalists. Despite his and his family's pervasive criminality and unpopularity, he was a divisive figure who still commanded a number of supporters, through fear or favour. The 'bampots' knew what was happening at Chirnsyde was wrong but many others were too scared to speak out. Lyons' presence at Chirnsyde had become a taboo subject which people dared not speak about, as they were not sure who might be listening or where the comments could end up.

Those living in the community frequently heard about many other incidents at Chirnsyde in which the thuggish Club Boys were linked to beatings, the sale of drugs, including cocaine, ecstasy and cannabis, and other criminality.

PC Cameron had been moved away from Milton by his police bosses not long before the crack cocaine death of Michael Lyons in 1999 but he had since returned and was, in 2000, the chairman of Chirnsyde. It was suggested that he was allowed to return because Lyons preferred to deal with him – if not, that Lyons actually insisted upon it. To some in the community, there was a belief that the police were using Lyons to help control Milton. The rationale is that, if you can never stop crime, you may as well attempt to manage it by choosing who prevails. Such circumstances allow the police to garner intelligence about communities on condition that those they have empowered do not overstep the mark.

With the success of the playing fields campaign still fresh in their minds, the campaigners hoped that the authorities would act swiftly to remove Lyons once the perverse situation was drawn to their attention. They genuinely thought that it would only take a couple of phone calls to the police and council to explain what was going on and the situation would be fixed immediately. It should have been the case but the campaigners admit that they were naive. They misunderstood how things worked in Glasgow, where the Labour Party ruled.

The meeting with the police, the phone calls and the letters achieved nothing. It became quickly apparent that the council – still smarting from the costly and humiliating playing fields defeat – had decided that Mr Lyons, the occupant of their building, was entirely legitimate. The four 'bampots' called a summit at one of their homes. On a plain, white sheet of A4 paper, one of them wrote the name of Lyons at the top and from that drew five lines which linked to Strathclyde Police, Glasgow City Council, the Labour Party, the Crown Office Procurator Fiscal Service (Scotland's prosecution service) and North Glasgow Community Forum (a community project which directed public funds). They were all organisations from which Lyons either had explicit backing or with which he had formed legitimate connections through his community role. The most important of these, in terms of lending Lyons support and enhancing his status, were Scotland's largest police force and council but top of the list were the police. It had been Lyons' overt links to PCs Cameron and Glancey that had allowed him to get his foot in the Chirnsyde door in the first place and they had backed him ever since.

The police were the catalyst for all that followed. The council owned the building and, based on all the evidence already available, they could easily have evicted Lyons if had they wanted to.

Labour's influence seeped deep in Scotland's political, legal, cultural and media worlds and the city council was a party power base. Lyons was backed by Councillor Ellen Hurcombe and had enjoyed the patronage of the MSP Patricia Ferguson.

The fourth connection was to the Crown Office through an association with a fellow Milton resident and Boys' Brigade leader called Barry Dickson, whose day job was to prosecute criminals in Glasgow's courts. On one particular later occasion, when Lyons became involved in Milton Community Council, he bragged about being able to summon Dickson to a meeting with other residents. He duly appeared in a professional capacity. There is no suggestion that Dickson did anything untoward but Lyons gloried in the connection.

The final group on the list, North Glasgow Community Forum, was a taxpayer-funded community group with strong links to the Labour Party. It helped to decide which groups would be favoured in terms of the channelling of taxpayer funding.

With that simple scrawled illustration, the campaigners – ordinary mums and dads – began to realise the scale of the battle on their hands. It was not just Lyons they were taking on – it was the whole establishment. In order to bring this matter to public attention, they turned to the media but, while reporters were often sympathetic to their plight, they could not publish a story about Lyons at Chirnsyde as further checks yielded glowing feedback from official sources within the council, police and Labour. The message could not be clearer – there's nothing to see here, so please move along.

When the campaigners' pleas to the authorities and the press fell on deaf ears, they fired up their PCs and printers. Johnny McLean sent letters to the council, the police, politicians and anyone else he thought might listen. Often they were hand delivered and he would patiently wait for receipts from bemused council clerks or seething desk sergeants at Maryhill police station who bristled at allegations of corruption. The replies were usually frustrating failures to answer specific points, typical obfuscation generated by officialdom the world over.

A trickle of letters became an avalanche. The 'bampots' were relentless, driven forward because what they were doing was important and right. Every single incident involving Lyons and Chirnsyde was logged. Some advised that the letter-writing campaign was counter-productive as the sheer volume allowed the police and council to portray them as irrational and obsessive. But they felt that it was all they could do because doing nothing was not an option. One father said, 'I said to the rest of the bampots, no one's listening so the best thing that we can do is try to raise awareness. All we can do is keep telling the truth and record everything that is happening. We refused to be fobbed off and there's no doubt we became a serious thorn in the sides of the council and police.'

The council's position could be summed up thus – there was no evidence of any criminality at Chirnsyde and that Strathclyde Police had told them so.

The following year, 2001, saw the council defiantly further endorse Lyons. Then Education Director Ken Corsar decided that four Milton primary schools – St Augustine's, St Ambrose, Chirnsyde and Miltonbank – plus two special needs school from nearby, should send their children to Chirnsyde for sports lessons. It had been bad enough when Lyons had been in Chirnsyde on a voluntary, part-time basis. Now, all the children of primary school age from these schools would be compulsorily sent there as part of their weekly school curriculum. Lyons would take them there and back in the minibus. At a stroke, with the creation of the Milton Schools Outreach Project, Chirnsyde had become an extension of six schools.

It made financial sense for schools to pool resources by sharing a facility but the campaigners were shocked and furious that the council should think it acceptable to force other people's children into Eddie's Club. Around a dozen parents staged a boycott as they did not want their children to be placed at risk by being anywhere near the den of criminality. Johnny McLean went further. He completely withdrew one of his sons, Dean, from Chirnsyde Primary School in protest. It was an act which the campaigners felt highlighted how serious the situation was but conversely played into the council's hands as it allowed them to portray this 'bampot' as unreasonable and unrepresentative.

The schools waged a campaign of emotional blackmail on parents and told them that it was unfair to isolate their children from classmates. Not only was there the imposition of guilt about the child missing out on the opportunity and enjoyment of physical education, council officials also tried to make the parents feel bad by telling them that it was costing significant sums of money to keep the children in classrooms when the rest of the class was at Chirnsyde.

As well as saving money by sharing one venue for PE, the council benefited through some questionable financial chicanery. Rather than use money from the council's education budget to provide PE lessons – as it was obliged to do – they instead tapped into SIPs money to fund the project at Chirnsyde.

Meanwhile, the control of Chirnsyde had passed from Education Director Corsar's department to Culture and Leisure which was headed by Bridget McConnell, the wife of Labour MSP Jack McConnell, then the party's Education Minister in the Scottish Parliament. The MSP for Motherwell and Wishaw – nicknamed Lucky Jack – was on the brink of becoming Scotland's First Minister following the death of Donald Dewar and the resignation of Dewar's successor Henry McLeish in an expenses scandal. His wife had been thrust into the public spotlight in the role of the politician's cheated wife. She sat by her man as he confessed to an affair seven years previously. The former teacher's public pronouncement of infidelity was a PR tactic which he assumed could help clinch him the top job in the new world of Scottish politics. Nine days later, on 22 November 2001, he was elected Scotland's First Minister.

Mrs McConnell became a focal point for the campaigners

as she stubbornly defended Lyons' Chirnsyde regime. Who she was married to was not the issue. Six weeks before her husband landed the most powerful job in Scotland, she made her position clear when she stepped in to the furious row about the enforced sending of pupils to Chirnsyde for PE lessons.

The campaigners had successfully lobbied Education Director Corsar over the potential risk to children. Their concerns were enough for Corsar to stop sending children there – not for long, though. McConnell was having none of it. She dismissed the parents' concerns in a lengthy letter to Corsar, dated 5 September 2001. At the heart of McConnell's letter – copies of which she also sent to Lyons and Councillor Hurcombe – was an admission which flew in the face of the council's long-stated position over the following years that there was no evidence of any criminality at Chirnsyde. McConnell admitted that she was aware of both the arson and vandalism attacks at the venue. She wrote:

Two incidents occurred which are the subject of enquiry. The first was an alleged wilful fire-raising on the roof of the building and the second was an apparent deliberate vandalism to the centre's minibus.

In the case of the first incident Strathclyde Police with the fire service are still investigating. In respect of the second incident I have been informed that a suspect has been charged by the police.

The suspect being Robert Daniel.

McConnell then informed Corsar – whose department was at that time under the control of her husband Jack's ministerial department – that her council officials had held a meeting with Lyons and his management committee. Her letter continued:

The result of that meeting was a recommendation by my officers that the Chirnsyde Community Initiative commission an independent risk assessment of the premises and its operations.

Chirnsyde selected a company called HSE Options to carry

out this work and they have carried out a full risk assessment and a training programme in the following areas: fire, evacuation, assessment of staff, weight equipment, hazardous materials, fire extinguisher courses to be set up in the near future.

HSE Options will provide a full written report within ten days but they have said that in their opinion there is no obstacle to this centre operating as normal.

Furthermore, Chirnsyde has asked Strathclyde Police to carry out a crime prevention survey of the building and this is in progress.

I am therefore satisfied that Chirnsyde should continue to operate as normal. I would hope that education services are willing to review the decision not to use the centre at the earliest possible date to allow it to function as normal.

It was an astonishing letter. McConnell candidly accepted that, despite Chirnsyde having been firebombed and its minibus trashed, her co-director Corsar should change his mind and overturn his decision not to send children there.

In addition, her proposed solution – the appointment of a firm to asses health and safety matters such as fire procedures and the use of gym equipment – completely failed to grasp the point at the heart of the issue – namely, whether a council centre run by a man like Lyons was a suitable place for young children to attend.

Exactly one week after McConnell's letter, it seems that Corsar's wobble had been corrected. In another letter, dated 12 September 2001, the council's then chief executive, James Andrews – the boss of both Corsar and McConnell – wrote to one of the campaigners. Andrews stated:

Education Services have discussed this with the head teachers in the area who use the Chirnsyde Initiative. They have stated that they are happy to continue to use the facility and do not believe that there are any dangers to the children concerned.

With regard to the recent allegations, the police have confirmed that there was one arson attempt at 2.30 a.m. one morning. They also confirm that a community bus was vandalised. At no time did this take place when any children were in the building or using the bus.

The director of Education Services [Corsar] is satisfied that the schools in question should continue to make use of this excellent facility.

These two letters written by McConnell and her boss Andrews, which endorsed Lyons in the face of the parents' legitimate concerns, only served to crank up the campaigners' letter-writing campaign. One parent, who sent the first of his many letters to McConnell in November 2001, said:

There were at least a dozen like-minded parents who were making a stand but I was lied to and told it was just me. Other parents got told that too and then we met we realised that was untrue – there were others. They hoped to keep us isolated. A few caved in under the pressure.

We were so determined that we never gave up. We ended up writing thousands of letters because we knew we were right. It took over our lives.

The more they told us that we were wrong and there wasn't a problem, the more it motivated us to keep going. There were times when friends and family members told us to give up because these people either don't believe you or they're not interested. But something kept us going.

I believe that we were doing something right – it might take time but it would happen.

Meanwhile, Lyons staged his own political manoeuvre to counter the campaigners by joining Milton Community Council in 2002. The council often struggled to find residents willing to become members so all Lyons had to do was find another resident to nominate him. He then flooded the council with his own supporters, including a friend whose son was a known drug dealer. He soon became its secretary while PC Cameron was usually in attendance at meetings. It was an astute move as it silenced the community council's dissent. Any attempt to raise the Chirnsyde issue was stifled. In protest, the campaigners resigned from the council en masse.

All they could do was challenge, cajole and badger those in power by churning out letters. They knew they were exposing themselves and their families to increased risk by standing up but it was the right thing to do and they knew they had to do it. That's what drove them. The campaigners grew increasingly bitter and untrusting of the council and police. They did not miss the irony in being ignored while putting themselves and their families at risk by standing up to crime in a city where the police routinely moan that too few people speak to them.

Another unlikely motive for at least one of the campaigners was the desire to see the Lyons boys themselves not become casualties of their father's criminal empire building. He said, 'They [the Lyons boys] later made their own choices but, in the early days, they were just out of their teens and under the spell of their father who was putting them in serious danger.'

The letter-writing campaign did score one victory with the resignation of PC John Cameron as Chirnsyde chairman. The issue had been raised at meetings and in letters, including one sent by Johnny McLean on 12 August 2001, to Chief Superintendent Margaret Barr. It stated, 'I would also appreciate written confirmation of the extent of your officer's [PC Cameron] involvement at this location [Chirnsyde] especially in light of the recent events and allegations of violent clashes between members of the management and other factions which some claim explain the fire which occurred on the roof of the initiative building last week amongst other things.'

Chirnsyde's minutes of its meeting on 7 March 2002, recorded that among the 10 people present were Lyons and his wife Josephine along with her sister Bernadette Gallagher, PC Cameron and Councillor Hurcombe. Under 'any other competent business', was the perfunctory note: 'Letter from John Cameron concerning his resignation. Committee thanks John Cameron for his many years of involvement.' By this point, the police had received numerous complaints about PC Cameron's connection to Lyons from the McDonnell family, the community campaigners and members of the force's own CID who had investigated the McDonnell stabbing.

Cameron's departure from Chirnsyde was also noted by Bridget McConnell in a letter written to McLean, dated 8 February 2002, in which she refused to make details of the lease agreement between Glasgow City Council and the Chirnsyde committee public. She wrote:

I have been advised that the issue of the lease to the general public would be a contravention of data protection regulations. As it is an annual tenancy base it is unregistered and to secure a copy would therefore require the written permission of Chirnsyde Community Initiative.

In respect of the chair of this project, Mr Cameron, he tendered his letter of resignation on December the 12th, 2001, and will formally stand down at the meeting to elect a new chair on or about February 21, 2002.

10

Gerbil Gunned Down

As Eddie Lyons Sr's confidence grew due to unwavering police and political patronage, Robert Daniel simply bided his time. He, along with the rest of the Daniel gang, had no intention of forgetting about the humiliating theft of their cocaine from the Milton house party or that it had ended up being peddled by the Club Boys.

Eddie Sr was pleased about the unofficial agreement, following the decision not to prosecute Robert for trashing the centre mini-bus, whereby trouble should be kept away from Chirnsyde but there was no truce elsewhere with ongoing simmering resentment, threats and violent flashpoints.

On the Daniel side were Robert, the ultra-violent Kevin Carroll and two of their close allies, Scott Bennett and Ross Sherlock. They were implicitly backed by Jamie and the elder generation. The young Lyons – Eddie Jr and Steven – were joined by Club Boys pals including Ross Monaghan, Andrew Gallagher and Paul McGuinness. They had the support of Eddie Sr, Johnny Lyons and, crucially, the veterans of the 1990s Paisley drugs war Robert Pickett and George Docherty.

The Daniels terrorised the Lyons as they competed to control the sale of drugs in the area. There had already been the botched attempt to shoot Steven outside Mallon's pub in late 2001 in the immediate aftermath of the cocaine theft.

From 2002 onwards, there were frequent car chases in which the Daniels played cat and mouse with the Lyons. Sometimes, the Lyons' cars were rammed in high-speed pursuits through residential streets. The safety of pedestrians was not a consideration. On at least one occasion, Eddie Sr was targeted for bumper-to-bumper contact as he drove the Chirnsyde minibus. Thankfully, no children were on board, as he was on a routine trip to a bookie's shop.

For the Lyons, it was very different to the one-way terror campaign they had inflicted on the McDonnell family three years earlier. They may have enjoyed an alliance with the McGovern brothers but that was just business. The McGoverns – who were still reeling from the murder of Tony – were not interested in fighting the Lyons' battles, especially those against the Daniels, and Pickett and Docherty could not be in Milton around the clock.

The next episode was a knife attack, what the military would term a 'blue on blue', when, at the beginning of January 2003, a young member of the Club Boys who peddled cocaine for the Lyons was slashed in the face. The good-looking victim, then in his early twenties and a close friend of Eddie Lyons Jr, joined the ranks of those in the city to suffer permanent facial disfigurement. The attack was not attributed to any of the Daniels but to Johnny Lyons – the swaggering, bragging brother of Eddie Sr, who loved to act the gangster and often reminisced about his brief time rubbing shoulders with the ex-pat criminals in Spain's Costa del Sol. Like his big brother, Johnny had never quite made the big time. It is not known whether the attack had taken place as a punishment for perceived disloyalty on the part of the victim or whether it had simply been an unjustifiable and cowardly liberty. Whatever the reason, the scarred victim – who later turned his back on crime to become a binman – decamped to the Daniels and worked for them instead.

For the Lyons boys, 'Uncle Johnny' was under increasingly intense pressure to help his besieged nephews by flexing his gangland muscle. Weeks after the slashing of the young coke dealer, the Lyons were to lash out against the Daniels in the most dramatic way with an act which massively escalated the seriousness of the feud and sparked a flurry of tit-for-tat attacks that helped shape the course of the decade-long gang war.

The Lyons went hunting and Carroll was in their sights. On 12 January 2003, Kevin 'Gerbil' Carroll was gunned down outside his mother Elizabeth's home in Mingulay Street, Milton. Carroll lived a short life filled with and ended by the most depraved, terrifying and extreme violence. Sometimes he was the victim – more often he was the perpetrator. His incongruous nickname of 'Gerbil' is derived from Kevin the Gerbil, a sidekick of 1980s children's TV puppet phenomenon Roland Rat. Carroll's long-term partner, and later the mother of his two sons, was Kelly Green, known by her nickname of Kelly Bo, who was a daughter of Jamie Daniel.

At the time of this first assassination attempt on him, Carroll was aged 22 and lived in Drumchapel, a sprawling social housing estate on the northern periphery of Glasgow, which was created in the 1950s to accommodate around 34,000 people. It was another area in which the Daniel family had strong connections and a firm grip on the drugs market.

On the day of the shooting, Carroll had left his mum's house with his Staffordshire bull terrier. As he put the dog into his friend Barry Kelly's car, in which Ross Sherlock was a passenger, a gunman sprang out from his hiding place in the garden. He chased after Carroll and blasted him twice in the leg with a sawn-off shotgun, sending him sprawling on to the road. Amidst the screaming victim, squealing car tyres and streaming blood, the gunman took off.

As expected, Carroll refused to co-operate with the CID officers. He, like the rest of the Daniel gang, wanted nothing to do with the police, many of whom reciprocated the loathing. Nonetheless, police enquiries led to the arrest of an 18-year-old suspect called Stephen Burgess, who was from Pickett's Paisley territory.

During the subsequent trial of Burgess, Carroll told the High Court in Glasgow, 'I was lying on the ground and the gunman was standing over me. He ran away when my mum came running out of her house. My leg was hanging off and I was taken to Stobhill Hospital.' Such was Carroll's volatile and argumentative behaviour at Stobhill, medical staff refused to treat him so he was taken instead to the Royal Infirmary where he underwent an operation on his leg. The jury were shown photographs of pellet wounds to his right leg and buttock and Carroll, like an old soldier, said that his injured limb was weak and seized up in cold weather as a result.

When asked by the prosecutor John Hamilton if he knew who had shot him, Carroll replied, 'No, he was wearing a ski mask.'

Asked if he knew why anyone should shot him, he gave the stock answer of gangland shooting victims: 'It must have been mistaken identity.'

Proceedings took an odd comic turn when, for some reason, the prosecutor decided to ask why he was known as 'Gerbil'. He replied that it was because he could run fast. He clearly hadn't run fast enough when the gunman leaped from the garden.

Sherlock, then 22, was next to give evidence. It was as sparse and unhelpful to the prosecution case as Carroll's had been and did nothing to implicate Burgess. He said, 'I heard a bang. We drove off. I thought the gunman was shooting at us in the car. I heard a second bang and we saw Kevin lying on the ground with the gunman standing over him. We turned the car. Kevin's mum was then outside and the gunman jogged away. I wanted to get to him and knock him down and kill him but we took Kevin to hospital instead.'

The car's 22-year-old driver, Barry Kelly, also gave evidence. He said that he drove forward when the shooting started then reversed as the gunman ran away.

The judge, Lord Menzies, had heard enough and he told the jury that, after two days, the Crown had abandoned its case against Burgess due to lack of evidence.

Just 11 days later, revenge was exacted for the shooting of Carroll when Eddie Lyons' brother Johnny Lyons was gunned down outside his home in Milton's Stornoway Street, a stone's throw from Mingulay Street. Two gunmen – one of them Carroll – pounced just as Johnny approached the front door of the home he shared with his partner Lynn McNair, a classroom assistant at Chirnsyde Primary School. Johnny, then aged 38, was peppered with shot across the top of his right leg.

In a bizarre move, he decided to speak publicly about what had happened and even posed for photographs in which he dropped his shell-suit trousers to show the ugly scarlet wounds across the top of his milky white thigh. In another photo, he squatted down and pointed glumly at the gunshot damage to his front door. It looked like the kind of photo that might be published in a local newspaper about a council tenant with a minor gripe.

Johnny also decided that it was a good idea to share with the readers that he was an associate of a major east-end drugs baron called Tam McGraw, who would die four years later. Described in the report as being unemployed, Johnny said, 'I'm not the nicest guy ever to walk the streets but my criminal days are behind me. The wallet in my back pocket caught around 40 pellets and the doctors think that may have saved me.'

It was thought that his brother, Eddie Lyons Sr, having enjoyed good publicity as the face of Chirnsyde, had urged Johnny to go public in a bid to dampen the growing press interest by downplaying the incident. It was not good advice from the supposedly smarter sibling as it would have taken a very gullible reader to swallow Johnny's proclamation of innocence, particularly when confronted with his forlorn demeanour, pasty face and panda eyes. The gunman who shot Johnny was never arrested.

Meanwhile, following the collapse of the prosecution of Stephen Burgess in October of that year, some Strathclyde Police officers briefed a court journalist with a different take on the tit-for-tat shootings. They claimed that the attempt to kill Carroll had actually been ordered by his de facto father-in-law Jamie Daniel and had not come from the Lyons camp at all. The rationale being that Carroll was shot because he had become too big for his boots and was making rash decisions without the consent of Daniel. It was also alleged that, for the time being, Carroll remained unaware of this secret Machiavellian plot. However, the Daniel gang – including Carroll himself – dismissed the police claims as propaganda, intended to sow seeds of mistrust and destabilise their operation. To confuse the picture even further, one theory is that the police unwittingly peddled this fake version of events because it had been planted in intelligence files by the deliberate spread of misinformation from the Daniel gang. They – and other gangs – know that feeding a line to a particular person or speaking over a phone line which is likely to be tapped will reach the ears of the police and help cloud, confuse and perhaps even derail a criminal investigation. As in a conventional war, truth is also often the first casualty of in the gangland variety. What was clear was that Carroll was a promising apprentice to Daniel and a useful asset because of his willingness to inflict extreme violence on rivals or those who had not paid their debts. Over the following years, he would become one of the most ruthless and dangerous criminals in the country, whose reputation terrified the established, older generation ensconced behind the gates of their suburban mansions.

Weeks later, the Daniels staged a second attempt to shoot Johnny. This time, it was a poor aim rather than a fat wallet which saved him. Witnesses claimed that he was walking on his street towards a phone kiosk when a car drove up and a gun was stuck out of the window. It was alleged that shots were exchanged between the drive-by duo and their pedestrian target but no rounds reached either of the shooters' intended destination. Johnny fled and, within moments, the area was buzzing with a swarm of black-clad armed police officers, their Heckler & Koch machine guns primed and ready.

One resident summed up the mood of the area, by telling the press, 'There was at least one shot fired. It was terrifying. There were wee ones out and mothers with babies. The streets were crawling with police officers within minutes. The sooner these madmen are put behind bars, the better.'

11

In the Spotlight – the Daniels

As the tit-for-tat gun battle between the Lyons and Daniels ensued, Jamie Daniel's world was about to be turned upside down. He and his family were to have their decades-long anonymity destroyed as a newspaper laid bare their criminal empire.

The *Sunday Mail*'s 'Crime Inc' investigation fundamentally changed the media's depiction of cops-and-robbers criminality typified by the tired sagas of old-timers like Arthur Thompson, Paul Ferris and Tam McGraw. Much crime reporting was either sepia-tinted or propaganda which glamorised thugs. Newspapers rarely looked beyond a handful of well-known criminals – who often courted and controlled publicity – and many other significant gangs that operated under the radar. But the new approach rejected the awestruck fawning previously directed towards the inhabitants of this most seedy and ugly of worlds. The mind-blowing financial scale of organised crime in the country, a black economy in which billions of pounds swirled around, was spelled out. The investigation revealed an underworld rich list of the country's top 10 wealthiest participants and staring out from the front page was an unfamiliar face – Jamie Daniel, gangster number one. This was the man whose name had last appeared in a newspaper two decades earlier when he was sentenced at Chichester Crown Court in 1983.

The tone struck and the language used to expose Daniel and others were gradually embraced and aped by other media, politicians and police chiefs who finally acknowledged the depth and sophistication of Scotland's multibillion-pound drugs trade and the money-laundering enterprises which spread out of the schemes into suburbia, big business, politics and private schools. A week after the exposé of the Daniels, a follow-up report carried a quote from a police source which, with its biblical analogy, summed up the received wisdom as to where the power lay between them and their rivals. The source said, 'We are aware of two groups actively pursuing each other. We're fairly certain neither side will back down and more shootings can be expected. Unlike the bible story when Daniel was thrown to the lions, on this occasion it's the Lyons who should be worried.'

Detectives knew exactly who was involved in the tit-for-tat shootings in Milton but neither side would play ball. Despite Eddie Lyons Sr's long, close and fruitful connections to police officers and his previous full co-operation when he was stabbed in Cadder in the 1980s, his sons and the Club Boys vocally denounced all 'grasses', unaware of the irony as it pertained to their own father.

The shootings in Milton began to make headlines which brought pressure on the police to do something about it. It's a truism that, when such acts take place outwith the media glare, they do not always receive the same level of a force's manpower and money as those that are played out in the public eye.

In February 2003, BBC Radio Scotland responded to events by staging an outside broadcast from Milton in a live show hosted by Lesley Riddoch. Guests included the Labour MSP for Maryhill Patricia Ferguson, Strathclyde Police's then Assistant Chief Constable Graeme Pearson, who became a Labour MSP eight years later, and Reg McKay, a social worker turned crime writer known for promoting various criminals. Due to the nature of live broadcasting and the stringent legal restrictions, no mention was made of the Daniel or Lyons families. To the 'bampots' like Johnny McLean, that was a let-down. A prime-time radio programme was being broadcast to homes, cars and workplaces across the nation and it was only happening because of the gang war. Yet, like an elephant in the room, no one could or would mention what it was actually about. At one point, a well-meaning contributor waffled on about a lack of buses.

The unfamiliarity of being in the media spotlight seemed to be getting to Jamie Daniel. It would certainly explain why someone so adept at staying hidden for so long would stage a vicious attack on a taxi driver, in broad daylight, in front of a number of witnesses. Taxi driver James Gallagher was a white-haired 60-year-old who thought nothing of it when his boss sent a message over the car's radio asking him to pop into the office of East Side Cabs in Kirkintilloch, a former mining town just north of Glasgow. He noticed there was a BMW with blacked-out windows parked outside but didn't give it a second thought. He was then confronted by Daniel, chest puffed out and bearing down. Gallagher was viciously assaulted. He managed to scramble to his feet and lurch through the front door and into the taxi office. Gallagher shouted at the company owner Derek Steel and manager John Wyvar for help but the attack continued.

The attacker then allegedly shouted to the taxi firm bosses, 'Get rid of that bastard or I'll have this place torched.'

Bloodied and shaken, Gallagher – who did not drive for the company again – was asked by Steel, 'Do you know who that man is?'

Gallagher had heard of the Daniels by reputation but he had no idea that it had been the boss, Jamie Daniel, the godfather himself, standing in front of him. He was oblivious as to why he had been attacked, only later discovering it was because of a minor incident in a Tesco car park when he had gestured at one of Daniel's lovers, Samantha Kerr, following a near miss as she walked in front of his taxi.

The punches to Gallagher's head caused him a broken nose and jaw, permanent disfigurement and breathing difficulties but he was no soft touch. Despite being well aware of the Daniels' reach, he decided to co-operate with the detectives who were very pleased indeed. It was the first time in decades that they had the chance to get Daniel in the dock but Gallagher's fighting spirit soon evaporated. He suffered a relentless campaign by the Daniels which chipped away at his resolve. His protection was compromised and he repeatedly received warnings about the consequences of going to court. By the time Gallagher reached the witness stand at Glasgow Sheriff Court, he had suffered a memory lapse and, crucially, failed to identify the man in the dock as his attacker.

During the three-day trial Daniel was defended by top QC and Labour MSP Gordon Jackson but the taxpayer-funded lawyer earned his fees easily as he did not need to get off his seat to cross-examine a single witness. The taxi firm's telephonist Dawn Leckenby and controller Nadia McElhaney said they could remember nothing about the attack that took place at their office. The trial was a farce. Sheriff Craig Henry decided there was no case to answer and Daniel was allowed to go free, to the fury of Maryhill CID officers who suspected that too many people had been got at.

After the collapse of the trial, a friend of Gallagher, who was placed under police protection, said, 'No one else was willing to speak. Even if he could point the finger, there would have been no corroboration. It was a no-win situation so he got amnesia.'

The detectives' anger increased when the police officers guarding the court – not usually among the force's brightest and best – took it upon themselves to grant Daniel special treatment by allowing him to slip out a back door in order to evade the cameras lying in wait. Daniel was sick of long lenses.

12

In the Spotlight – the Lyons

Johnny Lyons had flaunted his bullet-ridden backside for the cameras and his family's gun battle with the Daniels had been documented but, to the frustration of Johnny McLean and the other three bampots, Eddie Lyons Sr remained in the shadows.

However, McLean had different ideas and was going to do his best to ensure he couldn't hide there forever. During the St Augustine's playing fields battle, he became known for appearing unannounced at newspaper offices, wearing his trademark bunnet, long coat and thick glasses, to deliver towering dossiers of correspondence and other documents to reporters. This dogged persistence led to a breakthrough when the media attention swung towards Lyons at Chirnsyde and the potential risk to children's safety due to the ongoing drugs war.

It was the *Sunday Mail* that first shone a light on Chirnsyde with a story published on 23 February 2003. It carried a snatched photo of a startled looking Lyons, his mouth hanging open, in the Chirnsyde car park below the headline: 'Would you let this man look after your children?' The headline cut like a knife through the spin, denials and disingenuousness of the police and city council. When those nine words were put to those who defended Lyons' Chirnsyde regime, the honest answer was usually a firm 'no'.

For the first time, the story made public how Lyons was being bankrolled to the tune of £120,000 a year with taxpayers' money while his family were fighting a turf war with the Daniels over the heroin trade. Its key message was about the safety of children using Chirnsyde while Lyons remained in charge.

The story stated:

A MEMBER of a notorious crime family is picking up £120,000 a year of taxpayers' money to run a community centre.

Eddie Lyons – whose family is waging a violent turf war with Glasgow's most powerful gangsters, the Daniels – runs the centre in the city's Milton area.

But worried parents are boycotting the Chirnsyde Community Initiative because they fear their children could be caught up in the feud.

One dad said: 'I'm not sending my kids there and I know other parents are keeping their children away while all this is kicking off. My kids won't be going near this place while he's in charge.'

Lyons, 45, receives funding for Chirnsyde from both Glasgow City Council and the Scottish Executive.

Yet the centre has already been the scene of violent exchanges and Lyons himself was once charged with attempted murder when a man was brutally beaten at Chirnsyde.

The council say they are 'very happy' with Chirnsyde and that ending an after-school scheme for kids at the centre was due to lack of cash – not fear of violence.

Last month the Sunday Mail revealed how the Lyons – connected to multi-millionaire criminal Tam 'The Licensee' McGraw – were involved in a feud to control the heroin trade in north Glasgow.

Their rivals are the Daniel clan, recently exposed by the Sunday Mail as Scotland's wealthiest crime family.

The tit-for-tat battle began on January 13 when a Daniel gang member, nicknamed Gerbil, was shot and seriously injured. Eddie's gangster brother John, 38, was blasted with a shotgun 10 days later.

But locals claim there have been two other firearms incidents that were not reported to police.

And campaigners, furious at police failure to end the gun feud between the hated drug-peddling families, find it incredible that Lyons is allowed to earn a good living from money designated to help the community.

One local said: 'The Lyons are scumbags who have helped scar Milton for decades.'

Billy McAllister, chair of the Northwest Communities Alliance, said: 'For years we've questioned the suitability of this individual to receive such vast amounts of public money.

'However our greatest concern is the safety of children who are expected to attend a centre where a number of gang-related incidents have taken place.'

Lyons, meanwhile, enjoys a good lifestyle and is seen driving cars including an Audi and a BMW.

A Glasgow City Council spokesman said: 'This year Chirnsyde received £77,000. Eddie Lyons got kids involved to take part in clubs and after school activities. He encouraged local primary kids along.

'This no longer happens but violence was not an issue in any decision and the department was very happy with services provided by Chirnsyde.'

A spokeswoman for Glasgow Alliance – who monitor the distribution of the Executive's Social Inclusion Partnerships (SIPS) funds – said: 'In the past year SIPS allocated £11,000 to Milton Schools Outreach Project and £39,000 to Chirnsyde Community Initiative Schools Outreach Project.'

Lyons claims criticism of his role in running the centre is political, originating from SNP activists.

He said his relatives' actions could not be blamed on him and that local people had faith in his work.

Lyons said: 'This is a politically-motivated vendetta. I've got nothing to hide. I am not my brother's keeper.'

The families also clashed two years ago when Lyons' son Steven, 22, was attacked by the Daniels. Robert Daniel, nephew of the family's driving force Jamie, was arrested after hunting for Lyons at Chirnsyde.

In 2000, Lyons and several other family members were charged with attempted murder after Thomas McDonnell was attacked by a mob at the centre. The case against Lyons was dropped before trial.

It was the kind of publicity that Lyons was unused to yet he was cocksure enough to think that he could swat it aside. He distanced himself from his brother Johnny and ridiculously claimed to be the victim of political rivalry between the SNP and Labour. He even falsely claimed that people were getting his family mixed up with another unsavoury family of a similar name.

Councillor Ellen Hurcombe sprang to his defence. She told the *Sunday Mail*:

What's happening is the children are enjoying themselves play-ing and it's been like that all the way along.

If you'd actually spoken to the mothers of the children that use the facilities you'd hear that.

I was at a school board meeting the other day and people were horrified with what was going on.

This is a vendetta against one person. There's no violence in Chirnsyde.

When the trashing of the Chirnsyde minibus was put to her, she said, 'That wasn't in the centre it was in the grounds so I think you have to get your facts correct.' Hurcombe went on to reveal that she had no knowledge of the McDonnell attempted murder at the centre where she held her surgeries. She said, 'I obviously didn't know about this. I just want you to print the truth for a change. I have no problem with Mr Lyons. I have never socialised with him. I have never seen a problem in the centre.'

Asked about the ongoing violence between the two tribes, she added:

They're a concern only if it affected the centre and it doesn't. It's not Eddie Lyons that's involved in it.

Obviously you've got more information than I have. You should go to Maryhill police station and get the truth from them.

I think you're persecuting one person. Where do you get your information from?

If you're not prepared to tell me where you get your information from I'm not prepared to talk to you.

How many times do you think this person and this centre has been up under scrutiny (*sic*) by allegations made by four people continually.

You tell me who the senior politicians that have a problem with it (*sic*).

Just tell me what senior politicians in that area who actually know anything about the centre.

Hurcombe's stance led to unsuccessful calls for her resignation from Strathclyde Police Board, the elected body of councillors which holds the police force to account. One campaigner wrote to its convenor, saying:

She has recklessly dismissed concerns of many of her constituents, just like myself, in order to support Eddie Lyons, who is a member of a family that are well known to be one of the leading crime families in this area.

Her statement is at best highly unprofessional and my concern is further fuelled by the well-known close relationship that she holds with members of the Lyons family.

Two of Lyons' employees, Andrew McKay and Roy McPhail, wrote to the parents of children who used the centre. Their letter of bombast and denial stated:

The article published in the Sunday Mail was rather concerning to ourselves as sports co-ordinators based at Chirnsyde in the sense that it was clearly misleading and appeared to be aimed at upsetting and putting fear in the minds of local people and parents such as yourselves.

We are taking this opportunity to inform you that such allegations are completely unfounded and have been proved so on many occasions in the past.

In addition, during the some three years of the after-schools running there has not been a single incident that raises concern about the security or suitability of Chirnsyde as a centre for children's activities. Clearly, there is no reason for you to jump to any negative conclusions based upon the Sunday Mail article.

As part of the multi-pronged defence, Lyons instructed a lawyer to complain to the newspaper. He whined that linking him with the criminal activity of family members which had nothing to do with him was 'unfair and defamatory'. It was a hollow legal threat. The facts were beyond dispute. If anything, he was lucky that the story had not gone into greater detail, especially about the attempted murder at Chirnsyde and his alleged role in it.

Despite Hurcombe's staunch defence of Lyons, concerns were voiced by MSP Patricia Ferguson, who had previously visited Chirnsyde with PC Cameron as they pounded the beat for the glowing *Evening Times* feature back in 2000. Ferguson had become the Minister for Parliamentary Business – the Labour Party's chief whip in Holyrood. She had been appointed by First Minister Jack McConnell five days after he took office. McConnell's wife Bridget was in charge of Chirnsyde and her views on the matter were already very well known.

Ferguson requested talks with the council's Chief Executive James Andrews. Ferguson said, 'I do have concerns about this particular centre and for that reason I'm meeting with Glasgow City Council's chief executive later this month. I know about the allegations being made and that concerns me. I want to be assured that the monitoring and evaluation of the work going on there and funded by the council is appropriate. And I also want to make sure that they've taken every step possible to ensure the safety of any children that might be using the facility.'

The sentiment was echoed by Ann McKechin, the area's MP, who said, 'People have the right to be considered innocent until proven otherwise but on the other hand there are some concerns about safety and young people.'

Despite the promising words, the campaigners were unconvinced. They correctly predicted that public concerns would not result in action. The closed-doors meeting between Ferguson and council officials yielded nothing.

Given the Labour Party's support of Lyons' regime, the campaigners turned towards the SNP, the second largest party in the city.

At the time, Labour in Glasgow dismissed the SNP as an irrelevance. In 2003, there were 71 Labour councillors compared to just eight from other parties – three each from the SNP and Lib Dems with solo Tory and Scottish Socialist members. Labour seemed to think that it could do what it wanted and often did. But some opposition politicians vehemently opposed the possibility of children being put at risk at Chirnsyde. Sandra White, an SNP MSP, lodged eight parliamentary questions about the opaque world of SIP's funding of which Chirnsyde was a recipient.

She wrote to Labour's Social Justice Minister Margaret Curran to ask for a public enquiry into Chirnsyde and SIPs in general and added, 'The police have said there is a drugs war going on in Milton and Chirnsyde has been at the centre of it. I'm concerned about the council's funding and involvement. As far as I am aware the council is still sending children here.'

While the media and politicians had begun to take notice, the violence continued. The campaigners still hoped that the council would do the right thing and remove Lyons. To their dismay, but no great surprise, nothing changed. The young Lyons boys even started showing off newspaper clippings about their exploits to girls in nightclubs. They basked in their new public notoriety.

Most of the campaigners' bitterness was reserved for Ferguson whose public questioning promised so much but delivered nothing. The campaigners were utterly amazed when, one year later, the MSP wrote a friendly letter to Lyons which was addressed 'Dear Eddie' and signed personally by her. It asked for his views on which worthy individual should be selected to represent the Maryhill constituency at the official opening of the new Scottish Parliament building – ten times over budget and over three years late – towards the end of that year. She wrote, 'I am keen to ensure that as many people as possible are considered for this honour and I would encourage you to submit a nomination if you have not already done so. So there is still time for you to send your nomination to me at the address below and I enclose a further copy of the nomination form for your convenience. I am looking forward to hearing from you and can be contacted on 946-XXXX should you require any further information regarding this.'

Any hope that Lyons had lost his Labour Party patronage was binned. He was in with the bricks. This made the campaigners even more determined than ever and they continued to lobby the media, politicians, the police or anyone else who might listen. Their main weapon was still the relentless flow of letters which chronicled every single issue and event. They challenged individuals and organisations with a hand in what was going on. By doing so, they were each held to account. The police often pleaded with the campaigners to stop writing to them as they struggled under the deluge of correspondence. The campaigners refused as they suspected that the police were more interested in the vast number of complaints coming to an end than they were in tackling the problem. At this rate, the postman with Strathclyde Police HQ in Pitt Street on his round would become the next casualty of the gang war as the letters flowed faster than ever.

13

Kalashnikov Attack

Kevin Carroll felt the weight of the Kalashnikov AK-47 assault rifle in his hands and a grin spread across his face. The iconic Russian weapon, of which 75 million have been produced since the 1940s, has been used to inflict devastation and death in wars, acts of terror and criminal underworlds worldwide.

Through the Daniel family, Carroll was able to lay his hands on an arsenal that was numerous and varied. They constantly added to their stash of firearms which were kept in lofts, under floorboards or buried in fields, back gardens and waste ground, ready and waiting for action. They were vital tools of their vile trade. Carroll, however, held a particular fascination that seemed to go beyond what might be expected. He let it be known that he was always a willing buyer. If you had a gun for sale, Carroll paid cash. Almost fanatically, he amassed dozens of his own, separate to those owned by the Daniels. His favourite was a 9mm Glock pistol which he nicknamed 'Olly Green' because of its drab military hue. Made from a heavy plastic, the Austrian weapons are hugely desirable because of their ability to evade metal detectors and the difficulty in using ballistic tests to link individual weapons to fired rounds.

He was partly driven to buy so many guns because he felt that, if he snapped up as many of those being touted on the streets of north Glasgow as he could, it would mean there would be fewer available to fall into the hands of his rivals and which could potentially be used against him as had happened once already when he was ambushed outside his mum's house. It was paranoid and astute yet ultimately futile.

Three months had passed since the trial of Stephen Burgess had collapsed and Carroll was itching to hit back against the Lyons. Chasing them in cars was not good enough.

Under cover of winter darkness on 10 January 2004, an opportunity arose. This time, the shotgun used to pepper Johnny Lyons' backside was left in its hiding place and Carroll's beloved AK-47 had been brought out of storage. Carroll was not fussy about which of the Lyons or their pals to shoot. Steven and Eddie Jr topped his wish list but their Club Boys cronies were also fair game.

John Madden was one such person and, on the day in question, he was paying a visit to the home of brothers Brian and Andrew Ferguson, both of whom were Chirnsyde attendees. Elder brother Brian was a pal of Steven and Eddie Jr while Andrew was closer in age to the youngest Lyons boy, Christopher, then aged 14.

Madden was considered by Carroll to be a capable member of the Lyons team. It is unclear whether he had arrived or left the Fergusons' home but Carroll's intelligence that he was there – either based on a pattern of behaviour or a tip-off – was spot on.

Carroll strode boldly into Ronaldsay Street, a few hundred metres away from Chirnsyde and at the heart of the Lyons' territory. As he did so, he tightly gripped the AK-47 and stopped in front of a small, dark-coloured van in which Madden was sitting, trapped.

Thankfully for Madden, the weapon was set to semi-automatic meaning that single shots were fired rather than a scything burst of automatic fire which would have produced ten rounds per second. At least one round went through the windscreen and tore through the flesh and bone of Madden's shoulder. Blood from the wound started spouting through the interior of the vehicle.

Madden suffered horrendous injuries and was lucky to survive. Shortly afterwards, he moved 15 miles out of Glasgow to a small village in deepest Lanarkshire. His days on the frontline were over.

It was a bold act by Carroll and one which was not picked up by the media. The police decided to keep the incident out of the public eye so did not issue a press release although the detectives at Maryhill police station were fully aware of exactly what had happened and who was involved. When they discovered the type of weapon that had been used, their concerns rose further. The police eventually charged Carroll with the attempted murder of Madden but the Crown Office prosecutors decided that there was not enough evidence to bring him to trial and the case eventually fizzled out.

The shooting heaped more pressure on the Lyons who lived with the intense fear that, at any second of any day, a gun could emerge from the window of a passing vehicle and their lives could be snuffed out. It was enough to make them purchase bulletproof vests, the gangland equivalent of a life insurance policy. Within weeks of the Madden shooting, Eddie Jr was stopped in nearby Torogay Street by police officers who asked him why he was wearing a protective vest. He replied that it was because his pal Madden had just been shot and then pointed out to the officers that it was not illegal to own or wear such an item.

The gun used by Carroll has never been recovered but a year later police found a stash of 30 AK-47 cartridges in a house in Drumchapel. It was fortuitous as the homeowner was only caught because he had assaulted his girlfriend who had then shopped him. He did not reveal the identities of the underworld thugs who he claimed had ordered him to look after their prized ammunition but, given that they were for an AK-47 – rare on UK streets – and that they were found at a house in Carroll's Drumchapel territory, the police drew their own conclusions.

The campaigners fighting to remove Lyons from Chirnsyde and get it back to being run as a normal community centre were also fearful. Not only had the attack happened close to Chirnsyde, which the victim frequented, but the type of firepower marked an escalation in the violence. More bloodshed seemed inevitable. Who in the council, police or the Labour Party could possibly guarantee that no shots would be fired in or around Chirnsyde?

Yet, the campaigners thought the view from within the council was either dangerously dismissive or arrogantly indifferent.

What else could explain the letter which was sent out on 12 January 2004 – two days after the AK-47 shooting – to the parents of children who attended St Augustine's Primary, the school in which there was a plaque to the late pupil Garry Lyons? In it, the principal teacher extended the exciting offer to send 28 pupils to an after-school coaching club at Chirnsyde by Celtic Football Club. The kids were to be transported to and from the venue by Eddie Lyons Sr in one of the club's mini-buses. The letter stated:

> This course will be delivered by fully qualified Celtic coaches in the community halls at Chirnsyde Community Initiative centre. The programme will begin on Tuesday the 18th of January from 3–5pm and will last for eight weeks.
>
> Pupils will be collected from school at 3pm in one of the centre's minibuses (seating restrictions will require two journeys). Pupils will be returned to school (or home, at the parent's request) at the end of each session.
>
> Should more children wish to take part than there are spaces, the names will be put in a hat.

The campaigners immediately fired off letters to Celtic, the police and the council which resulted in the football club hastily withdrawing from Chirnsyde and finding an alternative venue in Springburn.

Eddie Sr was furious at the loss of hosting the Celtic event and angrily denounced the meddling parents who he branded – with some predictability and irony – as grasses.

The campaigners were later able to demand answers about the Celtic incident thanks to the Freedom of Information (Scotland) Act 2002 which provided them with a powerful new tool. Council officials and police officers, used to fobbing them off with vague and woolly letters of reply, were now obliged by law to divulge information, albeit with conditions and exceptions.

One resident asked Glasgow City Council Director of Education Ronnie O'Connor who, in the education department, had checked with the police to clarify the suitability of Chirnsyde and its staff to host kids at the Celtic training. The answer? 'No member of education services contacted the police on this matter.' The fact that the council had not sought police advice before hosting the prestigious and high-profile event did not surprise the residents. The answer again confirmed that the council were clearly satisfied with Lyons' regime at Chirnsyde, despite all that had happened.

14

Cash Crisis

Eddie Jr, Steven and their Club Boys had come a long way from ruling the roost as teenagers at their taxpayer-funded gang hut. After years of being nurtured by Eddie Sr, the young men were in their early 20s and had 'graduated'. They had been taken off the streets into a youth club ostensibly to keep them out of trouble only for the opposite to happen. Eddie Sr was more like the Fagin character of the Charles Dickens classic *Oliver Twist*. The Lyons boys had gained gangland kudos for withstanding the onslaught by the Daniels and Kevin Carroll, which stemmed from the stolen haul of cocaine three years earlier. Bulletproof vests were a necessity and they could never be alone in public but they had survived and were still visible and active.

Eddie Lyons Sr must have been proud. His boys were talking the talk and walking the walk at around the same age he had been when he was stabbed, branded a grass and spirited out of Cadder by the police. His boys were mixing with serious people, such as Paisley gangster Robert Pickett who, a decade earlier, had been jailed for his role in the drugs war that had gripped the town. The family's connections to the Paisley gang had become even stronger. Pickett and his crew were unconcerned by the reputations of the Daniels.

But, no matter what connections Eddie Sr had cultivated with police officers over the years, the activities of his two eldest sons had begun to come to the attention of senior detectives tasked with tackling Scotland's drugs gangs and their names began to feature heavily on police intelligence files. Within the space of two weeks, in the month of February 2004, they ran into some very big problems which could have prematurely ended their gangland aspirations.

It was a fortnight which cost them £264,000 of drugs and cash and which also put Steven Lyons and other Club Boys back in the dock of the High Court. The rapid chain of events began on 5 February 2004, when Steven was stopped by police while in a vehicle in Lanarkshire. Using the relatively new proceeds of crime laws, the officers were able to seize the cash he was carrying – a cool £14,980. It was a serious amount of money for most people to have in their back pocket, let alone a 23-year-old with no discernible source of income. It was not far off the annual take-home wage of Steven's father Eddie Sr as Chirnsyde co-ordinator. It was money that Steven seemed willing to lose as he did not bother to turn up at Hamilton Sheriff Court to offer any kind of story that the cash was clean and that he should have it back.

Nine days after Steven's drug money was seized from the car, he landed in much more serious trouble on a night out in the early hours of St Valentine's Day. He and several Club Boys, including Ross Monaghan, Charles McMurray and others, had driven to a nightclub called Tuscany in the town of Kirkintilloch, just north of Glasgow, perhaps with trouble in mind. Inside they put on a display of swaggering machismo. They arrogantly scattered their dirty cash as they leered at the women and sneered at the men. It was intimidating and ugly behaviour, guaranteed to provoke hostility. Like virtually any club where speed, cocaine and ecstasy are washed down with strong lager and potent, multicoloured shots, trouble was not exactly rare. However, what happened that night in Tuscany – an unlikely name for a sticky-carpeted, canal-side venue in the one-time mining town – went beyond the typical Friday night kicking.

It was a bloodbath. The Club Boys were relatively unscathed but six other men were hospitalised – they all suffered stab wounds. Of those, three were lucky not to end up in the morgue. One suffered 10 separate strikes with a razor-sharp fisherman's blade. As the scene of terror unfolded outside, the unarmed locals did not stand a chance. But knives were not enough for the Club Boys. Suddenly, a car was driven straight into two of the stab victims. The short burst of squealing tyres ended with a sickening, dull impact as human skittles were sent flying. Two men were struck while others luckily dodged out of the way. Four of the six victims still carry the physical scars from that horrific night and will do so until the day they die.

The scale and seriousness of the terror inflicted on innocent clubbers enjoying an evening out merited a significant police investigation. The Club Boys – in particular Steven and Monaghan – were in the frame from the outset. An attempt to intimidate one of the victims 48 hours after the attack only raised the heat on them as he provided the police with the car registration of those who had delivered the warning not to 'grass'.

Six days after the nightclub carnage, police crashed through various addresses linked to the Lyons family and their associates. The raids took place to hunt down those responsible for the Tuscany attacks, but the police got lucky. As they snared Steven and Monaghan, they also uncovered £185,000 worth of cannabis.

Steven was arrested over the Tuscany attacks while another Club Boy, 42-year-old Susan Paterson and her lover Gavin Harper were also taken into custody. The decision by Harper, then aged 25 and the deputy manager of a residential home for vulnerable children, not to inform his council bosses of his arrest in connection with a major drugs haul later led to questions being asked about his social work role.

That same day, the Lyons suffered another major blow when the police searched a house in Kelvin Crescent in the Lanarkshire town of East Kilbride. It was a home which Eddie Sr had bought for £140,000 the previous summer and where Steven lived, a safe 15 miles from the mean streets of Milton where he was preyed upon by the Daniels. The detectives were ecstatic when they found a bag containing £63,000 in cash. It had been a good day's work for the police – and a very costly one for the Lyons with five arrests and the loss of drugs and cash. It was painful lesson. Crazy, reckless and high-profile acts of violence, along with ostentatious shows of wealth, only attracted the attention of the police. The Tuscany rampage had cost them dear.

News of the drugs bust and the arrests soon spread to the campaigners in Milton. It was yet more evidence that the Lyons were actively involved in drug dealing at a significant level. What was more important to them was the issue of the cash which had been uncovered at Eddie Sr's property in East Kilbride. The *Sunday Mail* got wind of the cash seizure and phoned Eddie Sr on 14 April 2004, to try to establish the facts. Mindful of the damage such news could inflict on his Chirnsyde role, he gave terse and dishonest answers during the 37-second call before hanging up. This is the full extent of what he said when questioned about the cash seizure: 'Sorry, can't speak to you . . . Don't know what you're talking about. . . . Don't know what you're talking about . . . Don't know what you're talking about . . . Don't know what you're talking about . . . have a nice day, sir.' He could not admit the cash was his or that he even knew about it. One of his sons' friends – a long time Club Boy who can't be named for legal reasons – stepped forward and claimed that he was the true owner of the £63,000.

At the time, rumours swirled as to how much had been seized but the police and Crown Office steadfastly refused to make the information available to the public or even confirm the basic details. Their secrecy denied the public the right to learn about something they had every right to know about. It was great news for Lyons as it gave him two years during which he continued to pose as an honest community leader before he had to deal with the awkward question of what £63,000 of drugs money had been doing in his house. It was not until January 2006 that the public found out the truth when its supposed owner signed a mandate at the High Court in Edinburgh, forfeiting the cash, which was officially recorded as being the 'proceeds of drug trafficking'.

In the meantime, more legal chicanery had taken place in relation to the £185,000 worth of drugs seized on the same day as the cash. Heroin had been found by the police yet only charges relating to cannabis were mentioned on the indictment that was served on the unnamed Club Boy who, despite being one of four arrested, again took the fall alone. Three charges were levelled at him. Charge one was that he had been concerned in the supply of cannabis resin at his home in Ivanhoe Drive, Kirkintilloch, and at the Kelvin Crescent property owned by Eddie Sr. Charge two was that he had been in possession of cannabis resin on the day of his arrest. Charge three – subtly different to the second charge – was that he had been in possession of cannabis on the day of his arrest.

The Crown Office struck a deal with the accused's lawyer whereby he agreed to plead guilty to the first charge in exchange for the other two being dropped. One final legal flourish was required before everyone was happy. The Club Boy culprit laid down a condition. Court records reveal that he only pled guilty to the charge of dealing drugs at Ivanhoe Drive and that doing so from Kelvin Crescent should be deleted from the indictment. The Crown duly obliged. Such a demand had no bearing on the seriousness of the charge or on the severity of the sentence. It served one purpose – and that was to distance the drugs bust from Eddie Sr and his property. The fall guy was given a 30-month jail sentence.

Months later, it was the turn of Steven and Monaghan to look out their best suits as they prepared to appear at the High Court in Glasgow over the mindless orgy of violence at Tuscany. They had no plans to join their friend behind bars. Steven had already beaten an attempted murder rap over the stabbing of Thomas McDonnell at Chirnsyde three years earlier. He was charged with three more attempted murders which he also walked away from – an impressive record of four in four years.

It seems that Steven and Monaghan had at least learned some lessons in the value of discretion. They were dropped at court each morning in a BMW convertible and sent gofers as lookouts to ensure no cameras lay in wait. The pair covered their faces and even sprinted uptown from the Clydeside court into a maze of city centre streets and lanes in order to dodge the long lenses but the *Sunday Mail* eventually captured them.

Monaghan was charged with driving a car at two men – Graham Syme and Robert Anderson – and knocking them down. He was also charged with inflicting knife wounds on Michael McLaughlin to his 'severe injury and permanent disfigurement' while also injuring Brendan Ferns less seriously with the blade. Both Steven and Monaghan were charged with the attempted murder of Syme by punching, kicking and knifing him on the head and body. Steven alone was charged with repeatedly stabbing Garry Scullion, who was maimed for life. Finally, Steven was charged with the attempted murder of Anderson and Gary Brown, both of whom were also scarred for life. The trial was an utter farce tainted by strong suspicions of witnesses having been nobbled through intimidation. During proceedings, several of those who took the stand were warned by the judge, Lord Reed, for failing to identify their alleged attackers.

In an incredible twist, another Club Boy associate stepped forward and, under oath, incriminated himself. Charles McMurray, who had not even been charged with anything, claimed that he was responsible. It torpedoed the credibility of the prosecution case. The Crown was forced to drop the charge against Steven of attempting to murder Anderson. Most of the other, less serious charges also fell by the wayside. By the time the prosecution case limped across the finish line, all charges against Monaghan had been marked 'no case to answer' and he was in the clear. All that remained were two of the attempted murder charges levelled at Steven. The jurors – by a majority verdict – found him not guilty of the murder bids on Syme and Brown.

The police who had worked hard to put them in the dock were sickened, prompting one to say, 'They walked because the witnesses never spoke up. Many were afraid of the Lyons family reputation. Witnesses were taken to court by the police and these are decent people with jobs and families. They were scared and we offer witness protection but, to accept that, their whole families would have to move away from the area. But the system, being what it is, these people know it's not worth it to them. Some of them have risked going to jail themselves by not speaking in court. If they're more willing to go to jail than point the finger at these people, what chance do we have?'

15

Meet McAllister

Billy McAllister was a teenage apprentice welder when union leader Jimmy Reid famously warned the men of the Upper Clyde Shipbuilders that 'there will be no bevvying' during the work-in to save the yards from liquidation in 1971. One year later, the unprecedented campaign resulted in victory. The experience helped to shape McAllister's politics of honesty, fairness and fighting for the underdog.

His abrasive and high volume delivery (blamed on partial industrial deafness), coupled with a relentless determination not to be fobbed off, is how he got results. Conversely, his outspoken and often aggressive, street-fighting manner has made him deeply unpopular with many police officers, politicians and criminals. Most councillors enjoy tea and biscuits with the police top brass; they don't shout at them and brand them as liars.

In 1986, when Jamie Daniel was completing his jail time in England and Eddie Lyons Sr had set up home in Milton, McAllister returned home to Maryhill after seven years living in Australia. His home city had changed. Not only had heavy industry been decimated but heroin had taken hold. McAllister embraced causes which included the anti-poll tax movement and poor social housing while speaking out against the new generation of drug dealers sucking the life out of communities and making a fortune in the process.

He was voted on to both Wyndford Community Council and Gairbraid Tenants' Association as chairman, which led to bitter and frequent clashes with all-powerful Labour who controlled the city. During a stormy public meeting he chaired at Mary-hill's Burgh Halls, the Labour politicians were verbally mauled by unhappy residents. One councillor walked out with the jeers ringing in his ears. McAllister said, 'I could see how ineffective the politics in the area were. My family and I had always voted Labour but I started seeing the party for what it was, particularly in Glasgow where it was rotten to the core. It was a cabal of self-interest, wheeling and dealing and being cosy with criminals and dodgy so-called businessmen. Labour had taken for granted who they represented.'

McAllister was a noisy nuisance but one who refused to go away. He used incessant letter writing to raise concerns. In one six-month period, 1,600 letters flew back and forth between him and officials at the housing department. His housing office visits were heated affairs where he often hectored staff about the inexcusable state of the damp-ridden homes where many families were forced to live.

McAllister's tirades – verbal and written – prompted the council to engage lawyers to secure a legal ban on him entering the housing office or any other council building. However, McAllister won a seat on a council board as a tenants' repre-sentative which allowed him to walk into the city chambers HQ to take his place around the table, in defiance of the ban. He celebrated by mockingly posing in George Square for a news-paper story with his hands raised and mouth gagged below the headline 'Banned Billy's Back!' He said at the time, 'They claimed I had the place in a state of siege. But I'm no thug. Maybe I raised my voice sometimes and finger-wagged but that was all. I fought for people with damp houses.'

In 1994, as he posed outside the city chambers, a council official said, 'He may be on a council committee but he won't be welcome in the housing office again.'

McAllister said, 'I was the tenant from hell – I wouldn't roll over. When the council took out the interdict, I continued doing my business. It was ludicrous. Every time I went to the housing department, they contacted the police who sometimes man-handled me out. They never arrested me but I was occasionally charged. It was ammunition for the council's attempt to get a full interdict but the complaints were malicious. One accusation was that I kidnapped a housing officer by taking him away in my car. I took him and other officials willingly to show them houses that were damp. This was part of the concocted 'evidence' for their interdict.'

Despite the elements of farce, the hostility between him and officials turned much nastier when McAllister was subjected to a series of death threats. He received phone calls to his home saying that he would be shot and to watch himself as he was upsetting too many people. He said, 'The caller also said he knew my movements and that my house would be blown up. They went on for months. A couple of times I told him that I wouldn't give in to the threats and other times I hung up. They were happening at all times of day and night. It was very stressful and you had to take them seriously. When the phone company traced the caller it was discovered to be the same senior council official who had falsely accused me of kidnapping him. He had previously threatened to 'sort me out' at a meeting because of the campaign against his department. He was charged and I heard he got some minor punishment and was disciplined by the council but not sacked which was scandalous. A couple of years later, I bumped into him in the street and I told him that he was a despicable coward who had got off lightly and should be ashamed of himself. He had nothing to say.'

McAllister helped to establish North West Communities Alliance, an umbrella group which advised residents about legal rights, benefits claims and dealing with the council and police. His role in the volunteer-run organisation served to antagonise many in the council even more.

It was in 1999 that he learned about Chirnsyde after a chance encounter with a Milton resident. At the time, he had no idea that it would become more than just another issue. It was to occupy much of his time and change his life by thrusting him into the national media spotlight. It would lead to his election as a councillor and to serious clashes with police officers, gangsters, council officials and politicians – as well as to many more

Eddie Lyons Sr inside Chirnsyde alongside then Labour MP Maria Fyfe (standing), Labour councillor Ellen Hurcombe and PC John Cameron

The centre in Milton handed to Eddie Lyons Sr and run as Chirnsyde Community Initiative (SDR/SM)

Milton resident and community campaigner
Johnny McLean (SDR/SM)

SNP Councillor Billy McAllister suffered
death threats for standing up to drug dealers
(Daniel Gilfeather)

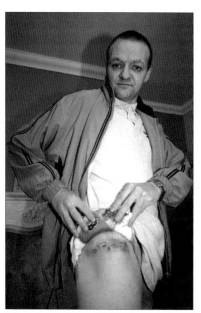

Johnny Lyons shows off his bullet wounds
following his shooting outside his home in
Milton, Glasgow (Spindrift)

Eddie Lyons Jr and Liam Boyle were handed
£30,00 by Prince Charles' Scottish Youth Business
Trust to set up a construction firm

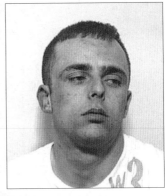

Above left. Applerow garage owner David Lyons gets behind the wheel of his Mercedes (SDR/SM)

Above. Paul Lyons after his arrest for killing innocent dad Mark Fleeman on the M74 motorway

Left. Chris Lyons poses with pals on his gang website

Ross Monaghan and Steven Lyons outside the High Court in Glasgow in 2005 as they stood trial for attempted murder (SDR/SM)

Above left. Publicity-shy organised crime boss Jamie Daniel is finally caught on camera outside his home in 2006 (SDR/SM)

Above right. Kevin Carroll outside the High Court in Glasgow during a heroin-dealing trial of some associates (SDR/SM)

Right. The grave of eight-year-old cancer victim Garry Lyons after it was targeted by Kevin Carroll (SDR/SM)

New father Michael Lyons Jr, 21, lost his life in the triple shooting at Applerow while his cousin Steven Lyons and Paisley gangster Robert Pickett survived

Police stand guard outside Applerow following the triple-shooting bloodbath which claimed the life of Michael Lyons Jr (SDR/SM)

The game is up for Eddie Lyons Sr as police finally move to evict him from Chirnsyde (SDR/SM)

Evicted Eddie Lyons Sr being escorted from Chirnsyde the day after the triple shooting in which his nephew Michael Jr was killed (SDR/SM)

Daniel gang hitman Raymond 'Rainbow' Anderson is serving 30 years for the murder of Michael Lyons Jr

A mugshot of Daniel family hitman James McDonald, who is in jail for murdering Michael Lyons Jr

Two armed police officers guard the taped off Asda car park where Kevin 'Gerbil' Carroll was gunned down (SDR/SM)

Hooded associates of drug dealer Kevin Carroll – including his partner Kelly's brother, Francis 'Fraggle' Green – at the scene of his murder at Asda, Robroyston (SDR/SM)

Detectives begin their investigation into the murder of Kevin Carroll whilst a forensic team painstakingly gather evidence to build a case (SDR/SM)

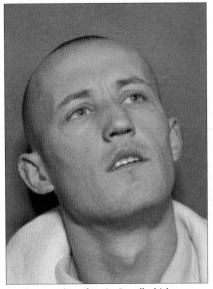

A police mugshot of Kevin Carroll which was released after his murder

Kevin Carroll's partner, Kelly Green, arrives at his funeral service (SDR/SM)

A mass of floral wreaths on Kevin Carroll's grave, including one of his car registration G3 RBO and a can of Red Bull (SDR/SM)

Carroll's coffin makes its way through the streets in a horse-drawn carriage, four months after his murder (SDR/SM)

Justice Secretary Kenny MacAskill poses with an Audi which was seized by police probing Kevin Carroll and his gang(SDR/SM)

threats to his personal safety and a vile and cowardly email smear campaign waged against him.

He said, 'I was already aware of the Lyons as criminals so the decision to give him [Eddie Sr] the keys to Chirnsyde was beyond belief. Chirnsyde was a gang hut where he recruited and groomed youngsters into criminality. Many youths who went through his hands in those years later committed serious crimes including murder and large-scale drug dealing. There were many reports made to me about people being set upon at Chirnsyde that were never reported to the police. That didn't mean the police were unaware. The victims would not talk to them because of fears of more violence being meted out and because of Lyons' connections to officers.

'Myself and others like Johnny McLean started an awareness campaign. We wrote to politicians from all parties and to Bridget McConnell who was the council official in charge of Chirnsyde and its landlord. We eventually wrote thousands of letters over the years as it is a way of logging every single incident and of holding the officials to account.

'PC John Cameron's role as chairman was a serious issue. I will never understand why a community police officer would have such ties to a man like Lyons and be so out of step with the people in his community.

'There was a meeting at Milton Community Centre where PC Cameron approached me outside and said, "You really don't want to be going there – you don't want to be complaining too much as I could make your life a misery." He said Eddie was a good guy. I told him to fuck off and told him not to intimidate or threaten me and that I'll do what I see fit – I'll fight injustice whether it's Lyons or anyone else. He backed off and looked a bit lost and sheepish. He couldn't get away quick enough. We complained to the police about PC Cameron's connection to Chirnsyde and, very soon after, he resigned as chairman and was removed from the area.

'From the police, council and Labour we were mostly dismissed – there were closed doors everywhere. I think some of that was because of who was involved. They despised me because of my previous run-ins and they had also had problems with Johnny and the other campaigners who had humiliated them over the St Augustine's playing fields. They had long memories. For many years, the council parroted the line that there was no evidence of criminality at Chirnsyde which, to a blind man, was demonstrably untrue. There were many proven acts of crime and violence – not least the attempted murder of Thomas McDonnell in 2001.

'There was a collective smear campaign made against us from within the city chambers and the police's Pitt Street HQ.'

Yet another police officer's connections with the Lyons family had come to the attention of McAllister and the campaigners. The name of the officer in question cannot be revealed for legal reasons but the Lyons referred to him as 'the cousin' despite there being no discernible blood link. For around two years, the campaigners had heard whispers about the officer and his friendship with the family. It took that long before they were certain enough about it to explain their concerns about his bond with the family in a meeting with Ruaraidh Nicolson, a senior Strathclyde Police officer who was one of many given the task of liaising with them over the years.

They revealed details of a house party in the city's east end, hosted by a relative of the Lyons. Also at the party were other Lyons family members and the off-duty 'cousin'. When one partygoer made an ill-advised joke about the shooting of Johnny Lyons that had happened several months earlier, another family member leapt to his feet to remonstrate. As the situation grew heated, the police officer intervened by pulling out his warrant card to defuse it.

By sheer chance, two days after the allegations about 'the cousin' and his behaviour at the party were made to the force's top brass, McAllister came face-to-face with him. The confrontation was explosive. It was May 2003 and McAllister had taken up the case of a family who were suffering a campaign of abuse by antisocial neighbours which had featured on the local evening TV news. He was in the family's Cadder home with a colleague when the police arrived to deal with their case. As the sergeant and two constables settled down in the living room, McAllister was oblivious as to who had joined them but his colleague's hackles rose as he instantly recognised the 'cousin'. Realising that it was neither the time nor place, the associate initially chose to say nothing.

McAllister launched a trademark diatribe about the police failure to tackle the criminal family who were making the lives of the law-abiding majority a misery. It was a typically heated exchange with McAllister in full flow, telling the police that their platitudes were not good enough and that they should be doing more to help the family. In the crowded room, McAllister's elbow accidentally clashed with that of the 'cousin' who immediately jumped up and ordered his colleague to arrest him.

In the melee, McAllister's until then mute colleague turned to the stunned policeman and calmly spoke his name. The officer was at once silenced and flustered. McAllister, now realising his identity, went off like a rocket. His fury prompted the astonished family to seek refuge upstairs in their own home. They were even joined by the bewildered sergeant who clearly wanted nothing to do with what was going on downstairs. McAllister accused the policeman of being in the pay of the Lyons, of leaking information to them and even snorting cocaine with them. It was an astonishing attack which fuelled the officer's demand that his colleague should handcuff and arrest McAllister who responded by calling his bluff. Who would blink first? The police. They beat a hasty retreat, leaving behind McAllister whose volume was restored to near normal levels. He remained untouched, un-cuffed but very angry.

McAllister said, 'I had been told by people who I trusted that this policeman had colluded with members of the Lyons family in order to do me harm and that he broke the law by feeding them confidential information. When he was confronted in that living room, he turned beetroot red and started shouting to arrest me. I encouraged him to do so while his own sergeant hid upstairs. What does that tell you? When my colleague said the name, I was furious that he was in front of me, especially as he knew who I was. He was sent packing with his tail between his legs.'

The campaigners had no faith in the police complaints system and, as they expected, the force eventually ruled that there was no proof to support the allegations against the 'cousin'. The fact that it was one of the Lyons family who phoned to tauntingly inform them that the officer was in the clear, only confirmed everything that they suspected.

Off the record, one senior officer later told McAllister's colleague who had been in the house that day that he would be moved out of the division and would be 'licking stamps' in his new role and that, if he was seen again, to let them know. In the opaque world of police discipline, they had no way of knowing whether that was true.

For McAllister and the campaigners, that was not good enough and they hatched a plan to distribute leaflets bearing the bold heading 'Public Warning' alongside the silhouette of a saluting policeman. They stated, 'If you are raising any concerns about the notorious Lyons crime family operating in the Milton area, make sure that you're not talking to PC [name withheld] as he is allegedly closely linked to the Lyons crime family. They are so closely linked to PC [name withheld] that they call him the 'cousin'. This is not the first police officer identified as having close links with his family. PC John Cameron was moved shortly after concerns were raised about his relationship with E Lyons and his questionable connection with the controversial Chirnsyde Community Initiative.'

McAllister said, 'The leaflet was very careful in that it told people to continue reporting issues to the police but that they should be aware of the concerns raised against this particular officer.'

As a courtesy to the police, McAllister's colleague forewarned their 'handler' Nicolson about their intentions. Nicolson shrugged and told him that it was 'only Billy going off on one' and said that they would not fall out over a few leaflets. They clearly did not expect 30,000 copies of the A5 poster to be distributed around Glasgow or for it to find its way onto the pages of a national newspaper.

McAllister said, 'A dozen of us put them through letter boxes, under police car windscreens and dropped them in police stations in Colston, Drumchapel, Maryhill and Kirkintilloch. This was over a period of weeks. They were also fly-posted around the entire city, including the doors of the main procurator fiscal office in the Gorbals one Sunday night, at the sheriff and high courts and stuck to lamp posts, shop fronts and bus shelters. They were everywhere. Nicolson went ballistic. He had been delegated as our liaison officer, which seemed to be more about stopping our letters rather than properly addressing the perverse situation at Chirnsyde.'

The police were incandescent with rage and would not take the direct attack on one of their own lying down. The force decided to deploy plain-clothes officers of the Serious Crime Squad on the tail of the rogue fly-posters. McAllister was in a car with Johnny and another of the four bampots when an unmarked police car swerved in front of him. The officers jumped out and shouted at the occupants to get out. They then went into a huddle to discuss who they were going to arrest and came up with the conclusion that it would be the hated McAllister. The charge? Fly-posting. McAllister was handcuffed and bundled into the back of the car. Johnny and the other men were told to walk home.

McAllister said, 'They took me to Maryhill police station and several officers came from the back room just to mock me because I had complained about so many of them. A report was send to the procurator fiscal but it was later marked no proceedings. They knew that dragging me into court would open a can of worms as a court case would lead to the officer being identified and he would be asked some tough questions about his links to the Lyons.'

Relations between Strathclyde Police and the Chirnsyde campaigners had sunk to a new low. The campaigners not only mistrusted them but believed that far too many officers were active supporters of the Lyons.

A bizarre episode followed when McAllister was driving in Maryhill Road with a colleague when one of the rabble who had been making the Cadder family's lives a misery stepped on to the road, forcing them to stop. He then started attacking the car and shouting that McAllister was going to get 'done in'. The threats turned into a volley of saliva which landed on the vehicle.

McAllister drove to Maryhill police station to report the attack but, on entering, felt the hostility towards him from the two bristling, uniformed officers behind the desk. Two CID officers appeared from a back office and demanded that McAllister join them for a chat. It sounded more like a threat than an offer of assistance and McAllister – keen to stay within the scope of the CCTV system for his own protection – declined. Again they insisted but McAllister stood his ground and requested the right to be able to report the crime that had taken place. To no avail, the stand-off continued with the plain-clothes men apparently determined to lure him into a private spot. McAllister refused to go and explained that he was complaining about an incident and that the spit could identify the person who did it.

He said, 'It was face to face and no one was backing off. They started threatening to arrest me if I did not go in the back room. They told my colleague to beat it, in exactly those words. Their voices were raised and they were soon joined by maybe half a dozen more officers. It became insane. I tried to emphasise that the rain was coming on and I wanted to preserve the evidence. I would have spoken to them afterwards. They weren't interested, they got more authoritarian and aggressive towards me. I was looking up at CCTV knowing that it should be running and, if so, I was safe – they couldn't lay a finger on me.

'I feared for my safety. It ended up that an inspector intervened and said that he would get an officer to attend to my complaint but I did not feel comfortable and decided to get out. Around 20 minutes had been wasted so I left.'

Undeterred, McAllister went into a nearby pharmacy and bought a packet of cotton buds and some sealable plastic bags. Using his DIY forensic kit, he bagged samples of the spit from his car and took them to the force's Pitt Street headquarters where a receipt was issued by the bemused officer behind the desk. Remarkably, the makeshift forensic evidence helped secure the conviction of the man who had attacked the vehicle.

Elements within the police had grown to despise McAllister. Some were spurred on because of his criticisms levelled at them while others were close to members of the Lyons family. His complaint about the behaviour of the two CID men at Maryhill led to an even more sinister encounter. McAllister had come out of Kelvindale Post Office when he was approached from behind by two men, both of whom appeared to be police officers in plain clothes although they did not produce any ID. They told McAllister, 'You should drop any complaints or allegations you've made against the police. We could fit you up by planting drugs in your car and you could go away for a lot of years – we can do it.'

McAllister said, 'I don't think they were from Maryhill as I didn't recognise them. They had been called in from somewhere else to threaten me and deliver the warning that I could be fitted up. It was chest out, growly, like the old Sweeney 1970s cops. It wasn't subtle or nice, it was a serious threat.

'I went fucking ballistic and started ranting at them and told them that I'd had all this before, being stopped by police and threatened. I was deliberately shouting very loudly because it was a public place and I wanted passers-by to hear. I pulled my phone out to get some witnesses there but the cops didn't hang around.

'The thing with the cotton buds and the threat to plant drugs on me sound ludicrous but they weren't funny at the time. This type of thing happened on many occasions in the 1990s because I was standing up to drug dealers and challenging some of the relationships between them and certain police officers and politicians which, in Glasgow, meant Labour. As soon as you start questioning individual police officers, you become a target for the entire force. It's long been joked that the police are the biggest gang in the city.

'I know that I'm not blessed with diplomacy and I am loud but I keep reminding these people that I'm not a criminal. I've been telling them that for years. They still don't get it.'

16

Eddie Rules Okay

During her husband Jack's reign as First Minister, Bridget McConnell was one half of the most powerful couple in the country. As the director of Glasgow City Council's Culture and Leisure Services which included the city's museums and sports centres, she held the keys to Eddie's Club. She also signed the cheques for Cultural and Leisure Services which was later rebranded as Glasgow Life, an 'arm's length' organisation of the council.

As far back as 2001, McConnell had admitted knowing about the arson attack on Chirnsyde and the vandalism of its minibus. She and her colleagues had also been repeatedly told about the attempted murder in which a pack of thugs stabbed Thomas McDonnell and left him for dead. Yet she swatted away the letters of campaigners who became increasingly confused, bitter and frustrated. The same two recurring themes ran through the replies from McConnell and others in the council. They were that, yes, they used taxes to fund Lyons and that Chirnsyde was a council building but, if anyone had a problem, then they should take it up with him not them. Secondly, there was no evidence of any criminality at Chirnsyde.

Billy McAllister and others believed that Lyons treated Chirnsyde as a private club and thought it was incumbent on McConnell to ensure that it should meet the basic levels of accountability and transparency expected from any publicly funded organisation.

However, in a letter to McAllister, dated May 2004, McConnell stated that the council would merely 'expect Chirnsyde to operate with an open and inclusive approach towards its management arrangements'. She added:

> It should be noted, however, that there is no automatic or legal requirement on the management committee to issue information that may be of a sensitive or confidential nature to the public.
>
> Nor do Glasgow City Council have the authority to insist that the management committee pass information of this nature to a third party.
>
> The management committee of Chirnsyde have, however, stated that they are adopting a policy of openness and transparency regarding the management of the initiative. To this end they have indicated that they intend to make copies of all future management committee meetings available at reception or by postal request provided a stamped addressed envelope is provided. The committee have also stated that they will consider any requests from you at any point. The council are not, therefore, faced with a situation where the management committee have refused to supply you with any information. In order to avoid any confusion regarding correspondence, I would advise you to address all correspondence to Chirnsyde by recorded delivery.

The answer angered McAllister. Firstly, the letter six times cited Chirnsyde's committee which, to the campaigners, was a euphemism for Lyons himself, as many of its members were viewed as hand-picked cronies. It seemed that the council conveniently took the view that, despite Lyons being bankrolled with taxpayers' money while operating in a council-owned building, public scrutiny did not apply. The suggestion that McAllister should personally attend Chirnsyde and politely ask for documents or divulge his address to the 'committee' was a non-starter given the long shadow of violence cast by the Lyons and a series of threats and attacks made against the campaigners.

Johnny McLean demanded McConnell's resignation. He argued that she had 'failed to properly monitor and reasonably respond to the serious community safety concerns raised in relation to Chirnsyde in terms of public safety and the appropriate direction of public funding'. McConnell's boss, the council's then Chief Executive George Black, hit back and, in his response, parroted the line that 'there is no evidence of any criminal activity at Chirnsyde'.

For the first time, a new method of dealing with the campaigners was deployed. Rather than defend, the council attacked. The constant flow of letters – often repetitive, sometimes clumsy but usually containing inescapable facts and awkward questions – was a major headache. The council decided that the writers would be singled out as vexatious, unreasonable and unrepresentative troublemakers who were in a minority compared to the happy but silent majority – apparently numbering many thousands – who used Chirnsyde.

Black's letter continued, 'The mere fact of the same allegations being repeated constantly by a small number of individuals does not lend them any further credence. The constant repetition of unfounded allegations may have an effect, however, on the reputation of a valuable community resource and it is fortunate that, in spite of this situation, the local community continue to use Chirnsyde in considerable numbers.'

The letters did not stop. They went to the council, councillors, cross-party members of both the Holyrood and Westminster parliaments, police chiefs, the tax man, the media and countless others. The campaigners figured that the powerful officials who lived in leafy middle-class areas a world away from Milton would never allow their own children anywhere near a man like Lyons. Why should their kids be different? An example of the tetchiness flared up the following year when an irate press officer had attempted to dismiss the campaigners as 'four bampots'. It had become very personal and both sides were entrenched but worse was to come in a bombshell report by McConnell.

On 22 June 2005, she presented her document to the committee of councillors whose job was to vote for or against what she, as a senior official, recommended. Her report stated:

Over the past five years there has been a campaign of serious complaints and allegations made against Chirnsyde and one of its employees [Lyons].

The allegations can be summarised as follows: That children who attend the project are being 'put at risk' by their close proximity to the co-ordinator [Lyons] as he may be a target of violence.

The same allegations have been constantly repeated in correspondence and telephone conversations stretching back years with various council services, politicians, newspapers, ombudsmen, funders, the police and any organisation which innocently engages with Chirnsyde.

The allegations have also been mentioned in some national newspapers, where Chirnsyde and its co-ordinator are linked to lurid stories about drug wars and serious violence. The articles make it clear that the co-ordinator is related to a notorious criminal family who operate in the Milton area.

It should be noted that throughout this campaign, stretching over five years, there have only ever been four regular complainants who have generated this massive volume of correspondence with council services and other agencies.

It should also be noted that no parent or user of Chirnsyde has ever made a complaint to the council about inappropriate or criminal activity witnessed at the centre . . .

As a result of the endless allegations a number of agencies have carried out investigations into various aspects of Chirnsyde. These include Glasgow City Council internal audit section, Audit Scotland, Charities Commission, Strathclyde Police.

No investigations by any of these agencies has uncovered any evidence of criminal activity, misuse of funds or any wrongdoing on the part of either the management committee or any of the staff.

Strathclyde Police clearly have a major role to play in the formulation of a response to the allegations and the council have maintained close and regular contact with the police service on this issue.

When it comes to the allegations, the council in general are acting on the basis of the most up-to-date police advice.

The advice received from the police has been absolutely consistent for a number of years and forms the basis for the current council approach to this issue. Their advice is that: There is currently no evidence of any criminal activity or wrongdoing at Chirnsyde or on the part of any member of staff.

All allegations made to the police or passed on to them by other agencies are investigated thoroughly and yet, to date, no allegations have been found to have any substance. This includes the most recent allegations concerning the Chirnsyde minibus where it was alleged that the minibus was used in an attempt to run over a local child.

Under the section titled 'Future Action', McConnell stated:

As a facility which delivers key services to a community which desperately needs them, the council would like to continue to work with this organisation in order to develop and expand the services on offer. Plans to construct a new full-size synthetic football pitch on the site are being developed and there are ambitions to expand and improve in other areas.

There is no question, however, that the campaign being waged against Chirnsyde is currently having an effect on service developments and has the potential to negatively influence future plans.

The management committee are concerned that the campaign is having an impact on current and future funding decisions.

The relentless pressure is also having an effect on the morale of the committee, made up of local volunteers, and indeed council staff who have to deal with the often repeated allegations.

A meeting was organised by the director of Cultural and Leisure Services [McConnell] at the request of two of the four individuals who have been responsible for the vast majority of the allegations.

This meeting was also to be attended by representatives of the police service, Glasgow Alliance and members of the management committee of the Initiative. The meeting was intended to provide an opportunity for all the allegations to be aired and responded to and help to create a more positive agenda around Chirnsyde. This goal was not achieved as the two regular complainants declined to attend.

The report concluded:

By all of the measures available to the council, Chirnsyde is a successful community facility delivering quality services within an area of multiple deprivation. As a result of the litany of allegations and complaints made against it the facility has been subject to a much greater degree of scrutiny than any other facility funded by the council.

It has demonstrated, through numerous investigations, that it meets all of the current conditions required of it by the council and that there is no evidence to support any of the allegations. It is also a facility with an active committee who have aspirations to enhance the current service provision for their community.

And yet there is a very real danger that this facility will fail to develop. This could happen either as a result of the negative impact that the constantly repeated allegations, however unsubstantiated, are having currently and could have on future decision makers or through fatigue on the part of agencies who currently support the facility.

It is therefore important for the council to consider all the issues and determine whether it wishes to continue to support the development of Chirnsyde as a valuable community resource.'

Her recommendation was unequivocal:

The committee is asked to note the contents of the report and agree to the continued support for the management committee of Chirnsyde.

The councillors duly agreed with McConnell. Lyons was delighted. The campaigners felt like they had been punched in the guts. Particularly insulting was the sections of the report which sympathised with the 'management committee' and its poor morale. But they remained unbowed.

During that time, those who questioned the situation were told the same thing by Glasgow City Council – namely, that Strathclyde Police had repeatedly told officials that there was no evidence of criminal activity there.

The letter to McLean – sent by the council's chief executive George Black in August 2004 – revealed that McConnell 'kept in close contact with the police service in order to be made aware of any information which would give the council cause for concern'. The reply from Black suggested a long series of contact in which McConnell was personally involved.

The campaigners longed to know exactly which police officers had spoken to which officials and exactly what they had told them. It took two laser-guided questions by one campaigner, under freedom of information, to reveal the truth. In February 2005, he asked the council to reveal which police officers had stated that they held no concern about Lyons or his involvement with Chirnsyde and when these communications took place. The council officials were aghast. Not only would they not release the information, they refused to state whether it was even held – a stance they justified by claiming it was not in the 'public interest'. Citing the relevant part of the legislation, Section 18, they wrote that it would be 'contrary to the public interest to reveal whether some or all of the information requested exists at all or is held by it, then by virtue of Section 18 of the Act, the council is entitled to refuse the request without confirming or denying that such information is held by it'.

The campaigner appealed to the then Scottish Information Commissioner Kevin Dunion who ruled that the council's secrecy and public interest defence were a breach of the law and duly ordered the information to be released which it eventually was, months after McConnell had delivered her report urging councillors to keep funding Chirnsyde.

What follows is a breakdown of the entire extent of the contact between the police and the council in relation to Lyons at Chirnsyde:

1. Assistant Chief Constable Ricky Gray wrote to Mike Blair, assistant clerk to the Strathclyde Joint Police Board, on 30 April 2004.
2. Detective Waters of Maryhill police station spoke by phone to Billy Garrett of Glasgow City Council's Cultural and Leisure Services on or around 12 August 2004.
3. Superintendent Paul Main of Saracen police station spoke to Billy Garrett on or around 12 November 2004.

The campaigners were absolutely astonished. McConnell and others had long dismissed complaints on the basis that the police had told them everything was fine. Yet no such assurances had been sought until April 2004. Furthermore, McConnell's 2005 report had said the 'absolutely consistent' police advice spanned a 'number of years'. According to the council's own records, their first official request for information from the police came 12 years after Lyons first entered Chirnsyde, four years after the attempted murder there and 14 months after the *Sunday Mail* exposed the situation. Furthermore, the council's overwhelming endorsement of Lyons as a fit and proper person was based upon only one letter and two phone calls spanning a period of seven months.

The same freedom of information request also finally answered the thorny issue of whether or not Lyons had undergone the required background check for those who work with children. The campaigners knew that his murky past – not least the attempted murder charge – would have been contained in an 'enhanced' check which was necessary for anyone working with children. The council admitted that 'Mr Edward Lyons has been the subject of a disclosure check at an enhanced level. The council holds no information concerning the data and is therefore unable to comply further with this part of your request.'

It was a sensational admission. Had Lyons been a council

employee, officials would have seen the contents of his enhanced disclosure and then made a decision on his suitability for
employment in such a sensitive role. Yet, because he was an
employee of the arms-length 'management committee' – albeit
operating in a council building and funded with council money –
they admitted that they had no idea what the checks revealed. It
is surprising that the council did not routinely demanded sight
of the disclosure checks as a condition of funding. Surely, out of
curiosity, common sense, professionalism, back-covering or an
obligation to the community and other taxpayers, they would
have wanted to know what skeletons could be rattling around in
Lyons' closet before installing him and blindly backing him to
the hilt in the face of so many howls of protest?

Weeks after McConnell's report, two of the most vocal
campaigners were issued with mobile phones by the police
which – were they or their homes attacked – would have allowed
them to be put straight through to the emergency control room.
They had been given the handsets because they had been
threatened for raising concerns about Lyons. One of them also
had police-issue CCTV cameras installed in his home to guard
against attacks. Why, if Lyons was a respectable community
leader, would anyone need such police protection? The answer
was obvious and it was one that neither the police nor the
council could give as to do so would contradict their stated view
that Lyons was legitimate.

The campaigners often felt that their efforts were futile. It was
bad enough putting the safety of your family on the line by
taking on the Lyons family. It was even harder when faced with
the power of the police, Labour Party and council. Yet they
chipped away relentlessly and even emulated the detectives who
got the early twentieth-century Chicago mob boss Al Capone
jailed – by following the money.

In early 2005, they amassed a detailed dossier of information
about Lyons' lifestyle – the homes, the cars – which seemed
at odds with the modest wage of a community worker. The
detailed information was sent in a letter to Strathclyde's Police's
then Chief Constable Willie Rae with copies going to HM

Revenue & Customs and others in authority. The letter revealed that Lyons had just moved out of his Torogay Street former council house into a £165,000 property – registered to his son Eddie Jr and his partner – in suburban Cumbernauld. The letter also detailed that Lyons was the registered owner of a £140,000 property in another Lanarkshire town, East Kilbride. In addition, another £140,000 property in a third town, Caldercruix, had been bought in the name of his 19-year-old daughter Ashley. The letter stated, 'Therefore, over the past 19 months Mr Edward Lyons, his son and his daughter have purchased properties believed to be in the combined region of £500,000.' The letter went on to link him and his family to a fleet of six cars – among them his own SUV plus a BMW and Audi, some with Lyons-inspired vanity registrations.

The writer concluded, 'Given the belief that Mr Lyons has been unemployed for the majority of his adult life up until he took his position at Chirnsyde and given the fact that his recent salary is believed to be in the region of £23,000-a-year, in addition to the controversy in terms of links to criminality, that continues to surround him, I trust that you will understand my concerns.'

Even though the campaigners had done all the legwork involved in property searches and had provided the details of the various cars, no action was taken. The police had been handed evidence of Lyons' criminality on a plate but five years were to pass before they did anything about it.

17

The Graduates

The Club Boys had spent their teenage years at Chirnsyde under the watchful eye of Eddie Lyons Sr. His eldest sons Eddie Jr and Steven led the tight-knit circle and, in turn, were linked to the younger crew of their brother Chris, who was around 10 years their junior.

To many of them, Eddie Sr was as much a father as their own dads, if not more so. The wise-cracking Chirnsyde boss spoke to them on their level – he was like a pal. The youngsters were impressed by the power, the bragging, the scams, the contacts and the stories of days gone by.

Eddie Sr was known throughout the scheme and was frequently seen in the Chirnsyde minibus where he spent his time between the centre and the bookies' shops of Lambhill or Springburn.

In an age of consumerism and entitlement, he could get the Club Boys the latest Nokia phones, gold chains or Nike tracksuits – no question asked. Eddie got them earning a few quid running errands, ducking and diving around Milton. Many of the Club Boys came from broken homes where material goods were not in abundance – Eddie Sr's club opened their eyes to a world of excitement and opportunity and gave them a taste for quick, easy cash in hand. Chirnsyde also gave them a sense of purpose and belonging. It was a home from home and a refuge where they were protected not just from rival street gangs but also from the police, thanks to Eddie Sr's contacts. Their affection for him seemed to be deep and genuine.

Eddie Sr always knew exactly who was in 'his' club. The council owned the squat, off-white building while taxpayers paid his wages but *he* decided who would cross the threshold. On one occasion, he yelled, 'Get out of my car park!' at a council official who was accompanying one of the campaigners – he was like a country laird chasing away riff-raff. Chirnsyde was for members only and, if your face didn't fit or if you posed the slightest threat to his personal safety or status, you would be rejected. To maintain control, only members were allowed on the management committee. Any unknown faces attempting to get inside would be challenged by Eddie Sr who spent most of the time in his office, invisible behind the mirrored reflection of a sliding glass panel which gave him a sentry duty view of all those coming and going.

The familiar faces of the middle-aged women attending aerobics classes and the work colleagues enjoying an evening kick-about in the gym hall were nodded in by smiling Eddie Sr. They would have no reason to venture into the games room where the Club Boys ruled.

Among Eddie Jr and Steven's group were Liam Boyle, Ross Monaghan, Andrew 'Dumbo' Gallacher, Paul McGuinness and Brian Ferguson whose younger brother Andrew was part of the younger team led by Chris. There were others in the gang, including Charles McMurray, who had admitted committing the Tuscany nightclub attacks for which he wasn't even charged. He later drifted apart from his contemporaries. It proved to be a decision that would spare him the type of life which lay ahead for them.

Most of the Club Boys had attended the now closed St Augustine's secondary school where, unlike at Chirnsyde, theirs was just one of a number of predatory gangs. School did not offer them the same protection they enjoyed at Chirnsyde, as illustrated by an incident when schoolboy Eddie Jr, showing off in his dad's burgundy Ford Mondeo, was attacked by the slightly older Robert 'Birdman' O'Hara, whose girlfriend was a pupil. Possil thug O'Hara, who was jailed at the age of 27 for at least 20 years for ordering a drug rival's murder, stepped out of the taxi in which he had arrived to pick up his girlfriend and battered Eddie Jr, who was humiliated.

During the early years, the Club Boys had roamed Milton where they bonded during the teenage rites of passage of underage drinking, dabbling in drugs and showing off to girls. As the unfortunate McDonnell family knew to their cost, the Club Boys were not a typical group of teenagers. Their participation in low-level crime escalated into peddling drugs – cannabis, then ecstasy and on to cocaine, crack and heroin. Not that it was an easy journey from teenage troublemakers to a small but ambitious organised crime gang in their early 20s, attempting to steal a slice of the city's fiercely contested drug market.

Paul McGuinness, an imposing physical presence, had already shown his loyalty when he kept his mouth shut and became the only person to be convicted for the attempted murder of Thomas McDonnell at Chirnsyde. In what was to become a pattern, Eddie Sr and his brother Johnny, along with Eddie Jr and Steven, had walked free.

A flurry of other arrests and court cases over the following years are like pieces of a mosaic which when put together create a clear picture of how the Club Boys graduated from teen troublemakers into making some very serious money through drug dealing at a significant level.

Andrew 'Dumbo' Gallacher received a short, sharp shock about the reality of life as a drug dealer when he was given a four-year prison sentence at Hamilton Sheriff Court – four years for heroin and two for cannabis to be served concurrently. At the same court two months later, Steven forfeited £14,980 of cash which had been seized by police from a vehicle in which he had been stopped on the M74 motorway from England, the biggest drugs route into Scotland. Another Club Boy, who can't be named for legal reasons, held his hands up to the £63,000 of drugs money that had been found in the East Kilbride home of Eddie Sr, who had gone mute when quizzed about it two years before.

In a separate case, the same unnamed Club Boy was jailed over £185,000 worth of heroin and cannabis – drugs which had been found during the investigation prompted by the Tuscany nightclub bloodbath. There had been four arrested for the drugs. Yet again Steven – plus the other two – walked free while the Club Boy pled guilty to dealing cannabis. He was sentenced to 30 months behind bars at the High Court in Edinburgh.

Another Club Boys associate was Eddie Sr's nephew Paul Lyons, a loudmouth lowlife and frequent visitor to Chirnsyde. The son of Eddie Sr's brother David, he was a close pal of his cousins Eddie Jr and Steven and was also jailed that year for a relatively minor breach of the peace adding to his already sizeable rap sheet which would eventually include a conviction for killing an innocent man.

All drug dealers – no matter what level they operate at – need to be able to inflict violence or they will be crushed and ripped off. The Club Boys were no different and were willing and able to launch sickening attacks, usually mob-handed, using any weapons that came to hand. Like the victims of playground bullies, those on the receiving end were often the weak and vulnerable or in the wrong place at the wrong time. Sometimes, it was violence for the sake of violence, to serve as a reminder of what they were capable of. The more moronic revelled in the growing public notoriety of their surname, little realising that a higher profile made them a bigger target for the police and other gangsters.

The ability of Steven and Ross Monaghan to beat the rap over the Tuscany nightclub rampage sent out the message that they were serious. Ultra violence was futile if you ended up festering in a cell in Barlinnie while your rivals steal your business. Steven, in particular, seemed to have a magic touch when it came to beating criminal charges. It was always the other Club Boys who ended up doing the time. One day, the penny might drop. If your name was Lyons, you stayed out of jail.

Meanwhile, young Chris aped his brothers by surrounding himself with his own gaggle of cronies in Chirnsyde's gym hall. Moving with the times, Chris launched a website for Milton Young Thugz, the name given to his offshoot of the Club Boys.

It was created on the taxpayer-funded computers in his dad's centre and its pages were plastered with photos of Chris and his pals. They typically stood on Milton street corners – skinny kids with sneering, ferret faces lit by the sodium glare of street lights – often with Buckfast bottles defiantly raised and weapons flaunted. They traded barely literate online threats with rival gangs. Baby-faced Chris, whose nickname was Chips, had already been accused of raping a girl, only for the charge against him to be dropped. Despite their youth, these kids had access to guns. In one attack, shots were fired at three teen rivals in a street directly opposite Chirnsyde. Andrew Ferguson, outside whose home Kevin Carroll gunned down John Madden with the AK-47 in 2004, was one of two teenagers arrested but the case fizzled out.

Strathclyde Police's intelligence gatherers were keenly aware of the axis that existed between the Lyons mob in Milton and their Paisley buddies – Robert 'Piggy' Pickett and George 'Goofy' Docherty. In earlier years, the Lyons had flourished due to their links with the McGovern gang in Springburn. Now it was all about the Paisley connection. The Lyons enhanced their growing status in the criminal underworld through their contacts with the highly dangerous mob, with whom Jamie Daniel had clashed the previous decade. On a practical level, it made them stronger and gave them reliable drug supply lines.

Evidence of this connection – and of the large sums of money sloshing around – was seen in another court case which involved a £1.3 million haul of 276,000 ecstasy tablets found in Paisley and 79 kilos of cannabis. Among those arrested were Milton resident Billy Paterson Sr, who was to walk free from all charges, and Hugh Pickett, from Paisley, who was jailed for six years for the coke. Co-accused Gary Sorbie, another Milton resident, got three years for the cannabis. It was a major police investigation which stretched from addresses in Paisley and Milton and the seaside town of Stevenston in Ayrshire.

Drug dealing on the streets is lucrative enough but those controlling the supply inside prisons can also make serious money. The hard part is getting the drugs inside. Docherty ran a £5,000-a-week racket inside the city's Barlinnie prison. He had an unlikely supplier in the form of 31-year-old criminal lawyer Angela Baillie, who was a familiar face in the city's club scene and who was drawn like a moth to a flame by the seedy glamour of the underworld. Baillie used her status as a lawyer to secure private visits and smuggle heroin and other drugs into the harsh Victorian jail where Docherty was doing time.

The whistle-blowing con who shopped Baillie – which landed her with a 32-month prison sentence – could have paid with his life for doing so. The ensuing reprisal revealed how entangled the Lyons had become with the Paisley gang. When Docherty, who had been jailed with Pickett during the town's 90s drugs war, needed the 'grass' dealt with, he turned to Eddie Jr. The informant told that he was a 'dead man walking' in an interview with the *Sunday Mail* in which he also revealed his ordeal at the hands of Eddie Jr who had tracked him down in the street, knocked him out with a high-voltage cattle prod, beaten him, stabbed him and then written 'grass' on his head. Eddie Jr clearly wasn't aware that, two decades earlier in Cadder, his own father was the grass.

There's no doubt that the Daniels – including Carroll – had underestimated the Lyons boys and their crew. Having survived going head-to-head with the Daniels, the Club Boys walked with an extra swagger although bulletproof vests were still frequently worn and they rarely risked being in public alone. No longer did they need Uncle Johnny's gun-toting reputation as a calling card.

The elder Daniel generation of Jamie and his brothers had spent decades successfully evading the police but the younger members entering the family business were not so lucky or smart. In 2005, his nephew Robert Daniel – the alleged Chirn-syde minibus vandal – was given an eight-year sentence for dealing £300,000 worth of heroin. Oblivious to the long-term surveillance operation tracking his every move, he was snared after paying for and receiving the high-purity drugs from former soldier Christopher Bailiff in a car park transaction. Bailiff – who had the £61,000 cash payment in his car when he was arrested –

fled to the sunshine island of Tenerife but got five years following his extradition.

Robert's jailing was a coup for the police and a major blow to the Daniels as it helped erode the perception that they were somehow beyond the reaches of justice. To the Club Boys, it was a cause for celebration to see one of their main rivals and threats being sent away for a long time. When Robert was released, he seemed to drift away from the family's traditional areas of control while striking up loyalties with other criminal groups.

The police were acutely aware of the flashpoints between the Club Boys and the Daniels which had resulted in countless assaults and knife attacks plus the three non-fatal shootings in 2003 and 2004. The first shooting victim had been Carroll and he was followed by Johnny Lyons and John Madden on the other side. The police could do little to prevent the violence or prosecute the perpetrators.

Despite the Lyons' growing status, those with a handle on the dynamics of where the power lay still regarded the dominant Daniels as far more dangerous. Even the prolific punter Eddie Sr would have admitted the odds were stacked against his boys.

What followed at the city's trendy Tunnel nightclub on the night of 12 August 2005 was another test of that assumption. When Paul Trainer, a Daniel associate, was slashed across the face, Eddie Jr was there with brother Steven and fellow Club Boy McGuinness. The Daniel party included Trainer plus Robert Maxwell Jr whose dad Robert Sr was another high-level north Glasgow drug dealer. The blade attack in the club was never officially reported to the police but the detectives had a crystal-clear picture. One officer said, 'There are two tribes – the Daniels and the Lyons. The bottom line is that no one spoke to police so we don't have a victim.'

The Daniel gang did not take the latest attack lying down and, within 24 hours, a car was torched in Ronaldsay Street, the same street where Carroll had turned an AK-47 on Madden the previous year. Other low-level attacks took place against the Lyons and their interests but the biggest problem was getting close to Eddie Jr and Steven – the prime targets.

With the ever-present spectre of attack hanging over them, the brothers were forced to retreat from the streets where they and the Club Boys had ruled with fear. The games hall was no longer the gang hut and the Lyons family drifted away from the area, in a subtler version of the night-time exodus from Cadder in 1984.

However, Milton remained their power base. It was where they were known and feared and where their key gang members still lived. Yet they could only risk occasional and fleeting visits, always in numbers and wearing bulletproof protection. It was common sense – just basic survival instinct. They knew that they would be like sitting ducks in Milton for the well-armed Daniels and their many wannabe hit men.

While all this was going on – and every single incident was being logged in letters sent by the campaigners to the police and council – officials at George Square continued to see and hear no evil at Chirnsyde.

For Eddie Sr and his supporters in Glasgow City Council and the Labour Party, the peace was about to be shattered – Billy McAllister was to become an SNP councillor.

On 16 February 2006, a by-election took place for the Milton ward when Labour's Gary Gray had to stand down over questionable expenses claims. The essence of McAllister's campaign was simple – to get Lyons out of Chirnsyde. He mobilised local support, primarily the other three 'bampots' who were known and well respected, not least due to the playing fields victory. The feedback on the doorsteps was encouraging – many in the community wanted action on Chirnsyde. They too were sickened that a crime family was being propped up by the police and funded by taxpayers. Putting your name to a letter of complaint was asking for trouble. However, with polling booth anonymity, putting a cross beside the name of someone who promised to do something about it was a safer option.

McAllister got 773 votes to the Labour candidate's 623, which represented a 15.1% swing. A local council election rarely makes the headlines but so unusual was Labour's bloody nose in a Glasgow heartland that McAllister's win even merited a mention on that evening's *Newsnight Scotland* current affairs show on the BBC. It turned out to be a sign of things to come. A change in the voting system was to lead to a revolution at George Square where Labour's iron rule was to be smashed. When he entered the City Chambers, McAllister was one of four SNP councillors who were faced with 69 of the total 79 being Labour. A year later, due partly to the new system, the SNP's ranks swelled to 22 while Labour's shrank to 45. The following year, the national political landscape was to change in a similar but even more dramatic way as Alex Salmond's nationalists forced Labour and Jack McConnell out of power in Holyrood.

Ironically, McAllister had only gained his position thanks to the obstinate refusal of the council and police to address the Chirnsyde issue properly. Effectively, it was Labour who put him there. Yet his victory cannot be understated in terms of the campaign. He was no longer 'that bastard McAllister', the shouty activist who could be fobbed off by officials and threatened by police officers. He was now Councillor McAllister and, when he asked questions on behalf of his constituents, he was entitled to proper answers. Every violent incident made questions about Eddie Sr's status harder to justify. The ability of the authorities to defend the indefensible was rapidly eroding.

The escalating war between the Club Boys and the Daniels continued to flare. After years of grooming by Eddie Sr, the Club Boys had graduated from the Chirnsyde gym hall. Many had done jail time, they had stood up to the Daniels and they were doing some serious business with their Paisley contacts but was it enough? Were they ready for the future?

18

By Royal Appointment

Kevin Carroll had a burning hatred of the Lyons brothers Eddie Jr and Steven but he was virtually powerless. He couldn't get near them as they rarely ventured into Milton and were too smart to hang around waiting to be shot. On 18 April 2006, he was taking a drive. Most of the early-evening commuters, their car headlights twinkling in the dusk while streaming north on the motorway, were heading home after another day at the office. Unlike them, Carroll was on his way to work. He had decided to take the scenic route out of Glasgow, away from the eyes of the countless potential witnesses on the M80 motorway.

At any given time, the Daniels have access to stolen vehicles which are identical in model, age and colour to cars which they know to be legitimate, taxed and insured. By fitting copies of the clean cars' registration plates on the stolen motors, they can use the clones – or 'doublers' – to commit serious crime safe in the knowledge that they won't be flagged up as suspicious by the police's automatic number plate recognition system.

In the passenger seat beside Carroll was a close associate from Drumchapel – a ruthless, violent criminal called Raymond Anderson, who was nicknamed Rainbow. The pair left north Glasgow in a regular car and made their way to Auchinairn Road – a B road which snakes east out of Springburn and through the suburb of Bishopbriggs. They parked up and transferred into a cloned vehicle where a gun – free from prints and DNA – had been carefully secreted. They then continued their journey, taking a series of dark country roads before passing through the former mining village of Croy and then cutting south into Cumbernauld, a 1950s new town which had become the refuge of Eddie Sr and Jr since their departure from Milton. Carroll and Anderson's destination was Ratho Drive, a sizeable new estate of redbrick homes for aspirational families whose gleaming cars sit on monoblock driveways. As darkness fell, Carroll killed the ignition a short distance from the house which was then home to Eddie Jr, his parents and his brother Christopher. The Chirnsyde minibus was regularly parked outside overnight. Anderson slipped the black ski mask over his face and strode towards the half-glazed, white painted door and knocked. A neighbour looked out and saw the masked man, a bulky object tucked under his arm, standing patiently for an answer. Eddie Jr, then aged 28, came to the door and partially opened it. It was almost a fatal error. Realising what was happening, he quickly slammed it shut in the split second it took for the weapon to be raised and fired. Thankfully for him, the door took the full force of the blast although his face was peppered with the safety glass of the shattered pane. He could easily have ended up dead on his front step. It was the fourth shooting of the feud and the police intelligence files would show that the score now stood at Daniels 3 (Johnny Lyons, John Madden, Eddie Lyons Jr), Lyons 1 (Kevin Carroll). Carroll and Anderson drove calmly away from the estate as the gunfire brought neighbours edging out and the wail of emergency sirens began to fill the air. Once back at Auchinairn Road, the 'doubler' was torched, leaving forensic experts only a worthless, black-ened shell to examine. Detectives later reported 45-year-old, shaven-headed Anderson to prosecutors as a suspect in the attack but they ruled there was not enough evidence to bring him to trial. The shooting delivered a very worrying message to the Lyons – you can run but you can't hide. Carroll was willing to travel – nowhere was out of bounds. The next time Carroll and Anderson went hunting Lyons, eight months later, there would be a very different outcome.

The campaigners in Milton seized on the shooting as further evidence that the war between the two families was far from over and that there remained a real risk to children while Eddie Sr remained at Chirnsyde. If a gunman was determined enough to travel 15 miles to target his home, why would they stay away from the Club Boys' occasional gang hut?

Billy McAllister's election to the city council seemed to be having a sudden and tangible effect on Bridget McConnell and her officials. Just 12 days after he became Councillor McAllister, she ordered an independent investigation into Chirnsyde. The council agreed to award another £80,000 of taxpayers' money to the centre which was to be paid in quarterly £20,000 instalments, with the final two dependent on the enquiry's findings. The campaigners were hopeful. For the first time, the council seemed to be offering a glimmer of acceptance that there were legitimate concerns. But their hopes were dashed when the council eventually revealed that the Chirnsyde investigation was to be conducted by a firm of accountants, Scott-Moncrieff, whose remit was 'governance and financial stewardship'. Criminality and public safety was kept off the agenda. Why order an independent investigation which would ignore the key issue of the suitability of a man like Lyons to run a centre, backed with public money, while his family waged a gang war? It felt like a whitewash.

In June 2006, the Lyons family mourned the loss of Eddie Sr's father, also Edward, who had suffered a knife attack during his son's stabbing in Cadder 22 years previously. When the family gathered for the funeral, emotions were running high. One family member flashed a handgun at other mourners. It seemed to be for protection rather than intimidation. As the cortege made its way through Milton, Eddie Sr joined it behind the wheel of the Chirnsyde minibus. The following night, at 12.35 a.m., a campaigner's car was petrol-bombed in the street outside his home. The burst of orange flames illuminated the street but the craven fire-starters – one of whom was suspected to be Eddie's nephew Paul Lyons – had slunk into the night. The police were fully aware that this was the latest attack by the Lyons against the law-abiding people who were standing up to them and not a simple case of vandalism. All the campaigners could do was continue to write letters of complaint to the police.

Weeks later, campaigner Johnny McLean scored a remarkable victory over Glasgow City Council in a row over his son Dean's safety and schooling which had begun four years earlier in 2002. McLean was struggling financially and was forced to seek £10 a week from the council towards the cost of transporting his youngest son to the school which he attended outwith Milton and where his siblings had been educated. The council refused and told him he should instead attend one of the schools in Milton. Their proposal was inconceivable given McLean's long history of standing up to the Lyons and the links between Chirnsyde and the schools. In a letter to then education director Ken Corsar on 12 September 2002, McLean wrote:

As the education services are involved with directing a number of schools in the north of the city to Chirnsyde during school hours, I could not comfortably permit my son to enrol in any such locations. The fact that I have spoken out against such criminal elements in this area naturally aggravates the situation further.

Finally, I do of course wish to return my child to school as soon as possible and would ask you to consider the possibility of at least in part meeting the transportation expenses involved.

McLean threatened to sue but it was an empty gesture because he did not have the money to do so. The council applied its own legal thumbscrews by threatening to prosecute McLean for refusing to send the boy to school. He was charged with breaking a law that states it is a parental duty to provide 'efficient education'. The Education (Scotland) Act 1980 also stipulates that, if a parent withdraws a child from school without 'reasonable excuse', they are guilty and can be jailed for up to one month.

The stand-off lasted four years. McLean believes that the reason the council took so long to take him to court was because the officials wanted to keep the whole messy saga under wraps. By the time the case reached Glasgow Sheriff Court in July 2006, McLean had gone through three different lawyers. He dispensed with the services of one when he refused to follow the advice to plead guilty.

SNP MSP Sandra White backed McLean's plight and, in a letter to the sheriff, she described him as a 'public-spirited citizen and a devoted family man'. She added:

Mr McLean's fears for his son's safety is that the local schools are within the ambit, for the purposes of sport and leisure, of Chirnsyde managed by Mr Edward Lyons. Mr McLean has had a long-running dispute with Glasgow City Council over the suitability of Mr Lyons as a fit and proper person to be managing a publicly-funded leisure facility, and he has been the victim of a hit and run incident and had his life threatened. Dean has also been the victim of an attempted hit and run – as a result of which he was issued with a panic alarm by Strathclyde Police – he withdrew his son from school. During the period when Dean was being taught at home by his father there was no attempt by Glasgow City Council education department to test his level of attainment.'

McLean also submitted a written statement, powerfully setting out his position. He wrote:

All four of the local schools acted in conjunction with Mr Edward Lyons and utilised Chirnsyde of which he is co-ordinator. This meant that Mr Lyons had access, and still has, to the school buildings and that he was present outside them to transport children to Chirnsyde.

The thought of directing my son to a school which was interacting with Mr Lyons was quite frankly perverse given Mr Lyons' connection to serious crime. It flies in the face of what I was trying to teach my son Dean.

In addition to this was the fact that I had publicly spoken out against Mr Lyons, raising concerns about the suitability of the position that he held with children.

This is not just a perception that I hold, it's held by many and it was later a question that was asked in the *Sunday Mail* newspaper under the title of 'Would you let this man look after your children?'. My answer to this question is, quite simply, absolutely not!

My position and concerns are further fuelled by the fact that I have come under personal threat from Mr Lyons as a result of the concerns that I have raised. I have documented these threats with the police at the highest level. These threats have also extended to my family as I have been informed that I was going to be burnt out of my home if I did not keep my mouth shut.

I am charged with failing to send my son to school under the Education Act without a reasonable explanation. I would argue that I have a reasonable concern that prevents me from sending my son towards the locations on offer by the council and that the council has failed to acknowledge my genuine concerns.

I struggle to understand why the council education department continues to interact with such an individual given the level of concerns raised by so many thus far. I also sympathise with all the affected children and their parents who on one hand know all too well about the controversy surrounding Mr Lyons in terms of his links to crime and, on the other hand, have to sit back whilst the schools tasked with education and caring for children appear to mindlessly direct them to this location.

By the time the sheriff had heard everything, he came to a very firm view. McLean was given an absolute discharge. His obstinacy in the face of council threats had paid off. The prospect of a prison sentence would have been enough to break many other 67-year-olds but not McLean. Outside court, he said, 'I would rather have gone to prison than back down.' In the meantime, Dean had finally been able to return to school after a four-year absence thanks to the provision of a council bus pass.

Within weeks of McLean's victory, the council revealed the findings of the investigation by Scott-Moncrieff. Despite not being tasked with looking at Lyons' crime links or the potential risk to children attending the centre, the accountants had reached some stark and brutal conclusions about the way in which Lyons' den operated. Their lengthy and detailed report identified 32 areas of concern. Half of those were classed as 'significant control weaknesses which may lead to major financial, reputation or operational risk to the organisation. This weakness should be resolved as a matter of priority.' The report confirmed what the campaigners had been saying for years – the publicly funded council building was being run like a private club. Of the 32 concerns, 11 related to finance issues. The accountants also found that the two minibuses were registered in the name of Lyons himself, contrary to Chirnsyde's constitution. No records were kept of how they were used and nor was there any control of the Chirnsyde computers – which Chris Lyons had been busy using to create his gang website.

The council unveiled the Scott-Moncrieff report at a public meeting on 15 September 2006 at the City Chambers. In the view of the campaigners, the report presented ample evidence of ineptitude on such a grand scale that Lyons should be removed from Chirnsyde immediately. Given the farcical way in which he ran Chirnsyde, how had he been allowed to get away with it for so long?

The council officials saw it differently. They recommended to the councillors not to remove Lyons but instead to move towards month-to-month funding. In addition, the councillors also agreed to vote for the creation of a 'comprehensive scrutiny review of the issues surrounding Chirnsyde Community Initiative and its relationship with Glasgow City Council and make recommendations regarding the future nature of that relationship' – in other words, another enquiry. This time, it would be compiled by veteran Labour councillor Archie Graham, whose MSP wife Johann Lamont was promoted eight weeks later by Jack McConnell to become Deputy Justice Minister in his cabinet. In 2011, she was elected leader of the Labour Party in Scotland, to replace Iain Gray following his crushing Holyrood defeat by Alex Salmond.

McAllister, McLean and the other campaigners smelled a rat. They feared that Graham's enquiry would deliver the answers that the council was seeking and would conclude that the status quo should remain at Chirnsyde. After all, he who pays the piper calls the tunes.

A preliminary public meeting of the scrutiny committee prompted a protest by McLean who unfurled a poster stating 'shame on you' beside Bridget McConnell. Others held up enlarged copies of news stories about the Lyons family's gangsterism.

Days after that protest, Councillor McAllister was told by council officials that the scrutiny committee witnesses would only be allocated 20 minutes each to give evidence – an arbitrary and unnatural condition. He was also informed that they would begin taking evidence in November. One person invited to give evidence asked what security measures would be put in place, given the family's previous use of intimidation to derail criminal trials. No answer was forthcoming so he refused to take part.

The campaigners had rejected previous requests to provide testimony to the council because of the condition that Lyons and his management committee would be present. This time, Lyons would not be present but they still had misgivings owing to their complete mistrust of the council. Around nine people tentatively agreed to provide testimony to Graham and his committee. First up was Margo McDonnell, the wife of Thomas McDonnell Sr who had almost been butchered in the cowardly mob attack at Chirnsyde six years before. Margo took to her feet in a grand committee room of the City Chambers to deliver a moving and articulate account about the damage done to her family by Lyons and his family. As she spoke, Councillor Graham kept his head down and scratched away at his notepad with a pen. He seemed to shrink into his chair when she asked him directly why the Labour-controlled council was bankrolling and backing a man who had ruined her family.

The second day of testimony saw numerous people come forward, each of them with first-hand accounts which incriminated Lyons and painted lurid and compelling pictures of his connections to drug dealing and violence. Emotions were raw and tears occasionally flowed from those who found their voices – or, rather, were being listened to. This was no longer just the four 'bampots' as the council sneeringly referred to them. These were mothers and fathers, ordinary people who were determined that they should be heard. One campaigner believes that Margo's testimony alone was enough to spell the end of Lyons' reign at Chirnsyde.

It seems that the Lyons family, however, were not done with their quest of seeking friends in high places. This time it was the turn of Prince Charles to be duped. Eddie Lyons Jr and his pal Liam Boyle – one of the Club Boys who had terrorised the McDonnell family – had formed a construction company and had entered the fledgling business into a royal competition. The firm, WIT Construction, won Lanarkshire region's best young start-ups in the Prince's Scottish Youth Business Trust (PSYBT) and The Royal Bank of Scotland Business Awards in a ceremony at Chatelherault Country Park, just south of Hamilton. With the accolade came a loan from the prince's charity of £30,000 to set up in business. Councillor Billy McAllister noted at the time, 'Members of the Lyons family terrorise a community, yet they are rewarded and held up as role models by Prince Charles. He can rest assured, though, as he joins a list of respectable people who have backed the Lyons family, including politicians and police officers.'

Eddie Lyons Jr and Liam Boyle were among a group of eight finalists who then enjoyed a private lunch and a knockabout on the court with tennis player Andy Murray at a ceremony in Glasgow. Only Boyle attended the third and final event at the grand Strathclyde University venue, the Barony. Eddie Jr had more pressing matters to deal with.

19

Grave Wars

The cold, white glow of the full moon picked out the name of
Garry Lyons on the black headstone and the inscription:

> To the wee tough guy
> Love You Forever

It was where he had rested in peace for 15 years.

In the night's darkness, Kevin 'Gerbil' Carroll and two other
men were on the most sickening of missions. Attached to their
four-wheel-drive's tow bar was a rope which was looped over
the large headstone. The vehicle's engine revved, the rope went
taut and the stone crashed down. An angel statue, which formed
part of the stone, was smashed and two adjacent headstones
were also toppled while the surrounding pristine grass of Cadder
Cemetery in Bishopbriggs was churned to mud by the vehicle's
tyres. It was the early hours of 6 November 2006. The next
morning, the Lyons family were due to visit the grave on what
would have been Garry's 23rd birthday. They found desecration – and a declaration of war.

The attack prompted public revulsion. Even to those who lurk
in the sewers of the city's underworld, it was an odious and
indefensible act. Carroll had crossed a line and he did so fully
aware of the significance of what he had done. The 26-year-
old's self-justification for his actions centred on the abduction
and torture of a 15-year-old associate of his from Drumchapel –
a boy who was like a brother to him. The Lyons were blamed for
that cowardly and vicious attack and Carroll, unable to get at the

elusive Eddie Jr and Steven, perversely sought out the final resting place of their sibling. When Eddie Sr chose to bury his son in the out-of-town cemetery because of his 1980s feuds, little could he have realised that his fears of the grave being targeted would come true all these years later, albeit as a consequence of another feud with a different family.

Seven months after the shooting of Eddie Jr in Cumbernauld, Carroll's graveyard stunt was a brutal reminder to the Lyons that he would stop at nothing to do them harm. The message was picked up by the Milton campaigners who again pleaded with the council to evict Lyons Sr from the community centre before an innocent member of the public became caught in the crossfire. Councillor Billy McAllister told a newspaper:

> What happened at the cemetery is inexcusable. But if people are twisted enough to take their feud to a child's grave, then what's stopping them targeting the Lyons family at Chirnsyde?
>
> Glasgow City Council has been in possession of many good reasons to boot Lyons out of Chirnsyde but they continue to back him. It defies explanation.

In later years, the Lyons boys would tell people that their brother Garry had suffered taunts from Carroll when he was dying slowly from his disease. They claimed that Carroll, then their paperboy and 10 years old, had mocked the cancer victim's hair loss by shouting names as he passed their Torogay Street home. However, others firmly refute that claim. They point out that no such behaviour would have been tolerated and that Carroll had never even been the family's paperboy. They suspected that the story was cooked up and spun by the Lyons in an apparent bid to convince others of Carroll's repugnance – as if attacking Garry's grave was not enough.

Over the coming years, there was much speculation about who was with Carroll that night. Of the numerous names that routinely crop up, only two are correct but the perpetrators are unlikely to ever admit their presence.

Carroll was still not satisfied. Two days after the grave attack, at 6.30 p.m. on 8 November, he struck again. In April, he and Raymond Anderson had driven 15 miles north-east to get to Lyons in Cumbernauld. This time, he went the same distance south-eastwards to the town of Bellshill. He was acting, as the police might put it, on intelligence. A small-time dealer in the Lanarkshire town owed the Lyons money and Eddie Jr and fellow Club Boy Andrew 'Dumbo' Gallacher were going to collect. Despite the attack on his brother's grave, business continued. The pair, both wearing body armour, drove slowly into the town's Myers Court, a new-build cul-de-sac, where the debtor lived. Lyons pulled in and stepped from his black BMW X5 on to the pavement. Gerbil was lying in wait. He had been tipped off by the man who was expecting a visit from the Lyons. Why pay the Lyons when he knew that a call to Carroll could make the problem go away? Loyalty among drug dealers was clearly in short supply.

Like a jack-in-the-box, the masked Carroll popped up from behind a row of green wheelie bins and dashed towards the car, gun drawn. Lyons tried to jump back inside the steel cocoon of the X5 and gunned the powerful engine to life but it started to roll forwards before his legs got inside, causing him minor injuries. At least he managed to dodge the hail of bullets being unleashed by Carroll. Dumbo was not so fortunate and he was struck with at least one round before Carroll fled towards a nearby getaway car. Dumbo's vest could have been the difference between life and death and he was treated at Glasgow's Royal Infirmary before being released, having failed to tell the police anything. The shooting scoreboard now read Daniel 4 (Johnny Lyons, John Madden, Eddie Lyons Jr, Andrew Gallacher) – Lyons 1 (Carroll).

The Lyons knew that they had to fight fire with fire. Trigger-happy Carroll was out of control and, if they did not do something about him, he was clearly determined to kill them. Paranoia haunted their every movement.

In the aftermath, Carroll was subjected to a near constant and usually obvious police tail. He loved the attention and, for fun, would attempt to lose the surveillance team or wave at them with a grin on his face. He seemed to think he was in a gangster movie.

An opportunity to hit back against Carroll arose just eight days later when he and 25-year-old Ross Sherlock, also in a BMW X5, drove into Clelland Avenue, a quiet residential street off Auchinairn Road in Bishopbriggs, for a meeting with a violent red-haired associate Craig Gallagher, who revelled in the nickname of Rob Roy after the eighteenth-century outlaw. Carroll and Sherlock had no reason to feel edgy. After all, they were the hunters, not the prey.

This time though, someone had slipped Eddie Jr and his Club Boys the valuable inside track on Carroll's exact whereabouts. Gallagher, who was in a black Mercedes ML350, got out to talk to Carroll and Sherlock who remained seated in their vehicle. Gallagher's girlfriend – a social worker who worked with vulnerable young people – remained in the Merc with the couple's pet dog as the men got down to talking business. At around 9.55 p.m., two cars which had been circling nearby, swung into the street. Perhaps the unremarkable vehicles – at least one of which was a Ford – were initially mistaken for CID vehicles by the trio. Carroll later claimed that the surveillance officers who had been following him since the Bellshill hit were present at the time of the attack and that they sat and watched it unfold. Given that the police were unarmed, there was not much they could have done about it – even if they had wanted to.

The gunman emerged from one of the vehicles and started firing. Residents reported the sound of at least four shots, possibly five, in rapid succession. The target was Carroll who suffered serious injuries as he was blasted in the stomach from close range while Sherlock was hit in the legs. Carroll was rushed by ambulance to the Royal Infirmary. Guarded by armed police and treated by medical staff, his critical condition eventually improved to serious then recovery. Sherlock managed to scramble a few hundred metres to Stobhill Hospital before being transferred to the same hospital as Carroll. The only fatality was the bull mastiff owned by Gallagher. Armed police and dog handlers swarmed into the street. Flags went up in police circles warning that this was the latest in a series of tit-for-tat shootings between two armed and dangerous gangs although the information issued to the public would omit those details. Terrified residents gave sketchy and conflicting accounts. The victims refused to say a word. Yet again, the police knew everything but could prove nothing.

What was obvious was that the Lyons were sick of being hunted and had hit back in spectacular style with the score now Daniel 4 (Johnny Lyons, John Madden, Eddie Lyons Jr, Andrew Gallacher) – Lyons 3, (Kevin Carroll twice, Ross Sherlock).

The demands for immediate and decisive action from the terrified residents of Milton reached fever pitch. Councillor Archie Graham took members of his scrutiny review group and clipboard-wielding council officials to pay a visit to Chirnsyde where they would meet the co-ordinator. The expected whitewash was soon to become nothing more than a sideshow.

20

Massacre at Applerow

Hitmen Raymond Anderson Sr and James McDonald had been on a Christmas shopping trip. First on their list were two powerful handguns and ammunition, acquired via their Daniel paymasters from soldiers of the Royal Regiment of Scotland's Argyll and Sutherland Highlanders. Next were several pay-as-you-go, unregistered mobile phones purchased from St Enoch shopping mall in Glasgow's city centre. On 4 December 2006, they paid cash for an eight-year-old, pale blue Mazda 626 from a classified advert placed by a Mr Young in the southern suburb of Clarkston. The final items, bought on 5 December, were two 'old man' masks and wigs from Tam Shepherd's magic shop, a city institution founded in 1886.

Kevin Carroll had just got out of hospital after several weeks of slow and painful recovery from taking a Lyons bullet in the guts. Due to his stomach injuries, he still walked with a stoop and was in too much pain and discomfort to deal with his hated adversaries personally. Instead, he ordered immediate revenge. He and the elder Daniels were willing to pay large sums of cash to make it happen. The criminals who knew no boundaries were about to stage another spectacular that would shock Scotland.

The cocky young Lyons – and their protector-in-chief Robert Pickett – had been crowing since the double shooting of Carroll and Sherlock in Bishopbriggs. During Carroll's convalescence in a hospital bed, the Lyons routinely staged public meetings on the forecourt of Applerow Motors in Balmore Road, Lambhill, during which they bragged loudly about the demise of Carroll. They were no longer running or hiding. They were even bold enough to casually hurl abuse in the direction of a Daniel family member who was resident nearby. It was a very visible show of chutzpah and defiance which the Daniels could not allow – look at what happened to Frank McPhie when he dared to cross them.

On 6 December, the day after the trip to Tam Shepherd's, the Daniel hit squad was primed and ready for action. Lookout Raymond Anderson Jr was in the vicinity of Applerow Motors when he made a mobile phone call to his father Raymond Sr just before 2 p.m. At that point, Raymond Sr and McDonald were in the Mazda, cruising steadily along the M8 motorway from the east end towards the garage on Balmore Road, Lambhill.

At 2.10 p.m., the 21-year-old made a second call to his father which lasted just four seconds. The hit was on.

At 2.12 p.m., Anderson Sr, 45, and McDonald, 33, pulled up the Mazda outside the entrance of the garage run by Eddie Lyons Sr's younger brother David. Wearing long, dark trench coats, like Wild West gunslingers, they slid on their masks and readied their pristine, military hardware.

Michael Lyons Jr – a nephew of Eddie Sr and David – was visiting the garage to fill the water tank for his mobile car wash business. It was a typical day in the bustling and noisy MOT station, where tinny music blared over the clatter of metal and shouted banter. David saw the gunmen first and shouted a warning to his family members. Michael Jr began running but a British Army bullet cut him down in mid flight. David went towards his screaming nephew but realised that, unless he wanted to be next, he should take cover.

Moments before the gunmen had walked in, Steven Lyons, 27, and Pickett, 42, had driven into the small yard in a Ford Focus. They – not Michael Jr – were the real targets. Just as David shouted his warning, Steven had glanced in the Ford's rear-view mirror and seen the two men – their faces hidden by the grotesque latex masks – walking quickly towards the back of the stationary car. Steven brought his foot down hard on the accelerator as a shot blew out the Ford's back window in an explosion of glass. In the confines of the yard, he had nowhere to go. He almost crashed into his cousin, Mark Lyons, another of David's sons, before slamming into the garage's metal perimeter fence which forced a sudden halt. A second bullet penetrated the Ford and grazed Steven's back, from where a fragment was later recovered by medics. He then scrambled from the vehicle and attempted to seek refuge inside the shed-like building but one of the gunmen picked him off with a round as he ran, snapping a bone in his leg. It was the final shot.

Pickett had also scrambled from the Ford and he took two rounds into his back and gut from as close as two feet away.

Anderson Sr and McDonald were not jittery amateurs. They had spent plenty of time coolly honing their shooting skills on an old railway line and at other secluded spots. During the rampage, the two men unleashed round after deafening round, moments after taxis had collected special needs pupils from St Joan of Arc primary school next door.

The peaceful winter afternoon had been shattered by the roar of gunfire which brought panic, pain and terror. By 2.15 p.m., it was over. It had been three minutes of carnage. Blood drenched the concrete.

David returned to Michael Jr who had stopped screaming. The colour had drained from his face. A 999 operator offered medical instructions but the bullet hole in Michael's stomach confirmed to David that he was dead.

Steven lay stricken on a growing scarlet circle on the ground while Pickett sat on a chair, bent double in agony with a serious stomach wound. He spent three weeks in a coma at the Royal Infirmary where he lost a kidney due to his injuries and became infected with the MRSA superbug. By the time Pickett was well enough, the parole board decided that he should be sent back to prison from where he had been freed early from his 12-year sentence for the triple attempted murders of the Rennie brothers, imposed in 1996 during the Paisley gang wars. The police were delighted that he was taken off the streets.

At the age of 13, the dead man Michael Jr had lost his father Michael Sr to a crack cocaine overdose during the police drugs factory raid. When Michael Jr was shot dead, he was the father of an 11-month-old daughter called Ellie. A week before the murder, he had celebrated his 21st birthday and had also recently become engaged to his partner Nicola Stevenson. The year before the Applerow massacre, he had been charged with a brutal knife attack in nearby Scapa Street but the case was dropped by prosecutors. Despite this violent episode, he was not on the Daniels' wanted list. Most likely, he was a victim of mistaken identity on the part of the gunmen who, looking through the masks' peephole eyes, thought the running young man was either Eddie Jr or Steven.

Anderson and McDonald, adrenaline surging through their bodies and their hearts thundering in their chests, jogged back towards the Mazda and slipped into the traffic of Balmore Road. They drove north before turning left into Skirsa Street in Cadder. The emergency sirens of police and paramedics streamed towards the garage while the police helicopter, scrambled from its Clydeside base, was soon overhead. The Mazda's final destination was to be Vaila Street, half a mile and three minutes away from the shooting. Having dumped the car, Anderson and McDonald split up and continued their getaway on foot. Anderson Sr walked across a patch of waste ground and, at 2.20 p.m., made his first phone call since the shootings to his son. Over the next 18 minutes, he made several other calls to his boy as he tackled the 1.3-mile walk south down to Maryhill Road, determined not to do anything that would cause witnesses to notice him. At 3.02 p.m., he was back behind the wheel of another car and on the M8 heading to his home in Jerviston Road in the east end. Within days, Anderson Sr was seen driving around in a sleek, black Mercedes SUV. It was a part payment from the Daniels.

For the hitmen, the job was not yet complete. Committing murder was one thing – getting away with it was quite another. They realised that it was only a matter of time before the Mazda was found. It didn't take a fan of TV detectives to know that the car could provide police with a trove of evidence. Immediately, the police officer in charge of the investigation, Detective Superintendent Campbell Corrigan, issued appeals for information on the pale blue vehicle. On Friday, 8 December, the police wrongly suggested that it may have been a Subaru Impreza. That same evening – realising how important it was for the car to be destroyed and emboldened by the police's apparent confusion – Anderson Sr returned to Vaila Street. Mindful of being spotted by witnesses and tuned in to any hint of police surveillance, he walked quickly past the Mazda, giving it the slightest glance. He pulled out his mobile at 8.34 p.m. and hit McDonald's number to tell him that the car was still there and the coast appeared to be clear. As Anderson Sr departed from the scene, McDonald arrived, cloaked by the midwinter darkness. The car was soon engulfed with flames while acrid, black smoke rose into the night's sky. The first 999 call to the fire brigade was at 9.41 p.m. When the detectives arrived, the smoking vehicle was largely intact – McDonald had botched the torching. Realising the Mazda was still potentially incriminating, the Daniel mob decided to have another go. Given their involvement in the scrap metal and used car trades, they had the inside track on where the Mazda had been taken – a privately run vehicle recovery yard in the Queenslie area which had a contract with the police to store vehicles.

On 22 December, the Mazda was torched for a second time. It was a bold move by the Daniels and an embarrassment for the police that a murder gang should be able to stage such an audacious attack on a vital piece of evidence from a high-profile crime in a supposedly secure compound. The police claimed that no evidence was lost as a result of the attack but, during the later trial, no forensics from the car were led by the prosecution.

On the day of the massacre at Applerow, word spread rapidly through the city and in newsrooms across Scotland about the atrocity. The Lyons and Daniel families were about to enter the mainstream.

Months earlier, Councillor Billy McAllister had arranged a public meeting within St Joan of Arc School for 6 December, to air concerns with the police about crime in the area. Suddenly, a routine meeting that may have attracted a few dozen residents was the only show in town. Strathclyde Police attempted to have it shut down. They ordered McAllister to postpone but he refused. At one point, McAllister was circled by black-clad uniformed police officers who told him the event could not happen due to the health and safety difficulties caused by so many people in attendance. They even threatened to arrest him but the presence of the BBC TV news cameras and newspaper journalists was enough for them to back down.

When Chief Superintendent Bernie Higgins had agreed to attend all those weeks before, he would have had no idea about what he was to face. McAllister was in the chair and it was standing room only. McAllister spelled out in graphic, undeniable detail all about the police support of Lyons – the catalogue of violence at Chirnsyde and the six-year gun feud between the Lyons and the Daniels. The meeting went on for two and a half hours and the police took a verbal kicking. Reeling off crime stats and offering soothing police-speak platitudes did nothing to placate the rapid-fire questions from angry mothers, fathers and grandparents who demanded tough action on the gangsters who operated with apparent impunity.

21

Eddie Evicted

His nephew Michael was lying in a morgue, his bullet-ridden son Steven was fighting for life in a hospital bed and lurid headlines about the triple shooting were plastered on the front of every newspaper in the country. Eddie Lyons Sr, however, was determined that it would be business as usual and, the following morning, he opened Chirnsyde as if it were any other Thursday.

Around 2 p.m. – 24 hours after the Applerow bloodbath – a convoy of eight council and police vans filed into the pot-holed Chirnsyde car park. Eddie Sr, his wife Josephine and a handful of others inside the centre were given a few minutes to take what was theirs and get out. The police stood silently as the message was delivered by council officials. The myth of Eddie Sr, the self-styled community leader, was finally over.

That morning, eviction rumours had circulated around Milton which prompted a small group of residents to gather expectantly on the pavement of Ashgill Road. They were not to be disappointed. Dressed in a T-shirt and jogging trousers and with a woollen hat pulled down to his eyebrows, Eddie Sr grabbed a few fishing rods and scurried out the back door, with the residents' jeers and catcalls ringing in his ears. He drove away, at high speed, in the taxpayer-owned Chirnsyde minibus, never to return. The humiliating eviction came 22 years after Eddie Sr and his family had been given a police escort out of Cadder for being 'grasses'.

That night, there was a palpable sense of relief in Milton. The only dissent came from the up-and-coming Club Boys, lads aged as young as 12, who were loyal to the Lyons and who voiced their anger. Under the glow of streetlights, Councillor Billy McAllister did not try to duck their criticism and shared a robust exchange of opinions with the latest young apprentices.

The campaigners were happy and relieved but they did not gloat. Not only had a young father lost his life but each of them had suffered during the past six years. They had risked their personal safety, relationships, family cohesion and sometimes their sanity.

On the day of the shootings, moments after the final round struck Steven Lyons' leg, one of the campaigners had raced to the scene and spotted the Chirnsyde minibus parked on Balmore Road, across from the garage gates. Had Eddie Sr got there quickly in response to the shootings or had he been due to attend the family summit and missed the attack by sheer good fortune? Both these scenarios presented problems for his backers in the council and Labour Party. Inside the City Chambers, they realised that Eddie Sr's position had become untenable.

Yet the council still could not bring itself to admit it had been wrong and instead issued the following statement: 'As a precautionary measure, Chirnsyde Community Initiative has been closed with immediate effect. A meeting of the council's review group will take place tomorrow, followed by a report to the executive committee.' In other words, Councillor Archie Graham and his officials would continue wandering around with their clipboards. Despite the council's weasel words, newspapers, which had ignored what had been going on in Milton, finally found their voice. On 8 December, the *Evening Times* published a damning leader column which stated:

Three more people shot in the street and a community living in fear. And once again the finger of blame was pointed at Chirnsyde Community Initiative.

Repeatedly the centre has been linked to the notorious Lyons crime family, two of whom were gunned down.

And, given that the facility is run by Eddie Lyons, uncle of the man shot dead, it was no surprise questions were asked about why the council was funding the centre.

Thankfully, and at last, the council has now closed the centre after six years of probes failed to find evidence that it was being used by criminal elements.

However, it was inexcusable that it took so long to act on a facility which most local people believed had gangland links.

Such centres are supposed to benefit residents. But anyone walking in Lambhill could have had no doubts that Chirnsyde is where locals have long believed the gang wars are centred.

And, given the level of public belief about such criminal links, Chief Constable Willie Rae must examine the effectiveness of investigations in an area which has seen so much violence.

What's more, given his curiously low profile in dealing with an incident which has made national headlines, Mr Rae, personally, should declare how his force is going to bring peace and security to Lambhill's streets.

The council must also scrutinise its handling of the affair.

Public cash should never be handed to any organisation which has even a whiff of suspicion about it. At Chirnsyde that whiff had become a stench.

Councillors had no more powers yesterday than at any point over the past six years. So why did it take so long to act?

Chirnsyde may have a positive role to play in Milton. But, it must not re-open it until all trace of suspicion is removed.

The following day, the same newspaper supplied a detailed breakdown of how much public money had been funnelled into Chirnsyde over the past 11 years – £1.38 million with £438,000 of that coming from the council since 2001.

Days later, the *Sunday Times* journalist Joan McAlpine, who later became an SNP MSP, wrote a column with the headline, 'This is a nasty stink you cannot just ignore, Jack'. She wrote:

Jack McConnell is publicly committed to fighting crime, reducing violence and improving the prospects of young people in deprived urban areas. Yet his wife's department, and his party organisation in Glasgow, has given a man with high-profile criminal associates £1.4m in public funds over 10 years to run a community centre used by children.

Since 1999, local people have begged that Eddie Lyons be sacked as co-ordinator of Chirnsyde Community Initiative in Milton, north Glasgow. Their pleas have been contemptuously ignored by both the council and Strathclyde police, until a triple shooting this month.

Lyons's family is involved in a long-running feud with another group of villains, the Daniels, and at least 11 people have been shot since 2003 as a result of this vendetta. Last week the community centre was finally closed when Lyons's nephew Michael was shot dead and his son Steven and another man were critically injured.

Steven Lyons has been charged with attempted murder several times, but never convicted. In 2001 Eddie Lyons, his sons Steven and Eddie junior, his brother Johnny and a friend called Paul McGuinness were all charged with the attempted murder of Thomas McDonnell, who was attacked outside the community centre. Only McGuinness was convicted, though Eddie Lyons Jr and his father received not proven verdicts. Two years ago £63,000 was confiscated from Eddie Lyons's home by police investigating the alleged drug dealing of his son's friends.

It sounds like something you might expect to find in the slums of Rio, but the astonishing aspect of this debacle is the authorities' complacency. I first came across the story in 2003, when I heard that local parents were complaining that the council was forcing them to send their children to after-school fitness classes at Chirnsyde.

McConnell was, perhaps not surprisingly, inundated with letters. Yet nothing was done until 2005, when she produced a report claiming there was no evidence of criminal activity or misuse of funds. This is beside the point. Ordinary parents cannot help out at their local Brownie pack without submitting to official checks by Disclosure Scotland on their character. Why was Lyons thought a suitable person to run activities for young people? McConnell then changed her mind and recommended closure earlier this year, but Labour councillors refused to follow her advice. She should have resigned then. But that would have embarrassed the party her husband leads.

Glasgow Labour had already been humiliated when Billy McAllister, the SNP community activist who campaigned against Chirnside, unseated them at a local by-election. Perhaps this explains the failure to act. Did the Labour party dig in its heels because political opponents made the issue their own? Despite his democratic endorsement, McAllister was excluded from the council review group investigating the affair. The secrecy of this approach was condemned by Kevin Dunion, Scotland's information commissioner. He was astounded the council refused to give local people the names of the management committee that ran Chirnside in their name.

It's easy to dismiss these events as a tale of the underworld in one of Glasgow's less salubrious corners. But it should concern anyone who cares about crime, young people and democracy. Teenagers in Milton risked Asbos if they stepped out of line. Meanwhile, they watched the local hood handed taxpayers' money, and official endorsement from Scotland's first lady.

Due to the unprecedented nature of the crime, Jamie Daniel was also about to feel the heat. A highly skilled *Sunday Mail* photographer, using a long lens and a lot of patience, captured the first contemporary picture of the crime boss at a large family home in the city's leafy west end. Alongside Daniel was John McCabe, the sniper suspected of gunning down Frank McPhie. For Daniel, it was unwelcome and unfamiliar to be under the microscope.

Within days of the shootings, the police went looking for Kevin Carroll and Ross Sherlock. On 15 December, they raided the Milton homes of Carroll's mother and that of Sherlock along with the home in Torrance of an associate who can't be named for legal reasons. Sherlock was arrested on an outstanding warrant for minor offences of threatening behaviour the previous month.

Carroll – possibly to avoid his mother's door from being battered in again – handed himself in to police three days later with a lawyer in tow. The following day he appeared at the city's sheriff court accused of causing 'stress and alarm' due to threatening behaviour towards a woman, also in November. He was bailed and back on the streets where he could continue inflicting damage.

One consequence of the Chirnsyde closure was a decision by Strathclyde Police that the committee of councillors who had voted to evict Eddie Sr would be the subject of risk assessments. Councillor McAllister – the man who the Lyons blamed most for the closure – was unsurprised that the police's concerns did not extend to his welfare. Several days later, that changed when the SNP's deputy leader Nicola Sturgeon met with the Chief Constable Willie Rae to demand protection for the brave councillor, which prompted an appropriate response.

McAllister felt as much at risk from the Labour Party establishment and some elements within the police as he did from the Lyons. Three days after the Applerow massacre, he and another campaigner were walking through the grand marble lobby of the City Chambers when they fleetingly crossed paths with Bridget McConnell who, for so long, had dismissed their concerns. The campaigner turned to McConnell and made a spontaneous but ill-advised comment about her having blood on her hands.

A version of the story was spun from within the council to a *News of the World* reporter. The now-defunct paper's front page claimed that McConnell had suffered threats from gangsters – apparently in the form of a single, anonymous and unspecific text message to the council switchboard. The paper then erroneously claimed that McAllister had been 'interviewed by cops' in relation to his City Chambers encounter with McConnell. The report quoted an anonymous source as saying: 'McAllister confronted Bridget. He was in her face, shouting at her, with one of his pals by his side. They accused her of having blood on her hands for the way the situation was handled. Bridget was frightened and called in the police. She also reported him to the council's Standards Committee.' It took eight months before the *News of the World* published a retraction – albeit on page 40 – which admitted that their report of McAllister being questioned by police was fiction.

McConnell did lodge a formal complaint with the Standards Commission for Scotland which investigates alleged breaches of the councillors' code of conduct. The findings by chief investigating officer D. Stuart Allan paint a very different version to the one peddled to the *News of the World*. McConnell had accused McAllister of invading her personal space and shouting at her for one and a half minutes. CCTV footage of the incident proved that the encounter lasted seconds and that the pair were not even in the same room at the time. Of the four employees asked to give evidence to the councillors' watchdog, only one stated that McAllister had shouted.

Allan wrote:

It was a chance meeting, not having been premeditated by Councillor McAllister who had come into the council's office to meet with police officers in connection with threats which he had received. Although the CCI [Chirnsyde Community Initiative] had been closed, both Councillor McAllister and his companion had outstanding concerns that minibuses from the centre were still in the control of the CCI co-ordinator . . . Councillor McAllister said he has a naturally loud voice and this was supported by his companion who thought Councillor McAllister was not any louder than usual when he spoke to her that day. The CCTV images showed that, while addressing Mrs McConnell, Councillor McAllister remained entirely within the hallway and did not cross over the threshold into the Gatehouse office where she was located. There was nothing in the CCTV images to show Councillor McAllister and Mrs McConnell standing face to face or even in the same picture frame, and therefore nothing to show that he invaded her personal space. His companion stood further back at the open door across the hallway, and none of the images showed him standing beside or behind Councillor McAllister as he spoke to Mrs McConnell.

The evidence of witnesses was enough to confirm that Councillor McAllister's voice was raised and that he spoke loudly. Only one of the witnesses referred to it as shouting. It was certainly loud enough to upset Mrs McConnell. However, while understanding her reasons for feeling upset, I have noted that, on examination, the nature of the encounter was somewhat different than was recollected by her. There was no evidence that Councillor McAllister came within her personal space and there was differing evidence as to whether he was shouting, as opposed to speaking loudly. His address to her did not last the length of time that she and other witnesses described, and he was already walking away even as the duty manager came to investigate.

For many months, the campaigners had been attempting to attract the BBC Scotland investigation show *Frontline Scotland* to take an interest in the tangled tale of the Lyons and the Daniels and the murky nexus between criminals, police officers and the political class. The Applerow murder heightened the BBC's interest but relations with the campaigners became strained when, following an in-house risk assessment, one of the corporation's journalists told a campaigner that the crew could no longer visit his home. On a previous visit, the twitchy hack visibly jumped from the sofa when an automatic air freshener in the corner issued an unexpected blast of scent. There was frustration but no real surprise when the BBC eventually conceded it would not investigate.

22

Cocaine Councillor

Steven Purcell was a Labour councillor at the age of 22. By 32, he had become the modernising leader of Scotland's largest city council and was being hailed by Tony Blair as a visionary. That he would one day be anointed First Minister of Scotland was a matter of destiny. Blair turned to his young protégé after lunching with a group of businessmen who helped bankroll the party north of the Border and stated, 'Steven, they really are a horrible bunch.' – 'they' were the Glasgow businessmen who held the real power in the snakepit of the city's Labour Party. The oligarchs – a word derived from 'oligarchy' which comes from Greek and means 'rule by the few' – decided on the winners and losers. Purcell, with his hands on the city's £2-billion annual budget, was their man. In their eyes, he was a superstar. Camera-friendly, youthful and with a smooth delivery, he was miles better than the rest. At least, that was the smiling, clean-cut version of Purcell which had been fed to the voters.

The reality was somewhat different. Purcell was a troubled young man who had lived a lie about his homosexuality for years during which he deceived his wife, family, friends and colleagues. While in charge of the city's 30,000-strong workforce, he was secretly a frequent user of cocaine. A heavy drinker whose weekends started at Friday lunchtime, he kept some very questionable company. He and Katrina, his wife of five years, had been hailed as the next Jack and Bridget McConnell in a gushing political magazine profile. Few cared about his sexuality but what did matter was the duplicity.

The timing of Purcell's announcement that he was gay is interesting. He believed that he was about to be outed, not least because of this snippet by a political columnist which appeared in the *News of the World* six days earlier:

The things you hear at the Labour Party conference. At last week's gathering in Oban, what was the big topic of conversation? The war? The election? Andy Kerr's hair? No, it was this: Which Labour councillor is considering leaving his wife after deciding it was a bit naughty to wed her when he prefers male company? And they say politicians are dull . . .

But the timing of Purcell's revelation, three days after the triple shooting, adds weight to another theory – he was being blamed by factions within Labour for having meddled in the Chirnsyde affair. Purcell's enemies were furious that First Minister Jack McConnell's wife Bridget was getting the flak when, in fact, it was Purcell who had vetoed an attempt by her to evict Eddie Lyons Sr four months earlier. McConnell's supporters claimed that she presented a report to a private 'pre-meeting' of Labour councillors on 11 August 2006, ahead of the full, public meeting one month later. A copy of McConnell's unseen report was leaked to a newspaper on 11 December. McConnell stated that her department had 'now lost confidence in the management committee to operate Chirnsyde Community Initiative in the best interests of the local community'. It recommended that the council 'does not award any further grants to the management committee of the Chirnsyde Community Initiative, further that the current lease is revoked and the facility is closed, at least temporarily'. However, the secret and un-minuted meeting chaired by Purcell rejected McConnell's plea to close Chirnsyde. Instead, her report was watered down to recommend month-to-month funding rather than closure and the creation of Councillor Archie Graham's scrutiny committee.

One strange aspect of McConnell's claim worth noting is that her 'secret' report which recommended Chirnsyde's closure was almost word-for-word the same as yet another report which she had presented to the council more than a year previously, in June 2005. Entire tracts of her August 2006 report are identical to the earlier one yet, inexplicably, they came to polar conclusions. The June 2005 report ended with a call for councillors to give their 'continued support for the management committee of Chirnsyde Community Initiative'. However, the August 2006 report recommended closure. No one within the council has ever offered an explanation.

When Councillor Graham and his scrutiny committee finally finished their investigation, the report he presented to the council in May 2007 contained no surprises. He did exactly what had been expected of him. One strange excerpt stated, 'It is not the role of the scrutiny committee to determine "the truth" amongst the allegations.' Graham then rounded on the police for failing to co-operate with his committee while adding that they told the council no allegations of criminality were 'substantiated' – despite the inconveniently undeniable attempted murder, fire attack and vandalism, not to mention the myriad other areas of concern.

Graham also admitted that the council had never set eyes on the Disclosure Scotland background check on Eddie Sr. They had, instead, blindly trusted Lyons and his committee's claim that the check 'does not provide any evidence that would debar him from working within the centre'. Graham also backed McConnell's claim that she had attempted to shut Chirnsyde but had been blocked by a mysterious unidentified force, presumably Purcell. He added, 'The director [McConnell] came and provided a verbal report to us which suggested that, in light of Scott-Moncrieff report and other reports in the past talking about governance issues, perhaps the administration would want to close the facility for a temporary period. The administration took the view at that time that, rather than close immediately, we would ask this committee to carry out a full scrutiny review.'

Graham delivered his 20-page findings to a room filled with officials, councillors and journalists. When McAllister rose to his feet to respond, the Labour councillors started chatting to one another like naughty schoolchildren. They did not want to hear

McAllister's criticisms of Graham's 'whitewash' and nor were they interested in his tribute to the campaigners who had fought for so long. He said, 'These brave people risked their safety because they did not think it right for the council to send their children to Eddie Lyons Sr. They spent five years standing up to a dangerous crime family while also fighting against the council and police who ought to help ordinary people. The fact that Lyons was evicted and will not return vindicates everything these people have said. You have to ask, "Would any of these people who insisted Lyons was a fit person to run this centre have sent their own children there?"'

Weeks later, a new voting system and a diminishing support for Labour produced a political earthquake in Glasgow. Labour's 71 councillors were cut down to 45 while McAllister and his two SNP colleagues saw their ranks swell to 19. For the first time in a generation, the people of Glasgow had a proper opposition that would hold to account a Labour Party which had ruled unchecked for so long.

Purcell maintained his smiling, clean-cut pretence for two more years and then the wheels came off in spectacular style. In May 2009, he welcomed two visitors to his grand office within the City Chambers. They were Assistant Chief Constable Johnny Gwynne and Detective Chief Superintendent Allan Moffat of the Scottish Crime and Drug Enforcement Agency (SCDEA), often dubbed Scotland's FBI. They told him that he was the target of an underworld cocaine blackmail plot and that one dealer may have incriminating mobile phone footage of him. Weeks after the bombshell warning by the police, Purcell confided in close colleagues that he had used cocaine but no longer did. It made a mockery of a 2006 interview in which Purcell hypocritically said, 'We all have a part to play in teaching our children about the dangers of drugs – and it's our responsibility to provide alternatives to an often destructive and chaotic way of life plagued by both legal and illegal drugs.'

The blackmail warning and Purcell's dramatic confession remained secret for another nine months. He then lost the plot and, after a bout of erratic and boozy behaviour, suddenly resigned as council leader. During a tumultuous week, Purcell checked into an addiction clinic, went missing and was fought over by lawyers, media groupies and the wealthy men whose vested interests were at stake. The *Sunday Mail* finally revealed the reasons – the SCDEA warning and the cocaine confession. Two days later, he stood down as a councillor and fled the country, leaving an opened Pandora's box spewing out lurid claims of cronyism and corruption.

The fall of Purcell added weight to the campaigners' belief that he had been compromised by the Lyons or other gangsters in a city where the lines are often blurred between organised criminals, mainstream business people and politicians. The Chirnsyde campaigners knew of another Glasgow councillor, who also happened to be gay and who frequently bought cocaine from a dealer who worked from a flat in the city's Hamiltonhill area. The dealer was supplied by the Lyons. This same councillor was a friend and ally of Purcell and was routinely at the forefront of attacks against Billy McAllister, the Lyons' enemy number one. McAllister held the view that the other councillor was being blackmailed by the Lyons because of their knowledge of his coke habit.

In the months before the implosion of Labour's great hope, Councillor McAllister had attempted to put a motion to debate the links between organised crime and the council but Purcell had personally thwarted him by doing everything possible to block it from taking place. In sheer frustration, McAllister had even cornered Purcell in a corridor and asked him, 'Steven, are you on drugs?' It was meant to be a joke.

23

Next Generation – the Daniels

They were schoolboys with baby faces but they hunted in packs and were deadly. The latest Daniel recruits seemed capable of even more extreme violence – and at a younger age – than their predecessors.

William Brown was a 44-year-old drug addict who routinely bought tenner bags from the Daniels' network of teenage street dealers. When Brown heard a whisper that some of their heroin was stashed in a small triangle of parkland between Milton and Possil, he and his girlfriend Carol Lawrence went foraging in the undergrowth on 19 July 2006. The couple were spotted by 16-year-old Joseph Bennett and Stephen Dunn, 15. As they swigged from bottles of Buckfast, the pals realised what they were doing and made a phone call to their Daniel gang contacts, prompting backup to arrive. Brown and Lawrence ran but, in the night's darkness, the feral pack swarmed from all directions, ready to teach them a lesson. They took in turns to dart forwards and inflict blow after blow. Lawrence was pulled to the ground and punched on the head but she managed to break free and escape from the park. Brown desperately attempted to stay on his feet, fend them off and keep running. Exhausted, terrified and confused, he eventually fell on to a path. In their frenzy, the mob jumped and stamped on his face, head, torso and limbs. Brown was struck with a wooden pole and, once down, they rifled his pockets and stole his phone and a small amount of cash.

His lifeless body was found at 7.15 a.m. the next day. Maybe he was killed instantly when one of the Nike trainers slammed down on his head or perhaps life ebbed away at some point in the hours before dawn. When the pathologist conducted the post-mortem, he discovered skull fractures, brain damage and all but four ribs broken. The police described the attack as 'sustained and brutal' while the trial judge opted for 'vicious and brutal'. It seems they had run out of adjectives to express the horror of that summer's night adequately.

Detectives quickly rounded up five suspects. The sixth arrest was a 17-year-old son of Jamie Daniel called Zander Sutherland who was finally apprehended at Christmas time after five months on the run. The six charged with murder were Bennett, Dunn and Sutherland along with Jamie Byrne, Darren Taylor and Mick Brazier who, at 36, was by far the oldest. In previous eras, such a shocking crime and the subsequent trial would have been subject to in-depth reporting but, in an age where news is often supplanted by celebrity tittle-tattle, the Brown murder barely registered. With six men in the frame and a lack of media interest, the conditions were ripe for the fine legal minds at the Crown Office in Edinburgh to start cutting neat deals, behind closed doors, with the half-dozen, taxpayer-funded defence teams. What they agreed was that Bennett, Dunn, Byrne and Taylor would plead guilty to a reduced charge of culpable homicide in exchange for the murder charge against Brazier and Daniel's boy Sutherland being dropped. Heroin dealing charges against Sutherland and Taylor were also abandoned, as was a charge against Brazier, Bennett and Dunn of assaulting Brown's partner.

Bennett, having turned 17, was jailed for seven years and eight months, Dunn, then 16, got six years and nine months while Byrne, 21, and Taylor, 20, were each given eight years. The Crown Office was made aware that some of the four who held their hands up and agreed to the deal had only done so because they had been offered cash. It was yet again suspected that the system had allowed the footsoldiers to take the fall in exchange for the officers going free. Not that there was any outcry or enquiry into the stench of alleged result rigging. After all, the Daniels had been attempting to buy justice for half a century, when Jamie's brother Billy failed to bribe his pals into taking the rap for the murder of police officer George Gates in the late 1960s.

Another incident involving some of the same teenage rabble generated ten times more publicity than the Brown murder. On this occasion, their victim was not a human. It was a hamster. The police admitted that the hamster killing garnered much more help from the public than had been forthcoming over the slaughter of Brown.

Police had discovered a 90-second, shaky video clip – filmed on a phone – which showed cackling teenagers laughing and joking as they tipped the small pet from a box. As the furry creature tried to wriggle free, one of them excitedly joked that its eyes looked as if they were going to pop out. Young hands were then seen tightly clutching the hamster as it was taped to a large, rocket-style firework which was planted in the turf. A lighter was then steadied under the fuse which moments later fizzed into life. One of the gang shouted, 'See you later!' just as the rocket screamed into the night sky. The firework and the hamster were blown to bits. The sadistic act sent the feral youths into howls of uncontrollable laughter. Police knew who they all were but the grainy footage only allowed them to pinpoint two of the half-dozen perpetrators. One of them was 17-year-old Steven Gordon who was identified, with no trace of irony, due to his 'mouselike features and pointy ears'. The other was Taylor who, nine months later and in the same park, took part in Brown's murder. However, criminal proceedings against Taylor over the hamster incident were dropped and only the shaven-headed Gordon was convicted. Turning up in court in a hooded top and with a sneer on his face, he was ordered to do 220 hours of community service.

The final word went to the Scottish Society for the Prevention of Cruelty to Animals whose spokeswoman advocated the adoption of the US system of psychiatric assessment of those guilty of animal cruelty. With a degree of prophecy, she added, 'Significant research indicates that this level of violence to animals can often progress as teenagers get older.'

24

Next Generation – the Lyons

Having lost their Chirnsyde gang hut with the eviction of the paternalistic Eddie Lyons Sr, the young Club Boys were determined to silence their gloating rivals from Milton's 'back end'. The lives of the Club Boys and the Backend Boys were mirror images but the invisible dividing line roughly along the east–west-running Liddesdale Road through the scheme's grey streets was as important to them as a country's border on a map. In the territorial mindset that dictates much of Glasgow's youth gang violence, such differences are worth fighting – and even dying – for.

Across Glasgow, such divisions are common. Some motorway bridges spanning the M8 are a no-man's land where running battles are waged. Teenagers and children – wielding bats, blades and makeshift weapons – take part. The gang's crude, home-made websites and uploaded YouTube videos of drinking, fighting, threats and tributes to dead members, appear to emulate US street gang culture with a dark Glaswegian edge. Community police officers trawl the internet to get a handle on who's who while seeking out incriminating photos of knives on display and attempting to make sense of the myriad jumble of gang names and torrent of barely literate taunts and threats. To the outsider, it seems illogical but such territorial violence runs deep for many of the city's estimated 170 teenage gangs. Under any other circumstances, the Club Boys and Backend Boys would have probably been friends but the quirk of living either side of the Liddesdale Road 'border', ensured otherwise. Since Lyons had been installed at Chirnsyde, the Club Boys had adopted their name. Chirnsyde is almost directly south of Liddesdale Road so it was a powerful show of strength against the Backend Boys who had no such facility. There is no doubt that the abuse of the community centre in this way strongly enhanced the perception that it was not inclusive. The gang kids from the 'backend' would never have been able to set foot in the place, even if they had wanted to.

With Eddie Jr and Steven having graduated from street level, it was their 17-year-old brother Chris and his pals who roamed the streets at night. Weeks after Chirnsyde's closure, the teenage Club Boys hatched a plan to track down their rivals one by one. Their hunting spree lasted two hours and left five youths – mostly schoolboys – in hospital suffering from blade injuries inflicted with razor-sharp samurai swords and kitchen knives. This was not the usual recreational, weekend violence.

The violence began at 10 p.m. on 14 January 2007 when a 16-year-old Backend Boy was attacked outside St Ambrose Primary School. His mobile phone was stolen and his attackers used it to call his sickened and terrified parents to brag that their boy had just been knifed. The cackling thugs went on to issue a vile threat that any police co-operation would result in their daughters, aged nine and eleven, being raped as punishment.

The Club Boys, some on foot, other in cars, continued stalking slowly through the streets, picking off their enemies. By midnight, one 15-year-old, two 16-year-olds, a 19-year-old and a 26-year-old were in hospital. Four of the five were victims of the Club Boys. The fifth and final victim was 15-year-old George Docherty, a pal of Eddie Jr whose own dad Joe Docherty was among Eddie Sr's closest and long-standing friends. Docherty was part of the Club Boys mob who were in the process of subjecting one of the 16-year-olds, pinned down on Scaraway Street, to a blade attack. By complete chance, the victim's father turned into the street and saw the flash of steel plunging into his son. The dad instinctively grabbed the blade and turned on Docherty who, of all the victims that night, suffered the most severe injuries. The dad who inflicted the wounds felt some guilt but that eased whenever he thought of the likely outcome had he not appeared. Docherty's mother dismissed the bloodbath as being 'just wee lads messing about'. In a city where a police study found that a 13-year-old had been given a machete as a birthday present, perhaps her despicable view should not surprise.

Hovering around the vicinity after the bloodbath in Milton was Eddie Sr – still defiantly driving the Chirnsyde minibus owned by the council.

Even by Glasgow gang standards, five young men suffering knife injuries in two hours of butchery was unusual. But there was not a single prosecution. When the police attempted to obtain statements from the victims, they were flatly turned away. They had zero trust in a police force which, for so long, had been Eddie Sr's protector and promoter.

The Club Boys weren't finished. Two months later, the blades were out again. This time they did kill someone – a 17-year-old new father called Jamie McColl who was stabbed in the heart in the early hours on the morning of Saturday, 10 March 2007. By any measure, it was mindless. Being from Cadder, McColl had clashed with the Club Boys from neighbouring Milton. It was a typical postcode feud played out across the city but with the added edge of the history of the Lyons being driven out of Cadder in the 1980s. McColl's killer was a 17-year-old called James Murphy whose dad was another friend of Eddie Sr and, like Eddie, Murphy Sr was involved in the running of a community centre. Despite also being from Cadder, James Murphy had chosen to become a member of the Club Boys. Six months prior to the killing, he had smashed another youth – 17-year-old Ryan Stewart – on the head with a hammer. Stewart, scarred for life, was fortunate to survive. It was the hammer attack that led to the murder when McColl and his pals ran into Murphy in Cadder's Tresta Road.

As the pair exchanged punches, Murphy pulled out his hidden knife. In the flurry, he jabbed it into McColl's rib cage, causing him to yell, 'I've been stabbed!' The blade travelled just seven centimetres into his body – the length of a cigarette – but it pierced his heart and the paramedics could do nothing to save him.

McColl's 18-year-old fiancée Diane Campbell was at home with their three-month-old baby son Jay when she received a phone call from a friend who delivered the news. The child will grow up never knowing his dad. His dad's killer will most likely be a free man while still in his 20s.

Murphy was arrested within 10 days and was charged with murder but he admitted the reduced charge of culpable homicide. He was jailed for a minimum of nine and a half years by trial judge Lord Turnbull who railed against the 'the depth of the stupidity' of the turf war. He added, 'You have the whole of your adult life ahead of you. You have wasted that on account of the most petty differences between yourself and other youths. What is much worse is that this misplaced rivalry has taken the life of another young man, who, like you, had the future ahead of him. His family will have to spend the rest of their lives living with the consequences of what you did.'

25

Alien Abductions

Kevin Carroll was an unimposing physical presence. Slightly built and no more than 5 feet 10 inches tall, to his friends he was a happy-go-lucky joker with a smile on his face and often fuelled by Red Bull energy drink. Yet, by his mid 20s, the man known as Gerbil had become the most feared and loathed figure in Scotland's criminal underworld.

While many contemporaries aspired to nightclub VIP rooms to share cheap girls, overpriced champagne and fake friendships with Old Firm footballers, Carroll felt at ease prowling the grey housing schemes of Drumchapel, Possil and Milton. He was in a relationship with Jamie Daniel's daughter Kelly Green and, with the powerful backing of her family, he began generating serious sums of cash by peddling cocaine, heroin and other drugs. His network of dealers stretched 80 miles across the M8 motorway which divides the urban central belt, from Greenock in the west, through Glasgow, to Edinburgh in the east. Jamie Daniel had spotted the potential of his young apprentice at an early age. Daniel even respected that Carroll was bold and cocky enough to occasionally challenge his authority, something that few others ever did.

Carroll's drugs wealth brought him Audis, Prada clothing and designer watches to complement the WAG-style trophy blonde. He bought a new-build detached house in suburban Lennox-town. His conspicuous wealth drew misplaced admiration from teenagers whose lack of life choices presented gangsterism – or the fake glossy Hollywood version – as a glamorous way out. In a new era of proceeds of crime laws, he used a car-wash and mobile valeting business as means of laundering his dirty money and turning it into apparently legitimate income.

Drugs were lucrative but Carroll was not the first to realise that robbing other dealers – known as 'taxing' – also brought handsome rewards. Like playground bullies, the criminals with the muscle, weapons and higher propensity for violence target those lower down the food chain who don't have the means to protect themselves.

Carroll assembled a close-knit team who used extreme violence – or the threat of it – to strike terror into their victims and force them to surrender their drugs, guns or cash. Carroll took taxing and fine-tuned it. Before each mission, his team gathered at a farmhouse on a dark back road leading out of north Glasgow. They changed into skintight, scuba-style suits which hugged their ankles and wrists, covered their hands and sealed around their faces to prevent fingerprints or DNA traces in the form of hairs, sweat and skin from being left behind.

Because Carroll's tentacles spread into so many communities, he was never short of tip-offs about who to rob. Anyone was a potential target although usually it was drug dealers who had piles of cash that couldn't be banked. Not only did the thefts benefit Carroll financially, they also served to put rivals out of action – and, if they were associates of the Lyons family, so much the better.

The usual method was for the gang to approach the target's home and hammer at the door while shouting that they were armed police officers. The panicking householder would usually open the door only to be dragged outside and have a hood pulled over his head. He would then be forced into a waiting vehicle. Carroll even came up with his own 'invention'. He struck upon the idea of pushing a folding anchor – used for small boats and jet skis – through a letterbox with the rope attached to a vehicle's tow bar. As the vehicle shot forwards, the door would be ripped from its frame. Perhaps not a business pitch for *Dragons' Den*.

Carroll's gang carried guns and knives but power tools and blowtorches were also used because they could be just as effective and having them would not result in a jail sentence.

Sometimes, the money or drugs would be handed over quickly and with little resistance while other victims held out. Often they suffered acts of torture. One dealer in Drumchapel had a kettle of boiling water tipped over him. It took the threat of a second kettle to reveal the whereabouts of his hidden £5,000.

Carroll's main Edinburgh ally, Mark Richardson – a major force in the city's underworld – lined up victims in the capital. Richardson's gang sold five kilos of coke to a buyer for £60,000. Once the deal was done, Carroll's west-coast team turned up and 'taxed' the cocaine from the buyer without any violence being inflicted. A dealer in Glasgow's Balornock was taken away in his own VW Golf R32 and kept in a cupboard in a dingy safe house. After 48 hours of beatings and torture, he was threatened with infection from junkies' used syringes. He then decided to hand over his £30,000. A dealer who worked for his father, who was based in Spain, returned to Glasgow Airport after collecting £50,000 from the family business only to be robbed in Auchinairn.

Paul 'Kirky' Fleming, 25, was targeted at home in High Blantyre, Lanarkshire. When he opened his front door, he wished it really had been the police. Fleming had a hood placed over his head and was driven away as the thugs fired pot shots at an innocent neighbour who attempted to intervene. He was driven for 45 minutes and taken to a disused building where he was forced to sit with his face between his legs and with the gun's cold, steel barrel pressed into the back of his head. After suffering a barbaric ordeal, Fleming eventually gave them £60,000. He was later dumped in the street, wearing only his underwear. Many others were stripped near naked and abandoned in public places, often deeply traumatised, badly injured and utterly humiliated. No one ever said that drug dealing was easy. It earned Carroll's crew the nickname 'the alien abduction gang' because victims 'vanished' from their homes at night before they were found wandering the streets half naked the next morning. They also told the police they had no memory of what had happened to them. Given the business they were in, how could they?

Most of the victims were impotent when it came to any thoughts of revenge but others were well connected to other high-level gangs who did not take kindly to having their employees robbed by a bunch of mercenaries. Although there is no gangland code, many people in the underworld did not approve of Carroll's anarchic tactics. Carroll kept a list of potential targets and the thought of being on it caused sleepless nights for many a drug dealer or cash-rich businessman. One person Carroll took a keen interest in was the ex-boxer Barry Hughes who loved to flaunt his wealth by cruising through the city centre in his Rolls-Royce, Ferrari or Hummer. Carroll often joked – or hinted – that he would look good behind the wheel of one of the prized cars. In a terrifying twist of 'it could be you', another potential target for alien abduction was a £10-million lottery winner called John McGuinness. The plan was ditched when the gang realised the jackpot was gone and McGuinness was bankrupt.

The scale of the gang's violence, their disregard for public safety, the casual use of guns and torture, their impersonation of armed police and the wide geographical spread of incidents all caused the police increasing concern. Carroll had become public enemy number one. Jamie Daniel was proud.

One alien abduction gave police their biggest-ever breakthrough in their war against the Daniels. Five weeks after the Applerow massacre, Carroll learned that the Lyons were plotting to buy a gun which they planned to murder him with in a revenge attack. Carroll was told that the weapon was being held by Christopher Logan, a low-ranking but ambitious heroin dealer in his early 20s. Late in the evening of 10 January 2007, Logan was in his flat in Springburn when Carroll and two other masked men – armed with two handguns and a blowtorch – burst through the door. They bundled Logan into a VW Golf and took him on a long, dark drive into the countryside. The physical beating which Logan received was presumably easier to endure than the terror of being told that his face and genitals would be torched with the blue-orange flame and that a bullet would be fired into his head. He eventually gave up the golf bag containing a Heckler & Koch L86a2 LSW. He also surrendered £4,000 cash – which was the payment he had received from the Lyons for the gun. Traumatised Logan was dumped on the streets of Bishopbriggs in the early hours of the morning. He did not tell the police what had happened. Another one blamed on the aliens.

Used by the British Army, with a bipod for the battlefield, the magazine-fed automatic L86 LSW is prized for its accuracy and is capable of precision shots at up to 600 metres. It would be an understatement to say that such weapons were not commonly found in UK gangland. This one had been stolen by a corrupt band of soldiers of the Royal Regiment of Scotland's 5th Battalion, the Argyll and Sutherland Highlanders. They took it from their Howe Barracks in Canterbury, Kent, and sold it to Logan via middleman Andrew Quinn, an associate of Logan.

Carroll was delighted. Not only had he got a serious bit of kit for his collections but he had also got one over on the Lyons and neutralised a plot against him. As a bonus, he even had the cash the Lyons had handed to Logan. Carroll knew that the red-hot weapon should be stashed somewhere safe as soon as possible. He contacted one of the Applerow hit men, Raymond Anderson Sr, and made a handover.

Anderson Sr had an unusual domestic arrangement whereby he spent weekends at his Drumchapel home with his wife Rosemary and their children – including Raymond Jr – while during the week he lived with his girlfriend Margo Henderson and their daughter in Craigend, in the east of the city. Hours after the theft from Logan, Anderson Sr took the golf bag and its deadly contents from Carroll to the Craigend home of Margo's sister Georgette Bailey and her partner Gerard Elliot. However, Anderson Sr was unaware that he was already under police surveillance as a suspect in the Applerow shootings. The delighted detectives watched their target make his delivery on the morning of 11 January.

Anderson Sr's decision to handle the army gun was an act which ultimately brought him and James McDonald to justice.

Within hours of the drop, the police had secured a warrant and had searched every square inch of the home which was ripped apart. They recovered the stolen army weapon along with 9mm ammo similar to that used in the triple shooting at Applerow.

26

The Secret Policeman

He is a police officer who has never pounded the beat, worn a uniform or made an arrest. His identity is closely protected and his name does not appear on court witness lists. He went from basic training at the Scottish Police College in Tulliallan, Fife, straight into the ranks of the Scottish Crime and Drug Enforcement Agency. His job is to enter homes, cars and businesses of major criminals to plant bugs without leaving a trace. His highly specialised covert entry skills were learnt not at Tulliallan but during his career as a member of the British Army's elite special forces.

Within weeks of the Applerow Motors bloodbath, he had ghosted into the cars used by Raymond Anderson Sr and James McDonald and planted hidden listening devices. Days later, thanks to Anderson Sr leading police straight to the stolen British Army Heckler & Koch, other officers made a less subtle entrance into the home of Georgette Bailey, his girlfriend's sister. By raiding Bailey's home, the police effectively revealed to the killers that they were on their tail and, most likely, had them under surveillance. They had no choice because they could not risk losing track of such a dangerous weapon.

Carroll and the rest of the Daniel gang realised that they had a big problem. It was about to get bigger.

Bailey and her partner Gerard Elliott were arrested at gunpoint and taken in a high-speed police convoy to Maryhill police station for questioning. Elliott said nothing but Bailey burst under interrogation. She confessed that Anderson Sr – who she described as her 'uncle' – had delivered the golf bag and 9mm ammo to her home that morning. She also told the detectives that her home had been used as a safe house – by Anderson Sr and Carroll – to stash weapons for almost three years.

The gang were in a sweat. They had to get to Bailey. After five nights on remand at Cornton Vale, Scotland's only women's prison, Bailey received Anderson Sr in the communal visiting area while McDonald waited in the car. Anderson Sr whispered soothing reassurances to Bailey that they would look after her financially and that she should say nothing more to the police but the damage was already done. A deal was later struck which allowed her to go free in exchange for Elliott taking the rap, earning him a three-year jail sentence.

After leaving the prison visit and returning to McDonald in the car, the killers were oblivious that every word they spoke during the 60-mile round trip between Glasgow and the prison in Stirling was being recorded by the police. The recordings took place over three months and other suspects, including Carroll, were targeted with the same technology. As professional criminals fully conversant with police tactics and technology, they would have strongly suspected such methods were being deployed against them so they were very careful about what they said, no matter how familiar their surroundings.

They routinely spoke in their own indecipherable coded language in which the names of people, places and objects can change on a daily basis. To an outsider, it sounds like the ravings of mad men.

Tellingly, it was early in the investigation that some of the most incriminating snippets were captured. The police recorded many hours of conversations, much of it mundane chitchat with the occasional intimate moment. But buried within the transcripts were fleeting comments which became building blocks of evidence.

On the Cornton Vale journey, the trigger-happy pair revealed how dangerous they were by casually discussing, in their broad Glasgow accents, the possible need to open fire on any police officers who may be tempted to shoot them while attempting an arrest. The transcript reads:

McDonald: 'Aye they'll huv us doon as fuckin dangerous fuckers, know what Ah mean?'

Anderson Sr: 'Aye, they'll be thingmied in awe, Jamie, to shoot us.'

McDonald: 'Oh, Ah know they will.'

Anderson Sr: 'They make ah move, just shoot them.'

McDonald: 'Aye.'

Anderson Sr: 'Ah don't give ah fuck, Jamie.'

McDonald: 'Fuck them.'

The pair then incriminated themselves by discussing dumping cars and phones in order to beat the murder case that they knew the police were building against them.

Anderson Sr: 'Aye, fucking right up there, man. See wance we got oot in another motor, they're fucked.'

McDonald: 'Ah know.'

Anderson Sr: 'No matter what technology they've goat, fuckin leave wur phones an awe that behind. Aye, they're fucked'.

In a taped phone call, the strain began to show as McDonald voiced frustration at Anderson Sr, the senior partner in the relationship, for leading the police to Bailey's home. In the call to an associate, McDonald ranted, 'He got his girlfriend's sister to watch stuff, so he is fucked. It's down to me to try and sort stuff out, to try and get him out, which I will be able to do, know what I mean. I've not left any fingerprints or that, not on any of the weapons.'

In contrasting excerpts, McDonald talked hopefully about getting away with murder and pessimistically about the possible length of sentence if convicted. He said, 'No cunt gets away with them nowadays. You know that, don't you? Except us. That's because we are Kool and the Gang.'

In another exchange, he said, 'I am in deep, deep, deep, deep shit, know what I mean? I am looking at 15 years if I get caught.'

Both men knew the system almost as well as the legal professionals whose job is to keep thugs on the streets. They, and their Daniel paymasters, were willing to do absolutely anything to stay out of prison and were heard discussing how to get their hands on a witness list so that those on it could be nobbled with cash, threats or both.

The bugged evidence was crucial but, in isolation, it was of limited use to the Crown Office prosecutors. The police's biggest breakthrough came when they managed to 'turn' an associate of McDonald, a 43-year-old man called Billy Corkish, the Orkney-born son of a merchant seaman.

Witness protection may conjure up images of Mafia mobsters on TV but, in underworld Scotland, the same principles apply. In choosing to co-operate with the police, Corkish was forced to pay a huge price by accepting a new identity and having to live at a secret location with no contact with his family, friends or his former life. It was possible thanks to another specialist branch of the SCDEA, the Scottish Witness Protection Unit, which had been quietly formed that same year. It was long overdue. The unit's officers work to convince people like Corkish that their safety can be guaranteed, no matter how dangerous the people they testify against are. For far too long, justice had been undermined by gangsters who had got away with all manner of serious crimes by terrorising victims and witnesses who thought about pointing the finger. In the unit's first year, Corkish was one of 14 protected people but the numbers rose rapidly year-on-year with 72 witnesses given varying levels of support in 2010.

When Anderson Sr and McDonald learned that Corkish had become a 'grass', they were beyond furious. For McDonald, it was utter betrayal by a friend. Corkish told the detectives that he had helped to buy the Mazda used in the killing. He also admitted that he was with McDonald when he practised his shooting on waste ground in the city's Haghill area, near to a disused railway track. Corkish set the gun's sights for McDonald as he honed his shooting skills on bottles and cans placed on tree branches and a bridge. He was present when McDonald tested a handgun in a similar way. In addition, he conceded that he had agreed to McDonald's request to look after two 'old man' rubber masks similar to those used in the murder, if not the actual ones. Clearly, Corkish's evidence was damning even if his role in testing murder weapons, hiding masks and buying getaway cars raised questions about what exactly he knew of their plans.

With the bugged conversation and Corkish the supergrass, the Crown Office agreed that the police had enough to bring in the suspects. Given the taped comments about shooting the police, there was an added tension when the armed officers in body armour were briefed about who they were going to arrest. On 2 March 2007, one team burst through the door of Anderson Sr's Drumchapel home. Being in no mood to be shot, he followed the screamed orders to the letter. He and his son Anderson Jr were taken away. In a simultaneous raid, McDonald was apprehended at his home in the city's east end.

The three arrests were timely as the funeral of Michael Lyons was due to take place 15 days later. It has become increasingly common, in some murders, for the Crown Office to withhold the body as it is 'evidence'. Hugely painful for victims' families, it is seen as a requirement in the event of a defence lawyer demanding additional information that may be yielded from a corpse. The police had picked up intelligence which suggested that Carroll and the senior Daniels intended to defy convention by plotting to wreak violence on the mourners. It was a threat which they dared not ignore.

Carroll was next to be taken off the streets. On Tuesday, 13 March – four days before the Saturday funeral – armed officers raided Jamie Daniel's home in the upmarket west-end enclave of Jordanhill which is home to accountants, lawyers and ladies who lunch. Carroll was carted off in handcuffs and charged with using Bailey's home to store three machine guns, a bipod, a telescopic sight, flares and 5.56mm and 9mm rounds. If convicted, he would be thrown behind bars for many years. The case against Carroll was shaky and he was tempted to take a gamble by standing trial but his lawyer, the late Paul McBride QC advised him against it and managed to carve out a favourable deal with the Crown Office, away from public scrutiny. Prosecutors agreed to drop the three most serious charges relating to the machine guns. In exchange, Carroll held his hands up to possessing the ammunition which included the same 5.56mm rounds used by a Kalashnikov AK-47 which was used to gun down John Madden in Milton in 2004. The cherry on top for the jubilant Carroll was the jail sentence of 18 months handed down by Lord Menzies.

With Carroll and much of his gang behind bars, the funeral went ahead. The body of Michael Lyons was taken from undertakers in Springburn to Lambhill Cemetery where hundreds turned out to pay their respects. Eddie Lyons Sr chose to self-police the event by driving around and challenging anyone he thought might be a member of the press. At least he was no longer using the Chirnsyde vans, having been forced to hand them back.

As it turned out, the funeral was marred by trouble perpetrated by the Lyons themselves. Police were forced to shut down the remembrance celebrations of Michael's short life at a bar in Bishopbriggs when a fight broke out. The cause of the violence, which involved Steven Lyons who was still recovering from his shooting injuries, stemmed from an inappropriate joke about how Michael's death would mean that his seven-a-side football team was now a player short.

One month later, Corkish was spirited away from his home by the witness protection team, never to return. Strathclyde Police knew that the Daniel mob would do anything they could to 'silence' him. The case was solid but was utterly dependent on Corkish – who suffered from ill health and was scared out of his wits – going into the High Court in Glasgow, swearing an oath on the Bible and telling the 15 ladies and gentlemen of the jury everything he had shared with the police.

27

Judge Dread

Presiding over the trial of Raymond Anderson Sr and James McDonald for the murder of Michael Lyons was Scotland's toughest judge – Lord Hardie. The son of a textile mill worker, Andrew Hardie was state educated at St Modan's High in Stirling where contemporaries included uncompromising Scotland and Leeds United footballer Billy Bremner. A chance meeting with an Irish solicitor while studying modern languages in Vienna inspired him to follow a law career. His worst memory was his prosecution of 15 teenagers for the 1982 'Clarkston murder' of 18-year-old dental student Robert Howie who was slain by a blade-wielding gang. He got thirteen of them jailed, three for murder. On the way up, he was not afraid to clash with those in authority and in 1996, while dean of the Faculty of Advocates, accused Tory Scottish Secretary Michael Forsyth of judicial meddling which could lead to 'something akin to dictatorship'. As a QC, he has defended serious criminals. He rose to become the country's top legal figure, the Lord Advocate, a role he controversially quit 12 weeks before the Lockerbie bombing trial. Lord Hardie was the epitome of a no-nonsense judge, feared by criminals for dishing out very long prison sentences. Over the previous five years, 84 of his sentences were reduced on appeal which was more than any other judge, ten times the average and over twice as many as second placed Lord Dawson with 30.

It was bad news for Billy Corkish whose medical conditions included ischaemic heart disease, diabetes, angina, fainting, anxiety and depression. When he took to the witness stand inside Court Three at the High Court in Glasgow in March 2008, his body was rattling with a cocktail of prescription drugs which rendered him liable to anxiety, depression, confusion, low blood pressure, muscle pain and cramps. Corkish had been reassured by the Crown Office and his police handlers that he would be allowed to give his evidence either from behind a protective screen or by CCTV. When the star witness emerged into the packed and imposing, bombproof courtroom, there was no such protection and he squirmed under the intense scrutiny. There was nowhere to hide as the steely glares of Anderson Sr and his former friend McDonald fixed upon him.

The pressure, fuelled by the medication, proved too much for Corkish who dramatically deserted from the script. He perjured himself by failing to point the finger at Anderson Sr, prevaricated and spun a tissue of lies to the delight of the men in the dock but to the fury of Lord Hardie, the prosecutors and the police. Lord Hardie issued numerous warnings to the flaky witness who was sent back to his safe house for the weekend. Despite suffering angina attacks during the break, when Corkish returned to court on Monday morning – after a word in his ear from the witness protection team – his memory and resolve had returned. But a legal problem with the jury forced Lord Hardie to abandon the proceedings and order a restart.

During the second trial, Corkish was allowed to give evidence from behind a screen and this time he managed to keep it straight. Over two days, he delivered a clear account involving the masks, the guns and the Mazda getaway car to the prosecutor, Advocate Depute David Young. He then withstood robust cross-examination over the next five days by the highly experienced defence QCs – Edgar Prais for Anderson Sr and Donald Findlay for McDonald – to whom he admitted lying during the aborted first trial. Lord Hardie was not impressed and later took it upon himself to jail Corkish for one year for contempt of court. Corkish was only released thanks to the intervention of the Crown Office who had decided not to prosecute him and the police who were appalled that a judge would imprison a man who had risked everything in the name of justice.

Lord Hardie was not finished dealing with dodgy witnesses. When Paisley gangster Robert Pickett was lying in hospital after having been shot, his life in the balance, he broke with the supposed underworld code of silence to provide a detailed and signed statement to the police. Having survived and with no choice but to take the stand, he attempted to sabotage the trial. As he described the gunmen, Pickett began to smile, which prompted Lord Hardie to ask him why he was grinning. Pickett smirked and said, 'I find it a bit amusing that you have the wrong people in the dock. It's the wrong people.' Pickett went on to change his story from what he said in his police statement.

During an exchange with Findlay, he admitted that he was not a man who was easily scared and that he had previously faced firearms charges. His evidence was worthless. There are three main theories as to why Pickett would want to see the men who almost killed him to go free – he didn't want to be labelled a 'grass', he wanted them back on the streets so that he could inflict revenge, or he had been bribed. It may well have been all of the above.

When Lord Hardie later got round to jailing him for the maximum two years allowed for contempt, he urged parliament to increase the sentence available. He also suggested that Pickett only gave police the statement in hospital because he thought he was dying, and added, 'After your release from hospital, you clearly regarded giving such a statement to police as that offended your criminal code of non-co-operation.'

Another witness was Steven Lyons who gave a straightforward account of events which added nothing evidential to the case because he could not ID the masked men. He simply replied, 'Yes.' when Findlay put it to him that, 'In no [sic] view were these people coming into the garage to shoot up cars, to steal them or to carry out a robbery. They seemed to be fairly keen to shoot you. It is like a scene out of a gangster movie.' In another exchange, Findlay likened the incident to 'a scene from *The Godfather*'.

A specialist prosecution witness called Kenneth Coaker, who can pin down mobile phone calls through cell site analysis, gave detailed evidence which showed a series of incriminating calls between Anderson Sr, Anderson Jr and McDonald around the time of the murder as well as on the actual day of the murder.

Anderson Sr claimed he was on his way to sell a Honda at the time of the murder, a fake story cooked up to explain why his phone calls had been tracked around the scene. McDonald said he was tiling his kitchen when the murder took place.

During the trial, McDonald's phone was referred to as 'orange', Anderson Sr's as 'green' and Anderson Jr's as 'blue'. Suddenly, on the same day and just after the murder took place, all three of them stopped using the phones. It was a surprising and foolish mistake, especially given that they had already made the effort to acquire unregistered pay-as-you-go phones in advance, which they appear not to have used.

Much of the other testimony was pretty thin. A 15-year-old schoolgirl was in her mum's car when she saw Anderson and McDonald running from Applerow and fleeing in the Mazda. She failed to pick either men out of an ID parade but told police that McDonald could have been one of them because of wrinkles round his mouth and his big nose. The defence dismissed her evidence because virtually all the other evidence pointed towards the gunmen being masked when they fled.

The most bizarre moment of the trial involved the 'piper letter' which had been received in the post by Applerow owner David Lyons on 16 December 2006 – ten days after his nephew's murder.

The letter, typed in block capitals, stated:

DAVY LYONS

HERE'S YOUR CHANCE TO PUT A STOP TO THIS FEUD. THE BOYS OWE ME £25,000 AND I WANT WHAT'S OWED TO ME. IT'S FOR DRUGS THEY'LL KNOW WHAT IT'S ABOUT AS THEY'VE GOT TO PAY THE PIPER. THE MONEY DOESN'T MATTER TO ME BUT IT MATTERS TO THE PIPER. IT'S GOT TO BE PAID! I DON'T WANT THE POLICE OR THE

BOYS NOT EVEN YOUR WIFE KNOWING ABOUT THIS. IF YOU KEEP
THEM OUT OF THIS THEN ALL YOUR LIVES CAN GO BACK TO
NORMAL, AS WE'RE ALL LOSING MONEY THROUGH THIS IF YOU'VE
ANY TRICKS FOR MY PICK UP MAN THEN ALL DEALS ARE OFF. IF
YOU'RE A FAMILY MAN AND YOU VALUE YOUR WORD THEN YOU"LL
[*sic*] DO WHAT IS ASKED. AND REMEMBER TO KEEP YOUR MOUTH
SHUT. SO NO CAMERAS, NO SURVEILLANCE AS THE PICK UP MAN
DOESN'T KNOW NOTHING [*sic*] SO HE'S NO USE TO YOU. DROP OFF
4 PM SATURDAY. I'LL DRAW YOU MAP AND X WILL MARK THE DROP
SPOT.

THE PIPER

PS THE BALL IS IN YOUR COURT!

Lyons handed the letter to police but he dismissed it as a joke
– a view which made sense when no follow-up instructions were
received as to how to pay the supposed drug debt. One theory
some people with knowledge of the case had was that the letter
was dreamt up by the Daniel camp in an attempt to hamper the
early police investigation by sowing disinformation to throw
them off the trail. Others believed that 'the piper' was Jamie
Daniel and the £25,000 related to the Daniel cocaine which had
been stolen from a house in Milton five years earlier, sparking
the bloody gang war between the two families. That theory – or
at least the existence of someone nicknamed 'The Piper' –
gained credibility due to part of the bugged conversation between Anderson Sr and McDonald as they made their way back
from the visit to see Georgette Baillie at Cornton Vale prison on
16 January 2007. McDonald said to Anderson Sr, 'Oh well he's
got to pay the piper boy an' the piper's not a happy man.' If the
letter was a smokescreen and they were somehow in on it and
wanted to add to the confusion by deliberately discussing it in
the knowledge they were being bugged, they would obviously
not incriminate themselves during the same conversation. Conspiracy theorists may see some significance in the unusual
middle name 'Pyper' of Jamie Daniel's maternal grandmother
Agnes Grant but the letter remains an enigma.

The defence QCs argued that the letter was irrelevant but

Lord Hardie allowed it to be put before the jury – a view with which appeal judges Lady Paton, Lord Kingarth and Lord Philip later agreed. They stated:

> First, there is the obvious link in that someone called 'the Piper' is mentioned both in the letter and in the conversation, as is the concept of paying the Piper. It is in our view unrealistic to suggest that no weight could be placed on that link between the letter and the conversation.
>
> Secondly, the letter was received by one of the victims of the shooting only ten days after that shooting. It was open to the jury to infer that the contents of the letter related to the shooting: for example, it is suggested that if money is paid 'lives can go back to normal': at least one inference which might be drawn from that message is that if the money were to be paid, there would be no more trouble. It was further open to the jury to reject David Lyons' evidence that he could not explain the letter, that there was no question of drugs or money owed, and that the letter was a hoax.
>
> Thirdly, it was not in our view a prerequisite of the admissibility of the letter that the Crown should establish that there was indeed a particular person known as 'the Piper', or that there were in fact disputes about drugs and debts involving the Lyons family. The timing and content of the letter alone were sufficient to make it relevant. In our view therefore the trial judge was well entitled to admit the Piper letter in evidence.

Anderson Sr decided to give evidence in an attempt to try and counter the damage which had been done from the bugged conversations. He admitted that he, along with McDonald, had delivered a shoebox containing two smoke grenades, ammunition and a firing pin to a friend's address in Glasgow but had no idea what the contents were.

When asked to explain his comment that no 'cunt gets away with them nowadays. You know that, don't you – except us. That's because we are Kool and the Gang', he denied it was murder being discussed. He said, 'I was talking about steroids. I meant nobody knew that we were on steroids. Only one person knew that and that was the person who was giving us the injections.'

The taped conversation about shooting the police was dismissed as 'just bravado talk' while he branded McDonald as a 'fantasist'. Finally, he rejected his ability to run away from the Mazda by stating, 'I'm 46. I have bronchitis, scars on my lungs and smoke 45 a day.'

It would have taken a fairly gullible juror to swallow his explanations. After hearing seven weeks of evidence, they chose not to. It took them two days to reach a unanimous guilty decision on the possession of the army guns and ammo but they were split on the murder and two attempted murder charges, returning a majority guilty verdict.

The court – which had been built to stage terrorist trials – was suddenly swamped by police officers as Lord Hardie ordered the killers to be handcuffed. The judge had been tipped off that Anderson Sr had been furious towards the end of proceedings and had been mouthing off about meting out violence against various people including McDonald's lawyer, Findlay, who he believed had not performed well enough. In particular, his reference to Mafia movie *The Godfather* was seen as less than helpful.

Despite Lord Hardie's record of imposing long sentences, no one expected what came next. There was near universal shock when he jailed both men for a minimum of 35 years each, later reduced to 30 on appeal. It was a Scottish record and raised questions about sentencing consistency, especially when compared with the 27 years given to Lockerbie bomber Abdelbaset al-Megrahi for the murder of 270 innocent people in the 1988 terrorist outrage.

Hardie then turned the words of the pair's own lawyers against them as he delivered a damning criticism of their crimes and what was meant to be a clear message to the Lyons and the Daniels – this ends now. He told them:

Mr Findlay in his closing remarks said that the jury would be entitled to think that this was a premeditated murder involving the use of firearms and that nothing in life got more serious than this apart from terrorist activity. Mr Prais described your action as a cold-blooded and ultimately fatal attack. I respectively agree with these views.

I would only add that it is a matter of extreme concern for society at large that organised criminals should have access to firearms. It is even more concerning that they are prepared to use them. Such activity cannot and will not be tolerated in our civilised society. Decent law-abiding citizens are entitled to expect the court to remove you from society to afford them and their families the necessary protection from criminals such as you. That will not occur unless the public co-operates with the authorities in removing guns and gangsters from our streets. Failure to do so may result in death or injury to innocent people and those who stand by silently must bear some responsibility for such results. The court will do what it can to protect the public from you and your fellow criminals engaged in organised crime but the co-operation of the public is essential.

But Hardie also had something to say about how one of Scotland's wealthiest and most deadly organised crime gangs had been able to bring carnage on to civilian streets using British Army weapons. He added:

What is particularly concerning is that the weapons used to kill Michael Lyons came from the military. And it especially concerning because it comes at a time when our country's armed forces are conducting operations in Afghanistan and Iraq.

28

Gangster Regiment

When Andrew Quinn left school in Glasgow in 1996 at the age of 15 and signed up as a soldier with the British Army's Argyll and Sutherland Highlanders regiment, little did he realise how eventful his life would become – although not in the way the action-packed recruitment adverts promised.

Five years later, having been kicked out in disgrace for failing a drugs test, his career was in ruins. Back on the streets of his home city, the train driver's son was drawn into the heroin trade which bankrolled a comfortable lifestyle and taste for sporty Subaru Impreza cars. Living in Dennistoun in the east end, he became an associate of James McInally, a thug with connections to the McGovern crime family. Heroin soon become a sideline to the more profitable enterprise of arming the underworld. His customers included numerous criminal factions, not least the Daniel mob. His suppliers were three old friends in the Argylls – Colour Sergeant Garry Graham, Sergeant Kieran Campbell and Lance Corporal Martyn Fitz-simmons.

Graham had been a Sergeant Major with the Royal Highland Fusiliers and a qualified explosives instructor whose 22-year career included service in various danger zones. But he was kicked out of the RHF after being fined £80 for drunkenly abusing a police officer in Cyprus during a night out. He resurfaced in the Argylls the following year where he became second in command of its elite reconnaissance platoon.

Campbell was Quinn's best pal and drinking buddy and, by marrying his younger sister Lisa Quinn, the brothers-in-arms became brothers-in-law. Quinn was a doting uncle to the couple's three sons.

Fitzsimmons – a childhood army cadet friend of Quinn – had been lucky not to be jailed and kicked out of the ranks when he smashed a pint glass into another man's face during a night out in Edinburgh. His victim was left with two broken teeth and a face scarred for life. Fitzsimmons, then aged 20, was spared prison in order to save his army career and, despite going on to serve alongside the SAS in covert operations, it was an opportunity which he ultimately spurned.

Quinn was only 25 but he could get his hands on a steady supply of all manner of serious hardware – firearms, ammunition and explosives – from his crooked pals. As he and his girlfriend prepared for that night's Hogmanay celebrations to bring in 2007, the police were getting ready to spoil the party. Officers who smashed into the flat were pleased to recover two kilos of heroin worth £130,000. Quinn, hiding in a darkened cupboard, was clutching a shoebox containing £6,000 of cash. Littering the property was drug-dealing paraphernalia of scales, scissors and knotted 'tenner bags' of smack.

The police were utterly stunned at the real prize – enough ammunition to wipe out 2,273 people. In a black suitcase, they found 554 rounds of 5.56mm ammo, 977 rounds of 9mm, 742 shotgun cartridges, 10 smoke grenades, three parachute flares and a distraction grenade. Forensics also picked up traces of military plastic explosives in Quinn's flat and car. Scotland's biggest illegal gun dealer had been snared.

Given Quinn's army background and the discovery of Fitzsimmons' army ID card in his flat, it did not take long for the amazed detectives to deduce where much of the deadly haul had come from even though the serial numbers had been scratched off many of the objects.

Top-secret memos were fed up the line to those who work in the shadows of the Ministry of Defence, the Royal Military Police's Specialist Investigation Branch and domestic intelligence agency MI5. The seep of military firepower on to civilian streets and UK gangland was hardly new but Quinn's operation was on an industrial scale compared to squaddies who smuggled a trophy weapon from a foreign battlefield.

Strathclyde Police joined forces with their counterparts in Kent, where the Argylls were based at Howe Barracks in Canterbury. After six weeks of intense surveillance, they raided the barracks just as the Argylls were on the brink of deployment to Afghanistan. Fitzsimmons was asleep in his dorm while a simultaneous raid awoke Graham at his home in Kilmarnock, Ayrshire.

Kent police officer PC Martin Farrier used bolt croppers to burst open the padlock securing Graham's locker which was inside his barracks office. The police found seven sticks of British Army PE4 plastic explosives. In layman's terms, these greasy, putty coloured blocks were powerful enough to 'bring down a small skyscraper'. Also stashed in the locker were 60 firing wires and 96 detonators. A search of the platoon store-room uncovered a bag with five smoke grenades, plus more detonators and fuses in a metal container. Inside a wardrobe in Fitzsimmons' room were a smoke grenade, three training gre-nades and a belt storing bullets.

Graham was taken 500 miles south to Folkestone police station where he and Fitzsimmons underwent a series of gruel-ling interviews. Fitzsimmons claimed that he had found a 7.62mm round on Salisbury Plain during a training exercise but did not report it or return it by placing it in an 'amnesty box'. He added that he was superstitious and had planned to carve his name on it so he 'didn't get shot' in Afghanistan.

Graham, a married father-of-two who was three years away from receiving his army pension, admitted being in debt to the tune of £80,000. He claimed that he had found a metal box in his office just before Christmas but did not force it open until February when he found the 'sweating' plastic explosives inside. He told the detectives, 'I knew straight away that all these things together shouldn't be together because obviously they could create a big explosion, so I separated them.' He then spun the claim that he did not report the discovery because he thought he was being set up and – fearful of being branded a 'grass' –

wanted to confront his colleagues first to get to the bottom of it.

But their pleas of innocence looked to be in vain as Campbell decided to break ranks and co-operate fully with police. In doing so, he gave detailed statements which laid bare the extent of their trade between the Argyll and Sutherland Highlanders, the 5th Battalion the Royal Regiment of Scotland and the Glasgow underworld. His information provided a crucial missing piece of the jigsaw in relation to the Heckler & Koch which had been found 12 months earlier at the home of Raymond Anderson Sr's girlfriend's sister. Now the police knew exactly how such serious firepower had found its way to a Glasgow council house and how Applerow hit men Anderson Sr and McDonald had got their hands on military weapons and ammunition.

As police rounded up Quinn and the three Argylls, they also swooped in Dennistoun on a civilian associate called Christopher Logan who was found with £63,000 worth of drugs, mostly cocaine. Logan was the man who Kevin Carroll had abducted and threatened with guns and blowtorches in order to steal the Heckler & Koch which the Lyons had already paid for and intended to kill him with. It was the same gun which Anderson Sr had then taken to his girlfriend's sister's home. For the police, this drew a clear connection between the corrupt soldiers and the Daniel gang.

Following a weekend in custody, Graham and Campbell were taken to court in Kent while Fitzsimmons and Logan appeared in front of a sheriff in Glasgow. All four were remanded in custody. Less than 48 hours later, armed police officers raided two addresses in Drumchapel where they arrested Carroll and Anderson Jr. They were both charged with abducting Logan at gunpoint and forcing him to hand over the golf bag which contained the stolen British Army Heckler & Koch.

Logan was taken to Baird Street police station where Carroll and Anderson Jr were placed in ID parades. Given that Logan had not reported his 'alien abduction' at the time, the police feared that it was unlikely that he would – or could – finger his alleged kidnappers. In a combination of live and video line-ups, not once did he point at the two suspects. The police were bitterly frustrated as Carroll and Anderson Jr smugly skipped back onto the streets.

The prosecution of Quinn, Logan and the three soldiers was more simple – thanks mainly to the testimony of 27-year-old Campbell who pled guilty. Quinn, faced with his brother-in-law's devastating evidence, decided to do the same. They both admitted conspiracy to possess explosives and conspiracy to dishonestly undertake or assist in the retention, removal, disposal or realisation of stolen goods but denied the charge of conspiracy to steal explosives. As a result of his co-operation, Campbell received a four-year jail sentence. When 26-year-old Quinn was later sentenced to six-and-a-half years in jail at Maidstone Crown Court, Mr Justice Akenhead told him, 'Your involvement was a pivotal one. It involved procuring them from contacts in the Army, the paying of soldiers and selling them on. You knew that the people to whom you supplied would use them only for criminal purposes to spread death and violence.'

Graham, who arguably had the most to lose, and Fitzsimmons decided to tough it out and steadfastly refused offers of a deal. By standing trial, there was a chance they would be found not guilty but the odds were stacked against them. During their trial at the same Maidstone court, Campbell testified against the men who had once trusted him with their lives and vice versa.

He told the court that he once drove his in-laws – Quinn's unwitting parents Andrew Sr and Elizabeth – from Kent to their home in Glasgow with explosives in the boot of his car. He claimed that 28-year-old Fitzsimmons asked him to take the dangerous cargo 'up the road' in November 2007. Campbell and Fitzsimmons had the key to Graham's locker where the explosives were stored. Once he had dropped his wife's parents off, he delivered the sandbag containing the plastic explosives to Quinn who gave him £500 for himself and £2,500 which he handed over to Fitzsimmons back at barracks.

He said, 'It was £500 – it was coming up to Christmas, I thought I could make a bit of money to offset the bill.'

Following three weeks of evidence, the jury delivered bad

news for 37-year-old Graham and Fitzsimmons. It was a gamble which they lost with painful consequences. They were both found guilty of conspiracy to possess explosives and conspiracy to dishonestly undertake or assist in the retention, removal, disposal or realisation of stolen goods. As he sentenced them each to 12 years in prison, Mr Justice Akenhead echoed the revulsion felt by the members of the armed services who had risked their lives for their country and would never dream of handing weapons to gangsters. He said:

> You have dishonoured your battalion, your regiment, the Army and your country. If the explosives are used by those who wish to harm the people of this country, you will have betrayed them as well.
>
> The conspiracy is wider than the men in the dock, although they conspired to procure ammunition and explosives for sale to Glasgow gangs. You transported at least two caches of explosives and ammunition to Glasgow and probably more.'

Addressing Graham, he added:

> I do not belittle your service to this country. You have put your life on the line but you have betrayed the Army and you have betrayed your country. You must have known or been aware that these would be sold to criminal gangs in Glasgow and would have been used for criminal purposes and that these weapons could have fallen into the hands of groups committed to harming people in this country.
>
> These offences are extremely serious and among the most serious serving soldiers can commit. Fundamentally they stem from dishonesty and the motive was money – it was a very dangerous dishonesty.

At the High Court in Glasgow, Quinn admitted the £129,000 heroin charge and breathed a sigh of relief when judge Lord Brailsford ordered his four-year sentence to run concurrently with the six and a half years he was already serving.

The final member of the gang to be jailed was 21-year-old Logan who got four years for handling the stolen Heckler & Koch and an additional six years for the £63,000 of drugs. He was not as fortunate as Quinn as his sentences were to be served consecutively. In total, the jail sentences handed out on both sides of the border were a few months short of 50 years.

Remarkably, Logan was the seventh person to be charged in connection with the same Heckler & Koch, the others being Georgette Baillie, Gerard Elliott, Raymond Anderson Sr, James McDonald, Raymond Anderson Jr and Kevin Carroll. Of the seven, Baillie, Carroll and Anderson Jr were not convicted.

During the trial of Graham and Fitzsimmons, it emerged that Campbell and his family had been placed on a witness protection programme.

When approached, Andrew Quinn's father Andrew Sr revealed the damage which had been caused to his family with both his son and son-in-law in prison. He said, 'I'm not in touch with any of them. I can't get a message to them. I don't know anything. I took a stroke because of what happened at the time. Andrew has never even been to the Kent barracks. I wanted nothing to do with it then and nothing to do with it now.'

A worrying aspect of the case was that the police have yet to recover a single stick of the PE4 plastic explosives taken from Howe. Furthermore, the 9mm ammo found in Quinn's flat, did not come from the rogue band of Argylls, which pointed towards the possibility of other serving soldiers supplying criminals, a theory supported by Mr Justice Akenhead, who added, 'There can be no doubt that this conspiracy went wider than the four men in court – it's unlikely that the 9mm ammunition came from 5 Scots [the Argyll and Southern Highlanders, the 5th Battalion, The Royal Regiment of Scotland] – they must have come from wider criminal elements in the Army.'

A career criminal who lives in Milton is known in the underworld to have impeccable contacts in the Army, including a recently retired officer of senior rank. He is capable of acquiring virtually any type of weapon, ammunition or spare part . . . provided the price is right. So valued is he by the Daniels that, when his house was repossessed due to mortgage arrears, they bought it back for him.

At the end of the court proceedings, Mr Justice Akenhead issued the following plea to top brass: 'The Army needs to urgently conduct an inquiry into how this happened.'

However, it does not appear to be something which the men in suits at the Ministry of Defence in Whitehall are keen to discuss in public. A freedom of information request was made, seeking a list of all items stolen by the jailed soldiers which had not been recovered. Back came the answer that they did not know what was missing because the police 'investigation had been unable to determine exactly what material had been stolen'.

Another question – whether the judge's request for an enquiry had been granted and, if so, its findings – was also asked. No such enquiry took place but officials identified three documents relating to the issues of weapons storage. It took 12 months before the ministry released two of them. The main one was a 30-page audit about the control of arms and ammunition. Sections of the document were redacted but it identifies seven areas marked 'action required'. It begins with the acceptance that 'there are significant risks to the department should arms and ammunition continue to be lost and serious risk to reputation should they be used in the commitment of a crime'. It found that, in the main, the correct procedures were in place but agreed there was 'little awareness as to how such losses had the potential to impact on the UK's illegal weapons environment'.

One of the seven issues which required action involved 'non service weapons', many of which were 'acquired over a significant number of years as trophies and spoils of war'. The report found the recording and method of storage of these weapons varied between bases. An interesting revelation was that many civilian staff and ex-service personnel stored their privately held weapons in military armouries with one unidentified establishment holding 200 such firearms.

Another observation was that heads of establishments 'should be made fully aware of the guns and gangs environment and briefed to ensure that staff were treated sufficiently robustly as appropriate'.

It took an appeal to the UK Information Commissioner to rule on whether the ministry should release the second document based upon 'Protective Security Advisory Visits' to various barracks. The ministry told the Information Commissioner that to release it in full would reveal:

> . . . the weaknesses and vulnerabilities of 5 Scots [the Argyll and Southern Highlanders, the 5th Battalion, The Royal Regiment of Scotland], Howe Barracks' security and its arms and ammunition controls and accounting. This would allow individuals with wrongful intentions to potentially get hold of arms and ammunitions, therefore jeopardising national security.
>
> The reports also clearly outline the procedures in securing and holding ammunition and demonstrates the Army's capability and effectiveness in its weapon and ammunition management.
>
> The release of the redacted information in the report into the public domain would clearly demonstrate errors in accounting, control and storage of the arms and ammunition of the establishments reviewed allowing it to potentially fall into the wrong hands i.e. terrorists.

They added that it describes 'in detail the security vulnerabilities and identifies weaknesses in the unit inspected. This would give terrorists or criminals information that could be used to gain access to the Brigade HQs and weapons storage, potentially placing national security at risk.'

Quite what they found is likely to remain a secret. The Information Commissioner agreed with the men from the ministry that it was in the 'public interest' to withhold the report, as the risk to national security outweighed the public right to know. All but a handful of words contained on the five pages were blacked out by a censor's pen.

29

Land Grab

Now that Eddie Lyons and the Club Boys had been kicked out of Chirnsyde, Councillor Billy McAllister had questions to ask about Glasgow City Council's relationship with another member of the family, Eddie's younger brother David.

A major drug dealer called Alex Donnelly owned 730 Balmore Road, which comprised an industrial unit and a small piece of land beside the Forth and Clyde Canal in Lambhill. But the career criminal decided to make a grab of adjacent land owned by the council – which doubled the size of his plot. Council officials began legal action to evict Donnelly. For the council, it was a simple legal issue and their lawyers duly informed Donnelly that they would go through the civil courts in order to remove him from their public property. Donnelly realised it was a fight which would only generate fees for lawyers and one which he had no chance of winning. When David Lyons came along with an offer of £50,000 to buy the land in 2002, Donnelly took the money and ran. David launched his MOT station and garage, Applerow Motors, but still nothing marked the boundary between what was his and what belonged to the council.

In March 2004, McAllister wrote to Jillian Black, an 'enforcement officer' in the council's regeneration department, to request an explanation. McAllister asked whether the Lyons-owned plot extended beyond its perimeter and added, 'The perimeter fence may well now extend far past the actual perimeter of the site as sold to the current owner David Lyons, effectively encroaching on land that does not rightfully belong to him.' But, unlike when Donnelly had squatted on the council land, it seemed that the council had no inclination to raise the issue with the new owner so the case lay inexplicably dormant. The council did not even take an interest when their land and Lyons' became the scene of the triple shooting which resulted in the death of Michael Lyons. Eight months after the Applerow massacre, McAllister again asked why the council was allowing a business to squat on its land, rent-free.

David, much like his brother Eddie, tried to portray himself as hard working and honest. With his overalls and oily hands, he wanted the world to know that he had nothing to do with his family's criminality. But the police had begun to take an interest in his garage and the illegal sale of used cars. As a result of their visit, officers charged Edward McCandless, who was a friend of David and was once jailed for five years for guns, robbery and car theft. Interestingly, many of his lesser convictions took place in Paisley in the 1990s. The police sent a report about McCandless to prosecutors for allegedly selling vehicles without the required licence. Over the following seven weeks, he was reported twice more for the same reason.

McCandless realised that the police were not going to back down so his son Marc then applied for the licence which was required to sell second-hand vehicles. Marc was given an appointment to meet with Strathclyde Police licensing officers to discuss his application. It seems that he had either not been properly briefed on what to say, was too honest for his own good or was not very bright. He told the police that he had held a previous licence on behalf of his dad who believed he would have been rejected due to his long list of previous convictions.

Marc admitted that he was unaware of the motor industry's code of practice and could not answer basic questions about his supposed enterprise, even its turnover. He went on to reveal a curious arrangement whereby the business was leased to his father 'for free' by their close associate David Lyons. When Marc's licence application was put before the council, the police's dossier exposed him as a patsy for his gangster dad and the connection between them and Lyons. The police document, citing undisclosed intelligence, went on to state that 'David Lyons is involved in serious and organised crime including the trafficking and supply of class-A drugs'. Unsurprisingly, the council rejected Marc's application.

A simple and inexpensive check with the Land Register of Scotland provided McAllister with a very clear picture which showed that around half of the site was actually owned by the council. Given that it had been over three years since he had raised it with the enforcement officer, it was time to try again.

Council chief executive George Black admitted that the land was owned by the local authority and that no deal existed which allowed any third party to use it. He added that 'steps are being taken to ensure no unauthorised use takes place in the future' and that he was 'investigating the circumstances behind this situation'. Within weeks – four years too late – a metal fence was installed between the council land and Lyons' garage. The council feebly claimed they had 'forgotten' to take action earlier due to a 'breakdown in internal communications'.

Having seen his elder brother Eddie's Chirnsyde empire destroyed, David Lyons was not going to go down without a fight. The gloves were off and it was to become very dirty. He ordered his lawyer to turn on the *Sunday Mail* which had reported what was going on. The lawyer claimed that the used car business was 'next door' to Lyons' yard despite there being one entrance, one perimeter fence and no visible division between them. The same letter also traduced McAllister by falsely stating that he had been 'cautioned and charged' by police four months earlier during election day at the St Joan of Arc school next door.

Another politician who had taken an interest in the Chirnsyde campaign was the SNP MSP Bob Doris who secured a debate on the subject at Holyrood. It was the first time that the 'four bampots' had been named in public and they were entitled to feel proud. It was an unlikely coincidence that one of them had his car torched twice in the days either side of the Holyrood debate. This followed a first attack the previous year. On a later occasion, a petrol bomb struck his front door which became engulfed in flames while his family slept. No one was hurt and no arrests were made for any of these four craven attacks although Club Boys, including Paul Lyons, a son of David, were prime suspects.

The chamber was packed as Doris said:

Billy McAllister won the by-election on a ticket to clean up Milton. Following December's triple shooting, he received death threats for his attempts to do so.

Locals have put their lives on the line and their families in danger by taking a stand. Many are still living with the legacy of standing up against organised crime in their area. Indeed, on Saturday night, one local campaigner's car window was broken and his car was set on fire.

The courageous and tireless work that community campaigners such as John McLean, Alex O'Kane and Charlie Traynor have carried out to draw attention to the possible inappropriate use of the Chirnsyde initiative must not go unnoticed; nor must the support of newspapers such as the *Sunday Mail*, which championed their campaign despite attempts to discredit them. I have evidence that the Glasgow City Council media affairs team described the campaigners as 'bampots' to the press.

Criminals use fear to keep communities across Scotland under siege and on their knees. We should all be truly thankful that there are people such as John McLean, Alex O'Kane and Charlie Traynor around.

He added:

Locals knew that Edward Lyons Sr and other members of his family had been charged with the [attempted] murder of Thomas McDonnell in the vicinity of Chirnsyde and that the verdict was left at not proven amid fears of witness intimidation.

The fact that the centre has received more than £1 million of taxpayers' money in the past 10 years has only added insult to injury. The council pulled the centre's funding only after a tragic triple shooting last December at a garage on Balmore Road

owned by David Lyons, the brother of Edward Lyons Sr, where
Michael Lyons, nephew of Edward Lyons Sr, was shot dead and
Steven Lyons, the son of Edward Lyons Sr, and one other were
seriously injured.

The recently deposed First Minister Jack McConnell's face
showed no emotion as he heard Doris criticise his wife's role.
Doris stated:

> The police, the council – and Bridget McConnell, the council's
> director of culture and leisure – acted too late to prevent such
> an escalation in gang violence, of which the local community
> activists had repeatedly warned. Being proven correct does not
> give those activists pleasure, but their belief that they were
> brushed off by officials makes them angry.

During the 38-minute debate, six MSPs spoke, the only
Labour member being Patricia Ferguson who, four years earlier,
had sent the 'Dear Eddie' letter and three years before that
attended Eddie's Club with PC John Cameron. Her muted
contribution included the claim that allegations of criminality
at Chirnsyde were 'never substantiated'.

The council had planned to re-open Chirnsyde – renamed as
Ashgill Recreation Centre – in summer 2007 but the Lyons were
having none of it. If they couldn't have it no one could and it
suffered a spate of serious break-ins, thefts, fire attacks and
vandalism. On one occasion, the vandals betrayed their motive
by daubing internal walls with graffiti branding McAllister a
'grass'.

The campaigners allowed themselves a wry smile at the
admission from Councillor Archie Graham that these acts
now constituted evidence of criminality at Chirnsyde. He told
a local paper:

> The initial attacks in August took place just before the centre was
> due to be reopened and they were not carried out by your typical
> youthful vandals.

Criminals used heavy-duty implements to break through steel structures over the windows to gain entrance into an empty building.

I would question the timing of these attacks as we are trying to reopen the centre. This latest incident is very worrying.

The Lyons' apparent scorched earth policy ultimately proved unsuccessful when the new community centre was finally opened in 2008 – and, this time, it would be one that was for the entire community.

But the campaigners and the police were still concerned about public safety at Applerow and the fear that unwitting motorists might get caught in the crossfire of another shooting. During the parliamentary debate, Doris had stated, 'Organised crime needs a base in which to flourish. Chirnsyde might have been such a base, run at taxpayers' expense, but there is a fear that another base might remain.'

David Lyons decided to go on the offensive and was given a platform, on the front page of the *News of the World*, to whine about the perceived injustice he felt that he was suffering. The interview, under the self-pitying headline 'My hell living with the name Lyons', was a re-heat of what he had told the murder trial with the only addition being an attack on the police and McAllister.

Stating that he and his wife had 'had enough', David moaned, 'I'm taking legal advice. I want McAllister removed from office. I offered to explain my position but he refused. I want a meeting with police to explain what they said. I offered to show them any paperwork they want. I have nothing to hide. I've never been involved in crime or drugs as has been suggested. It's causing me and my wife distress.'

The police did not appear to take heed of this tortured plea as four weeks later and two days before Christmas, a team of officers staged a 5 a.m. raid on his Cumbernauld home, his son Paul's home in Bonnybridge, Stirlingshire, and five other addresses. In a separate raid on the same day, Lyons' ally McCandless also received a visit to his house in Bishopbriggs.

McCandless had been furious when his illegal used car business had been shut down by police and he blamed McAllister.

For months after the closure of the McCandless-run used car business, McAllister had been the victim of a cowardly smear campaign in which politicians and journalists had been bombarded with dozens of emails by someone hiding behind the fake name of John McColumn. The rants were badly written, rambling and spiteful. They contained claims that were not merely false but so wild and ridiculous that they portrayed the writer as some kind of foaming-at-the-mouth nutcase. According to keyboard crusader 'McColumn', McAllister was an 'evil little man', a 'drug councillor' with IRA and gang tattoos, a wife-beater who hung around with drug dealers, broke into property and had 'more criminal convictions than some of the crime family's [sic] he talks about in his sleep'.

One of the first recipients of the McColumn emails was the very same close council associate of the shamed Steven Purcell, who shared his fondness for white powder. This councillor, who was already suspected of being compromised by criminals due to his cocaine-buying trips up a close in Hamiltonhill, was quick to eagerly spread the word about the emails' contents and whisper the poison into the ears of anyone who would listen. Sensible people saw them for what they were while McAllister's many enemies wished them to be true.

When police raided McCandless's home, they took away his computer equipment and the emails stopped. Police reported McCandless to prosecutors but they took the decision not to put him in the dock. McAllister was not in the least bit surprised. Later, David Lyons would appear on TV and in newspapers to contend that he was not a criminal and to complain about his perceived ill-treatment. He then took his moans in the media to Scotland's highest civil court, the Court of Session, when he launched a £200,000 defamation action against Strathclyde Police's Chief Constable Stephen House. His expensive legal team argued that the police intelligence was little more than rumour and, as such, proof of nothing. The police argued that the intelligence was shared in good faith. The judge, Lady Smith, agreed. David lost his case and was left with substantial legal fees.

30

Motorway Killer

Paul Lyons was a thug, waster and snivelling wannabe who, as a peripheral Club Boy, aspired to be like his cousins Steven and Eddie Jr as they carved out reputations as gangsters.

The 27-year-old had swallowed powerful prescription tranquillisers washed down with strong lager and wine when he got behind the wheel of his van after a night out at a club in Manchester. With the alcohol and Valium cocktail coursing through his system, he continued to drink as he put his foot down on the near-empty M74, hitting speeds of 100 mph on 4 June 2000.

As Lyons headed to Bonnybridge, Stirlingshire, where he lived with his pregnant partner and two children, his passenger pals James Tulloch and Shaun McGuigan seemed untroubled that the driver was out of his mind on drink and drugs.

Mark Fleeman, nicknamed Flee, was a popular and hardworking 32-year-old with a doting wife, two daughters aged six and eleven and a loving extended family. He and his 17-year-old workmate Lee Allsup had decided to leave their homes in Uttoxeter, Staffordshire, in the early hours in order to beat the rush-hour traffic on their journey to a shop-fitting job in Fife. At 4.30 a.m., on a dark and quiet stretch of motorway, Mark became aware of Lyons' van rapidly approaching from behind. As Lyons raced past, Mark made a gesture towards the lunatic behind the wheel about his dangerous driving.

With the substances in his body undoubtedly fuelling his gangster fantasy, Lyons decided to teach him a lesson. He veered off the motorway and on to the hard shoulder then, like a Roman chariot racer, drew level with the white Ford Transit being driven by Mark. Both vehicles were travelling fast.

Lyons excitedly shrieked at his two friends, 'I'm going to sideswipe him!' before violently spinning the steering wheel to the left and causing his dark-coloured Transit to hit the other vehicle. Mark's van began to fishtail wildly from side to as he tried to call 999 on his mobile. The emergency operator heard only the unmistakable sounds of smashing glass and screeching steel followed by deadly silence. Mark could do nothing to stop his van as it veered across the northbound carriageway, violently struck the central reservation and then spun on its side into the southbound lanes. As the van overturned several times, Mark, who did not have a seatbelt on, was thrown free from the sliding side door. He died of chest injuries while being cradled in the arms of a passing motorist who had witnessed the horror near Larkhall, Lanarkshire.

Lyons, who was banned from driving at the time, saw the carnage in his rear view mirror and sobered up quickly. He got off the motorway and took a detour to Gartcosh train station where he abandoned the van and summoned an associate to come and collect him and his friends. He used his family's underworld contacts to dispose of the incriminating van. It was never found by police. Having warned his passengers to keep their mouths shut, he then joined summer holidaymakers on a plane to the Spanish sunshine. Unlike the tourists, he had no plans to return in a fortnight.

Within 24 hours of the crash, detectives went public to reveal that Mark's death had been 'more than a tragic accident'. Another terrified motorist had been so concerned at the erratic driving of the other van that he told police he thought he was going to be car-jacked.

Very quickly, on the streets of north Glasgow, the name of Paul Lyons was being whispered as the culprit. He drove a dark-coloured van, he had since seemingly disappeared off the face of the earth and it was the kind of mindless act of stupidity of which he was more than capable.

Two days after the tragedy, police arrested James Tulloch

over an unrelated matter and, when he spotted newspapers, asked the officers if there was anything in them about a crash. It didn't take much encouragement for him to tell them what had happened on the terror journey.

The *Sunday Mail* planned to reveal that Lyons was a suspect but agreed to a police request not to because it could have hindered their investigation. Although it was suspected that Lyons was in Spain, the detectives had been tipped off that he planned to meet his parents David and Yvonne secretly to celebrate his 28th birthday. Surveillance officers took up position around the family's caravan at Solway Holiday Village near Silloth in Cumbria but, if there was a party, the birthday boy didn't turn up.

Both of Lyons' passengers were placed under intense pressure to do the right thing and co-operate with police. It was a decision that was made easier when the Daniel mob got word to them that it would be in their interests to do so. Neither of the options were appealing – either grass on your pal and be targeted by the Lyons or keep quiet and have to answer to the Daniels. They chose to give evidence, with at least one being placed on witness protection as a result.

Lyons was lucky that he did not have another death on his conscience as the passenger Lee, who may have been asleep when the crash happened, made a slow but positive recovery. The college student underwent emergency surgery to save his shattered left leg while his right leg was also broken and dislocated. After many weeks in a Lanarkshire hospital, he was eventually transferred south where his recovery continued with therapy for a brain injury and – like Mark's utterly devastated widow Sandra – occasional, dark thoughts about suicide.

The breakthrough in the investigation came when the police learned that an associate of Lyons was going to take one of the fugitive's toddler sons to see him in Spain. Scottish police contacted their Spanish colleagues who were armed and ready for the anticipated rendezvous at Alicante airport. After 111 days on the run, Lyons was arrested as he turned up to see his son and friend. He was returned to Scotland and, faced with the testimony of his passengers, admitted culpable homicide and attempting to cheat justice by fleeing to Spain.

At the High Court in Glasgow, the man who aspired to be a gangster was exposed as no more than a pathetic and cowardly killer. Luckily for him, the trial judge was Lord Woolman rather than Lord Hardie. As Lord Woolman jailed him for 12 years and banned him from driving for life, he said, 'It was cruel fortune that placed these men on the same stretch of road as you that night. The lives of two men and their families – all total strangers to you – have been shattered. This has had an enormous impact.'

Lyons, whose previous convictions included violence, drugs and dangerous and careless driving, gave a feeble thumbs-up to the other Lyons as he was led away to the prison van.

Meanwhile, it seemed that the deterrent effect of Lord Hardie's record 35-year sentences for Applerow killers Raymond Anderson Sr and James McDonald had worn off. It was the Club Boys who decided to shatter the relative peace with the first shooting since the Applerow murder of December 2006.

This time, Kevin Carroll's associate John Bonner was gunned down in Springburn, Glasgow. The intended target had been Ross Sherlock, who had previously also been shot along with Carroll in 2006. Bonner, however, was considered fair game by the Lyons and he suffered serious injuries from the close-range shotgun blast while sitting behind the wheel of a VW Golf gifted to him by Carroll. This significant attack on 17 March 2009 was eclipsed by the M74 murder which took place weeks later.

The shooting scoreboard now read Daniel 7 (Johnny Lyons, John Madden, Eddie Lyons Jr, Andrew Gallacher, Steven Lyons, Robert Pickett and the dead Michael Lyons Jr) – Lyons 4 (Kevin Carroll (twice), Ross Sherlock, John Bonner). It also sent out a very strong signal to police and the underworld that the burning hatred remained undimmed by any threat of a lifetime spent behind bars.

It was clear that neither the Lyons nor Daniel were ready to walk away. The big question was, who would be next? The answer was to come 10 months later.

31

Asda Assassination

Kevin Carroll had survived being shot by the Club Boys twice but, on 13 January 2010 – seven years plus one day since the first hit outside his mother's house – his luck ran out.

At 1.23 p.m. and 17 seconds, a VW Golf screamed into the bustling Asda car park in Robroyston and slammed to a halt across the front of a black three-door Audi A3 in which Carroll was sitting in the back seat, trapped. Two men sprang from the VW and, in a pincer movement, stood either side of the Audi's rear side windows and raised their weapons using two-handed grips. In the following terror-filled moments, Carroll got only the briefest glimpse into the eyes of the masked men who had come to kill him. In a desperate final act, he grabbed the Audi owners' manual and held it up as a shield.

The hit men fired simultaneously. One of them emptied all five rounds from a silver-coloured revolver, with each of them hitting their target. Two entered Carroll's abdomen, one went into his groin and a fourth lodged in his back. The fifth smashed through his fingers.

The other gunman, using a pistol, unleashed eight rounds. One shot removed part of Carroll's skull and left his brain exposed. Others struck his chest, arm and hand, with one later found buried in the thick manual which had been held up so futilely. He even ejected two unspent bullets as the weapon briefly jammed, only to keeping on popping out shots.

The crashing sound of gunfire forced shoppers, some still gripping trolleys laden with groceries, to retreat into the refuge of the supermarket while others lay protectively on top of their children across the back seats of their cars. Some feared they were witnessing an indiscriminate killing spree or an act of terrorism. None could have grasped the extraordinary nature of what was happening in this most ordinary and familiar everyday scene.

At 1.23 p.m. and 42 seconds, the assassins were back inside the VW and moving away erratically and at high speed from the retail park in Robroyston, in north-east Glasgow. From start to finish, it had taken them just 25 seconds to end the reign of 29-year-old Carroll, the nemesis of the Club Boys. A life, during which many acts of extreme violence had been inflicted, had come to an end in the most brutal, terrifying and shocking way imaginable.

Carroll's reputation for 'alien abductions' and the taxing and terrorising of rival dealers was the catalyst of his demise. A dealer, 24-year-old Steven Glen, was low down Glasgow's drugs hierarchy but, by his own admission, he cleared £250,000 per year peddling cocaine. He claimed that he worked for and was supplied by Allan Johnston, nicknamed 'Babesy', who was a son of Paul Johnston, a wealthy former Strathclyde Police officer turned security firm boss with links to Glasgow's gangland.

On the night of 12 January, Glen's heart sank as his phone lit up – Carroll was demanding a meeting and intended to make him an offer he couldn't refuse. He also had something to say about Glen's 'boss', Johnston, whom he dismissively described as a 'bitch' and whom he threatened to 'pump' in a text message.

Glen tried to deflect Carroll by saying that he could not meet that night due to his commitments to a 'disabled aunt'. However, the aunt did not exist – it was just that Glen would never have agreed to meet Carroll in darkness. Glen convened a summit, which comprised a number of associates, at Johnston's flat. Perhaps some of the assembled dealers' product was chopped out into thin white lines and snorted to help fuel the excited discussions which took place until dawn the following morning, 13 January.

Carroll had run out of patience and, when Glen next looked at his phone, he saw he had two missed calls and another text which stated, 'You wee prick. You have no manners. If you don't phone me today I'll come to your door and I'll be using my feet to get in.'

Glen, feeling sick with dread and desperate to avoid being hunted down, duly contacted Carroll to agree to meet. Having suggested 12.30 p.m. that day at Asda as the time and place, Glen drove a Peugeot 406 to the supermarket car park and waited pensively. Convinced that he might end up being abducted by Carroll, Glen arranged for a friend, Jason McConnell, to arrive separately by taxi and to sit among shoppers in the glass-fronted Asda café, which overlooked the meeting spot.

Gerbil, running late, was picked up from his home in Lennoxtown by two friends – John Bonner, who had been shot by the Club Boys 10 months earlier, and Stephen McLaggan. The trio arrived at Asda at 1.20 p.m. and got out of the Audi to talk business with Glen while standing in the car park. When Glen told Carroll that he worked for Johnston, it prompted the reply, 'You're working for me now.' Carroll announced that all 'independent' dealers should work for him and offered Glen a wage of £10,000 per month, less than half what he already earned without Carroll's patronage. Carroll parted with the threat, 'Anyone who doesn't toe the line will be getting a bang.' They were famous last words.

With the two-minute, one-sided conversation over, Carroll and his two lieutenants strode back towards the Audi. Crucially, Carroll climbed into the back seat through a folded front seat. The two killers were poised, ready and watching from the stolen VW, parked in an adjacent car park. A third man was behind the wheel. The hit men pulled black balaclavas over their faces and held their guns firmly while their hearts thundered in their chests. The driver gunned the VW's accelerator and shot towards the Audi and neatly boxed it in. The hit men clinically completed their task.

The final score read Daniel 7 (Johnny Lyons, John Madden, Eddie Lyons Jr, Andrew Gallacher, Steven Lyons, Robert Pickett and the dead Michael Lyons) – Lyons 5 (Kevin Carroll – three times (once fatal), Ross Sherlock and John Bonner).

Carroll had been the first and last shooting victim in this diabolical drugs war.

As the paranoid survivor of two shootings who was routinely under police surveillance, Carroll was not someone who could be trailed easily. But the killers had not followed Carroll to the venue. The three-man hit team was in place thanks entirely to the terror instilled in Glen by Carroll the night before. The police and Carroll's Daniel associates are convinced that Glen himself had not passed on the information with any malevolent intent. They also believe he didn't even know that the shooting plot even existed. However, they are in little doubt that someone who attended the overnight summit of 12 January realised that such precise details of Carroll's whereabouts were of great value to his many enemies, in particular the Club Boys. Just days earlier, Carroll had got close to Eddie Lyons Jr yet again with another attempted shooting.

Bonner and McLaggan saw the masked men leap out of the VW and, within two seconds, they had both scrambled away from the Audi and run for their lives. Carroll did not have a door to get out of – not that it mattered anyway given the proximity and single-minded intent of the hit men.

As the horror unfolded, Glen watched and phoned Johnston to tell him that the man who had called him a 'bitch' was dead.

McLaggan – a friend of Carroll for 10 years – had run to a bedding shop called Dreams to seek refuge. When he edged back to the Audi, he was confronted with a nightmare. He did not need to be a medic to know that nothing could be done for the bullet-riddled figure, eyes and mouth wide open, slumped across the back seat.

McLaggan instinctively phoned Francis Green, whose father is Jamie Daniel and whose sister Kelly was Carroll's partner. Green, nicknamed 'Fraggle', had spoken to Carroll by phone just one hour earlier when they had agreed to hook up later that day. He got to Asda in his red Audi A3 even before the first police officers arrived. A police helicopter, which arrived at 1.42 p.m., captured the moment at 1.43 p.m., when armed officers spread around the Audi. The eye in the sky also filmed Green twice leaning into the back of the car where his friend lay dead. He grabbed Carroll's mobile in a bid to prevent it from landing in police hands. He, Bonner and McLaggan pulled their hoods up as the press photographers arrived. The armed police told them to sit inside Green's Audi which was within the taped-off crime scene. Inside his car, Green decided to have an unusual snack – the SIM card from his mobile phone which he judged was better inside his stomach than it was in the hands of the murder squad. Whether or not he also consumed Carroll's SIM card is unclear.

Other motorists had been forced to swerve as the VW recklessly screamed through roundabouts on to the eastbound lanes of the M80 motorway. The dark blue car had been stolen four months earlier in Rutherglen, on the south-east edge of Glasgow, and was a so-called 'doubler' as it bore the same registration of a nearly identical vehicle. Its burn out shell – with the copied plates carefully removed to decrease or delay the chance of it being identified – was found days later around 10 miles east of Robroyston in a rural road which skirts the village of Glenmavis, Lanarkshire. The forensic scientists' investigations yielded nothing from it.

The many shoppers who were caught up in the terror were told to remain in the supermarket where they recounted minutely detailed accounts to police officers. It wasn't until 7 p.m. that some of them, exhausted with emotion, were finally allowed to return to their families, with memories of a shopping trip that would last a lifetime.

The news swept rapidly through the underworld where the majority of the inhabitants were either pleased or relived – or both. Journalists in newsrooms across Scotland – who were largely clueless about the victim and the Daniel *v* Lyons feud – had to learn quickly. It was at the same supermarket that grinning Eddie Lyons Sr had directed his Club Boys to pack shoppers' bags to raise money for Chirnsyde. In a sign of the times, Asda tweeted, 'We're sorry to say there's been a fatal shooting incident outside our store in Robroyston, Glasgow, this afternoon. We don't know the full details yet, but the police are in charge and are dealing with the situation and we're helping with their investigation.'

To say that the Lyons were ecstatic at the death of Carroll would be an understatement. Some family members celebrated in an overt manner as champagne corks popped in one Cumbernauld pub while, in a corner of Milton, fireworks were reputedly set off. Inside his cell in Addiewell Prison, road-rage killer Paul Lyons was heard whooping and cheering as the news filtered through.

The two guns used to kill Carroll were a Sturm Ruger SP101, a compact, silver-coloured revolver marketed in the US for personal defence and a Croatian-made HS Produkt HS 95 pistol which fired 9mm rounds. The .357 rounds fired by the Storm were dumdums which expand on impact in order to maximise internal damage.

Thirteen days after the murder, the guns were found dumped in undergrowth behind a library in the Lanarkshire town of Coatbridge and less than a mile away from the construction firm HQ of Eddie Lyons Jr.

North Lanarkshire Council gardener Patrick McAuley was with five colleagues when he spotted a Marks & Spencer plastic bag concealed beneath some bricks. He picked it up and the guns fell out. To the despair of detectives, the weapons were passed around each of the six workmen, causing untold contamination. At one point, bullets fell out of one and they were picked up, again potentially wiping out or distorting whatever DNA may have been on them.

The police eventually took control of the weapons but, astonishingly, failed to take one of the two plastic bags in which they had been wrapped. It remained in a tractor being driven by Alex Wilson, one of the council gardeners, until he realised its potential importance and handed it in at a police station. It was an early indication of what was to come as the police investigation became tainted by farcical incompetence and poisoned by toxic police corruption, all of which would benefit the killers.

Meanwhile, Jamie Daniel was not in the least interested in the police's enquiries and ordered his own manhunt. Daniel was enraged at the slaying of Carroll who was effectively his son-in-law. Despite occasional clashes between these violent and unpredictable men, they had been close. On the night after Carroll's murder, a meeting was held at a house in a street in Maryhill, Glasgow, to which Daniel summoned senior members of his extensive criminal organisation. Cloaked by the dark winter night, the cul-de-sac quickly filled with prestige cars such as BMWs, Range Rovers and Mercedes before the entrance was blocked to prevent any unwanted attention from police or press. Daniel let it be known that money would be no object in his determination to avenge Carroll's death. He ordered that no stone should be left unturned. It was imperative that they should not to be seen as impotent. To do nothing might be construed as a fatal sign of weakness within the underworld. However, it was not that simple. The Lyons had spent years dodging Carroll and were most certainly not going to sit around waiting for Daniel's thugs to dispense his version of summary justice.

32

Godfathers Convicted

As a friend of policeman and politicians, self-styled community leader Eddie Lyons Sr was cocksure enough to believe that he would never be a common, convicted criminal. Other people got their hands dirty for him.

Jamie Daniel, last convicted of something more than a quarter of a century ago, was similarly confident because he too had minions to do his bidding. Even when he committed a crime, few witnesses would be willing to testify against him.

Lyons and Daniel, both aged 52, were in for a nasty shock and would learn a lesson to take nothing for granted.

During the fight to end the perverse, taxpayer-funded reign of Lyons, the campaigners sent information to the police and other official bodies on 28 February 2005, which raised serious questions about how a man earning a modest wage could fund such a lifestyle. Their letter revealed that Lyons and his children had embarked on a £500,000 property-buying spree in less than two years. To make it easier for the police, the campaigners helpfully included Land Registry documents showing owner-ship details and the prices paid. The dossier included a detailed breakdown of the family's fleet of cars – BMW, Mercedes, Audi and VW. It seems that the carefully constructed dossier was filed in the police HQ's bin. Nothing was done with the entirely accurate information. However, that was when Lyons was being protected by the police, council and Labour Party.

The headline-grabbing war between the two families had led to intense police scrutiny and, five years after the letter had been ignored, someone in the force decided to have a proper look at

Lyons. No longer their man in Milton, his protection was over, his licence expired. The force's forensic accountants trawled his financial records – wages, tax records, mortgages and loans. It may sound complex but it was simple – and the numbers just didn't add up. The information they uncovered mirrored what they had been told in 2005. Detectives arrested Lyons, his wife Josephine and John McMenemy, the 24-year-old partner of their daughter Ashley. The trio appeared at Glasgow Sheriff Court charged with fraud. In addition, Lyons faced a proceeds of crime rap. The parallel system of secret justice took over and in private talks between the Crown Office lawyers and his legal team, Lyons agreed to plead guilty to two fraud charges and a proceeds of crime charge. It is a common tactic of prosecutors to put a wife in the dock, knowing that the husband will often take the rap to get the spouse off. Not that all are as apparently chivalrous as Lyons. Deal struck, all charges against Josephine were duly abandoned. McMenemy too was in the clear.

The first fraud was committed when Lyons bought a house in Kelvin Crescent, East Kilbride – the same address from which police seized £63,000 of drugs money. He lied to the mortgage firm by stating that he earned £48,000 a year when his Chirnsyde wage was actually £20,000. That lie was enough for him to get the keys for the £140,000 house in July 2003. The proceeds of crime charge was that he made £74,000 profit from that first fraud when he sold the East Kilbride house two years later. Daughter Ashley was given £30,000 of those proceeds to open a tanning salon in Albert Street, Dundee. The second fraud was when he lied to another lender to obtain a £140,000 mortgage on his £220,000 home in Ashlar Avenue, Cumbernauld. He falsely claimed to be in receipt of a £45,000 annual salary.

Lyons was absolutely petrified at the prospect of being slung in prison where he would have been a very soft target. He spun a story to Sheriff Robert Anthony who was to sentence him. Either through delusion or desperation, Lyons ordered his taxpayer-funded lawyer Calum Ross to tell the sheriff all about his role as a community champion. To the hilarity of the people of Milton, the lawyer said, 'He directly contributed to his local community from 1992 to 2006. He worked tirelessly and self-lessly to achieve a benefit to a community blighted by social and economical deprivation.'

Sheriff Anthony had no evidence to the contrary and could only go on the facts and claims in front of him. Instead of jailing Lyons, he ordered him to do 300 hours of community service. Sheriff Anthony, who six months later became only the third to quit his post since 1945 after being caught drink driving, told Lyons, 'As far as I'm concerned, you are a first offender and a man of mature years who has never caused any trouble to society.'

It was a bittersweet moment for the campaigners. On the one hand they were delighted that the self-styled community leader – described as 'The Fraudfather' in a newspaper headline – was now officially a criminal. But the case raised a number of serious questions which neither Strathclyde Police and the Crown Office nor its then boss, Lord Advocate Elish Angiolini, have ever answered.

Firstly, just why had the police ignored glaring evidence of the same crimes five years earlier? Lyons, utterly confident of his protection, had been allowed to commit a six-figure fraud while the council parroted its 'no criminality at Chirnsyde' line. And why was Lyons allowed to plead guilty in connection with only some of the properties contained in the 2005 dossier?

In court, much had been made of Lyons meeting all the payments on his fraudulent loans but at no point did the Crown Office or the sheriff think to ask the obvious question as to how on earth a man earning £20,000 a year had been able to finance such an existence. As one newspaper headline put it: 'Where did you get the readies, Eddie?'

Councillor Billy McAllister said, 'The Crown Office must explain what discussions took place behind closed doors to the benefit of Mr Lyons. Justice should be transparent – not a secretive carve-up. Lyons did not have legitimate funds to pay his mortgages so where did the money come from? Was it from drugs or other crime? This case raises more questions than it answers.'

That same year also saw the police deliver a serious blow to Daniel's carefully cultivated status as an underworld untouchable – someone too big to get caught.

Daniel's money trail was altogether more complex than Lyons'. His downfall was due not to dirty money but to his ever-present propensity for violence.

The 52-year-old, a living embodiment of fury, was driving near his home in the west end of Glasgow, in October 2009, when he became angry at the way the car in front was being driven. Daniel, behind the wheel of his partner's VW Golf, flashed his lights and sounded the horn as the driver, Gerard Fullerton, attempted to turn right at a junction. Fullerton, a 30-year-old student, slowed down to see what the fuss was about only for Daniel to draw parallel and start making gestures. Daniel then pulled sharply in front of the stunned driver who was forced to slam on the brakes to avoid a collision. He had no idea that the scruffy, snarling middle-aged man who emerged from the VW, carrying a long, sharp metal pole, was, in fact, a major organised crime boss.

Terrified at the sight of the weapon, he reversed out of danger but Daniel wasn't ready to back down. He jumped back into the VW and continued the chase. On two more occasions, he chased and attempted to pen in his victim who eventually ran out of luck when he travelled down a cul-de-sac.

Daniel emerged from the VW and waved his weapon and like a more squat and less funny version of Basil Fawlty, proceeded to strike his victim's car while he remained trapped inside. Daniel trashed the bodywork and windscreen, while spitting out expletives, but was unable to get inside.

It was almost unheard of for anyone accused of such a crime to be kept in remand. Those accused of rape and murder are routinely bailed but, because of Daniel's status, he got special treatment. When he was arrested for the road rage attack four months later in February 2010, he was slung into a cell in Barlinnie prison. The timing of the arrest – a month after Kevin Carroll's murder at Asda – was no accident and nor was the agreement by a sheriff to keep him behind bars while awaiting trial. The police were desperate to keep him off the streets in the wake of the murder. He had made it known that there was a 'bottomless pit' of cash available to avenge the death of his daughter Kelly's partner.

His incarceration bought the police valuable time – the longer he was locked up, the harder it was for him to direct his gang and order revenge attacks.

During those eight months in Barlinnie, he was unable to attend the funeral of Carroll which took place in May 2010.

Simmering with rage, he got into more trouble inside. A Chinese inmate called Chang Di Hi – not aware of who he was talking to – told Daniel to 'fuck off'. Furious, Daniel followed the prisoner and then tried to throttle him for his cheek. The attack induced so much stress that Daniel keeled over, clasping his chest. He was carted off to hospital, where he was treated for a suspected heart attack.

Seven years earlier, Daniel had beaten the rap for the attack on a taxi driver, when the victims and witnesses developed amnesia. This time, he wasn't so lucky as enough people were willing to testify.

At Glasgow Sheriff Court, he admitted breach of the peace in relation to the road rage as well as two charges of assaulting the prisoner. Daniel's favourite lawyer, the former Labour MSP, Gordon Jackson QC, told the sheriff that he admitted 'losing it' and that 'he was having a bad day.'

Rumours of Daniel's ill-health were also confirmed when Jackson revealed that his client was 'extremely unwell' and that it was 'probable that he was in the process of having a heart attack' during the Barlinnie assault.

Daniel was jailed for 12 months during which time he was released pending an appeal before returning to prison to serve the rest of his time.

As he was led from the dock, he winked and stuck out his tongue to his pals in the public gallery.

33

Game Over?

The Lyons family had exploited and manipulated police officers for decades but their involvement with PC Derek McLeod of Lothian and Borders Police took things to a whole new level. He was able to access the Scottish Intelligence Database, a computer system holding a vast amount of information inputted by every Scottish police force, the Scottish Crime and Drug Enforcement Agency (SCDEA) and the Serious and Organised Crime Agency. It is a treasure trove of intelligence on virtually every crook in Scotland – from small-time scam artists, sho-plifters and sex offenders right through to those who operate at the sharp end of organised crime. It typically includes details of appearances, criminal convictions, associates, addresses, vehicles and movements. The authorities admit that this incredible and ever-growing who's who of crime is available at 'the touch of a button' to every officer in Scotland, from beat cops in the Highlands to deep-cover detectives of the SCDEA.

The problem was that PC McLeod was no more than a gangster in uniform. The former tyre fitter and lorry driver started his career promisingly when he was named best recruit during training at the Scottish police college in 1999. Eight years later, he felt let down by his colleagues who he accused of failing to investigate a fire attack on his family home properly. What-ever his excuses, nothing could justify the path he chose. Using knowledge gleaned from busting drug dealers, he turned his home into a cannabis factory and was soon producing signifi-cant quantities. It was easy enough growing it but, as a serving police officer, he needed to be more careful than most when it came to offloading his illicit crops. A friend stepped forward and offered to take the lot. His buyers? The Lyons mob. The lucrative relationship flourished but it quickly became apparent that PC McLeod's access to top-secret police files was of much greater value than his dope. He was only too happy to oblige. From offices within three West Lothian police stations – Livingston, Mid Calder and West Calder – McLeod began logging in to the police computer to steal tracts of information about the Lyons, their associates, their enemies and the code name of police operations. This flow of leaked intelligence from McLeod allowed the Lyons to keep several steps ahead of the police. Knowing what the police knew about them was hugely useful, but what PC McLeod could tell them about their rivals – in particular Kevin Carroll – was the greatest prize of all.

McLeod began harvesting stolen intelligence in January 2009 and continued through to and beyond the following January when Carroll was shot dead at Asda. Whether McLeod's corruption played any role in helping to plan and commit the fatal hit by serving up crucial information on Carroll or in any way helped the prime suspects foil the murder squad detectives may never be known. What is likely is that McLeod would probably still be doing it to this day were it not for the subsequent investigation into Carroll's slaying. A raid on the Glasgow home of one of the suspected gunmen in May 2010 unearthed handwritten notes about Carroll's haunts, cars, movements and associates.

The officer leading the enquiry was Detective Superintendent Michael Orr whose dad was former Strathclyde chief constable Sir John Orr. His uncle, Jim Orr, was the first-ever head of the SCDEA. The siblings were among the most prominent officers of their generation although, when John promoted Jim to assistant chief constable, there had been a few raised eyebrows.

At Orr's side during the Carroll murder enquiry was Detective Inspector Calum Young, whose own career was not without controversy. Previously, Councillor Billy McAllister and one of the 'bampots' had complained to Strathclyde Police about claims that Young had described David Lyons to them as an 'alright guy' and had dismissed the previous chief constable's letter branding him a drug dealer as 'spurious'. McAllister took particular exception because DI Young had been put in charge of investigating the email smear campaign he had suffered despite the fact some of the emails had named the officer as being hostile to McAllister.

When Orr and Young discovered the scrawled intelligence secrets in the home of one of their prime suspects, an audit of the Scottish Intelligence Database revealed that PC McLeod had been very nosey indeed. They raided his home in Breich, West Lothian, where they discovered 85 kilos of cannabis under the stairs and 70 plants – worth £35,000 in total – thriving in the garage.

McLeod was confirmed as the source of the stolen intelligence when his handwriting matched that on the notes found in the alleged hit man's home. As well as the murder prime suspect, another alleged recipient of McLeod's information was Andrew Gallacher, a long-standing member of the Lyons' Chirnsyde-based Club Boys who had been shot by Carroll in Bellshill in 2006.

Orr and Young made four trips to see McLeod at Edinburgh's Craigmillar police station but he was in no mood to help them. The Glasgow detectives' tactics also ruffled the feathers of some Lothian and Borders officers who complained that they had not followed procedure in their dealings with McLeod and produced CCTV evidence to prove it. Meanwhile, McLeod made a more serious allegation – namely, that he had been threatened by the pair who had told him that, if he did not admit that he had *personally* passed his notes to the prime suspect, rather than through a middle-man, then he would be up on a charge of conspiring to murder Carroll. McLeod was scared out of his wits by the threat and had no way of knowing whether or not it was a bluff, but he refused to co-operate with Strathclyde Police's counter-corruption investigation into the threat claims. Orr and Young were eventually reprimanded, albeit only over the breaches of protocol in the way in which they had approached and dealt with the drug-dealing officer.

McLeod appeared at the High Court in Edinburgh where he admitted dealing cannabis and breaking the Official Secrets Act by accessing the police computer for illegal purposes. The agreement to plead guilty allowed his wife and son to walk free from drugs charges. He was jailed for two years for drug dealing and 16 months for snooping.

The murder enquiry started badly but became a debacle which descended into farce. One drawback was that the killers and their associates were too smart to discuss their deed with each other or even their loved ones. They operated on the basis that every word they uttered was potentially being listened to. The SCDEA's secret policeman got busy just as he had after the triple shooting at Applerow, but this time his carefully placed bugs in homes, cars and workplaces – and numerous tapped phones – yielded absolutely nothing that could be used as evidence. In addition, the police did not have a single eyewitness who could identify the two masked killers and their driver at the scene.

Orr was under immense pressure to deliver a result. One of the suspected gunmen had left Scotland for Spain on 23 January – 10 days after the Asda assassination. The man, who cannot be identified for legal reasons, took a one-way ticket from Glasgow Airport to Malaga where he felt at ease among the Costa del Sol's ex-pat criminal fraternity. He hasn't been seen since.

Meanwhile, the Daniels were also causing headaches. Orr had already personally warned members of the family to forget any ideas about revenge and, in February 2010, Jamie Daniel was arrested and remanded in prison for the road-rage attack he had committed the previous October, in the hope that it would disrupt his ability to direct operations. He was handed a 12-month jail sentence four months later.

Any hope, however unlikely, that the Daniel mob would put aside their intrinsic hatred of the police was completely de-stroyed by a public relations stunt orchestrated by Strathclyde Police and the Scottish Government's justice secretary, Kenny MacAskill. In March 2010, a photocall was arranged in which

MacAskill posed beside a shiny, black £75,000 Audi Q7 AS7 which had previously been used by Carroll and his associates and was now bedecked in Strathclyde Police livery. To the police and the politician, it was a potent symbol that they were winning the war on organised crime. To Carroll's family and the Daniel mob, it was an outrage. Carroll's killers remained at large, and his body had still not been released for burial, yet the police were exploiting his death to score some cheap publicity. According to the PR spin, this unlikely police vehicle would be used in routine patrols through the Daniels' north Glasgow heartlands in what appeared to be the modern equivalent of an outlaw's head being placed on a spike as a warning to others. The Daniels had different ideas, and 10 days after the Audi was unveiled, on 18 March at 1.50 p.m., they launched a firebomb attack on the rear car park of Maryhill police station where they suspected it was being stored. A second volley of petrol bombs was launched over the perimeter fence at 10 a.m. the following day. Thankfully, no officers, staff or civilians were injured but the Audi – which had previously been linked by a Scotland international footballer with connections to the Daniel mob – was not seen on the streets again and was later disposed of at auction.

On 18 May, Carroll's long-awaited funeral finally took place. It had taken four months for the authorities to decide that his body should be released. Jamie Daniel was banged up in Barlinnie but he ordered a truly typical gangland funeral which was to be a show of strength and defiance. Carroll's coffin was placed in a glass carriage which was drawn by two black horses, resplendent with black plumes. His partner, Kelly, wearing Gucci sunglasses, read a poem in tribute to her 'best friend . . . lover and . . . soulmate'. Floral wreaths included one in the shape of a can of Red Bull while another spelled out Carroll's car registration – G3 RBO. More than 200 mourners were told that the deceased had a 'heart of gold', a view not shared by the many victims of his violence. Carroll's burial plot in a remote cemetery in suburban Bearsden remained marked only by flowers and cans of Red Bull for more than a year due to fears that a headstone would be targeted, just as he had trashed the resting place of Garry Lyons.

Weeks later, the net closed in on the other suspected gunman – Ross Monaghan, a Club Boy and close friend of Eddie Lyons Jr and Steven Lyons. A team of officers raided his home in Glasgow's Penilee at 4 a.m. on 30 July 2010. They removed a black Stone Island jacket which was later found to have a single particle of gunpowder residue in a pocket. In addition, the police had found Monaghan's DNA on one of the guns used to shoot Carroll. On the face of those two facts – the gun DNA and the gunpowder residue – a conviction seemed likely.

When the trial eventually went ahead at the High Court in Glasgow almost two years later, Monaghan was alone in the dock as his co-accused was still free, having frustrated extensive police efforts to catch him. Monaghan's defence was simple – he blamed eight other people, including his fugitive co-accused, for the murder.

By the time the ten women and five men of the jury were sworn in by the trial judge, Lord Brailsford, the Advocate Depute Iain McSporran who led the prosecution knew that there were major problems with both of the crucial pieces of forensic evidence. Monaghan's all-important DNA on the gun turned out to be essentially worthless when the forensic scientists admitted that it amounted to one-tenth of one-billionth of a gram – a miniscule amount which the average person sheds 400,000 times per day. The scientists further conceded that Monaghan's DNA could have been transferred on to the weapon through contact with another object and that he may never even have been in the same room as the gun – let alone to have touched it.

The other forensic evidence against Monaghan was the speck of gunpowder residue which had been found in the pocket of the Italian designer jacket seized from his home. The first problem was that the firearms officers who had swarmed through his house had been on a shooting exercise hours earlier and were still wearing the same clothes and carrying the same guns. The black bomber jacket was removed from a wardrobe *after* these gun-toting cops had searched it for weapons. Lord Brailsford agreed with the experts' view that there was a very real risk of contamination.

In addition, a report into the significance of the residue was produced by forensic scientists Alison Colley and Laura Wilcock which concluded that it was similar to that which had been found at the murder scene. Under oath, Colley dropped a bombshell when they admitted that it was against protocol to draw any conclusion from a single particle and that it was 'meaningless' in scientific terms. Lord Brailsford removed the jury and asked Colley who had ordered her to draw the incriminating conclusion to the report. She replied, 'We were requested to do so by the Detective Superintendent [Michael Orr] in charge of the case.'

Lord Brailsford stated, 'You are independent of the police and could have told the police officers to go away and get lost, could you not?'

She replied, 'We tried to give our advice but we were over-ruled and told "just do it".'

Lord Brailsford described her revelation as 'disturbing' and, consequently, the second major building block of forensic evidence turned to dust and was ruled inadmissible.

Meanwhile Orr was so tainted that the Crown did not even call him as a witness, presumably to save him from an inevitable savaging by Monaghan's defence team.

It's hard to ascertain how the Crown Office approaches different prosecutions. Relatively minor crimes can result in marathon trials lasting for months during which a vast array of witnesses – many with nothing evidential to say – are called. It seems that the celebrity of the victim may be the cause of such showcase proceedings.

During the Carroll trial, the decision by prosecutors not to call his partner Kelly was considered strange by some. She would have been able to portray a different side to Carroll, to humanise him in the eyes of the jury. Observers also considered it odd that the Crown's first witness was an ex-police officer who branded Carroll a 'nutcase' with many enemies.

The jury also heard from Steven Glen, the £250,000-a-year

cocaine dealer who had met Carroll at Asda, and from his alleged supplier Allan 'Babesy' Johnston – who denied Glen's claim that he was a drug dealer. Johnston – who joined his teacher brother on a skiing holiday in Switzerland in the weeks after the murder – was one of the eight men who Monaghan incriminated in his defence. The two others mentioned during the trial can't be identified here for legal reasons while the other five were not named in court.

Monaghan portrayed himself as a hard-working family man, but he was a criminal thug with convictions for violence and drugs. The jury had no idea he was wearing an electronic ankle tag – his sentence for cocaine dealing the previous year.

During the 17 days of evidence, Monaghan's lawyer, Derek Ogg QC, also produced a police intelligence report which had been handed to detectives at the beginning of the murder probe. It revealed a list of 99 potential suspects, and it took the lawyer almost three minutes to read out. The names included members of the Lyons and the Daniel families but Monaghan's name was not on it.

Once the prosecution case had come to an end, Ogg argued that there was no case to answer. Lord Brailsford agreed and Monaghan was acquitted. He walked out of the dock and stepped into the spring sunshine through the same door that he and Steven Lyons had walked through after they'd been freed following their trial on charges of attempted murder seven years before.

Lord Brailsford initially banned the reporting of his decision on 3 May to allow the Crown Office 48 hours to consider an appeal, but it didn't take that long. Prosecutor McSporran returned to court the next day to say that, following discussions at the 'highest level', the Crown had decided to accept the judge's decision.

Only at the end of the trial could the astonishing story of PC McLeod and his links with the Lyons be revealed on the front page of the *Sunday Mail*. A reporting ban had remained in place for 11 months, lest the details of McLeod's case prejudiced Monaghan's chance of a fair trial.

Lord Brailsford's comments about Orr's attempt to lean on the forensic scientists prompted Strathclyde Police's assistant chief constable, Ruaraidh Nicolson – who had previously been tasked with handling the 'bampots' in Milton – to state, 'Everyone at the force is deeply concerned by the comments made by his lordship and is determined to get to the bottom of what happened in this case.'

Tom Nelson, director of the Scottish Police Services Agency which employed the forensic scientists, said, 'I take very seriously the suggestion that undue influence or pressure may have been placed on an individual member of forensics staff to reach a conclusion.'

Politicians and legal figures joined the chorus of protest at the costly farce that had played out in the Clydeside court in the name of Crown Office boss, Frank Mulholland QC, the Lord Advocate.

Leading QC Brian McConnachie said, 'It seems to me that the Crown were heavily reliant on the firearm residue discharge evidence. Monaghan's DNA was on the gun but, given where it was found and how long after the incident, it didn't look like a particularly good case. I suppose they would have seen the challenge to that evidence coming, but I don't think they had any other evidence. The judge ruled that there was insufficient evidence and the Crown should have seen that.'

Perhaps the Crown realised the trial was lost before it began, and it had been easier for them to go through the motions than it would have been to make the more honest decision of dropping the case before it reached court.

Eleven years after a bag of cocaine was stolen at a house party, there are no winners. It can only be hoped that the men who seem grimly determined to continue down a path of death, destruction and revenge might stop and think. For the sake of their parents, partners and children, let's pray that they are brave enough to walk away.